A
History and Genealogy
of the
Descendants
of
Joseph Taynter

Who Sailed from England
April, A.D. 1638, and
Settled in Watertown,
Massachusetts

["Le Teynterer," "Taynterer," "Taynter," &c.]

Like leaves on trees the race of man is found,
Now green in youth, now withering on the ground:
Another race the following spring supplies,
They fall successive and successive rise.
So generations in the course decay,
So flourish these when those are passed away.
—Pope's Homer.

Prepared by
Dean W. Tainter

Member of the New England Historic-Genealogical Society

HERITAGE BOOKS
2015

HERITAGE BOOKS

AN IMPRINT OF HERITAGE BOOKS, INC.

Books, CDs, and more—Worldwide

For our listing of thousands of titles see our website
at
www.HeritageBooks.com

A Facsimile Reprint
Published 2015 by
HERITAGE BOOKS, INC.
Publishing Division
5810 Ruatan Street
Berwyn Heights, Md. 20740

Originally published
Boston:
Printed by David Clapp
1859

International Standard Book Numbers
Paperbound: 978-0-7884-5044-0
Clothbound: 978-0-7884-8350-9

TO

THE RISING GENERATION

OF OUR NAME

AND TO GENERATIONS YET TO FOLLOW,

THIS RECORD

OF AN HUMBLE BUT PIOUS ANCESTRY

IS RESPECTFULLY INSCRIBED.

———

MAY THEY

FOLLOW IN THE FOOTSTEPS

OF THEIR

FOREFATHERS,

EMULATE THEIR

GODLINESS, INDUSTRY AND PATRIOTISM,

AND TRANSMIT TO POSTERITY AN

UNTARNISHED NAME.

THE TAINTER FAMILY.

THE following history was commenced by the writer in 1855, and up to the present season it was intended that it should be published in connection with the history of the other Tainter family (which originated in Connecticut). For this purpose, its issue has from time to time been delayed, and would be delayed still further, but for the constant inquiries for the book. (See page 92.)

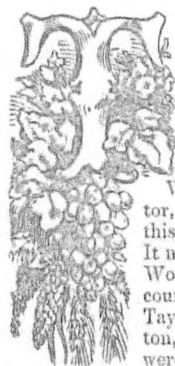

HE ship Confidence, a large vessel for those times, but no larger than an ordinary sized schooner of the present day, reached the shores of New England in the summer of 1638, with about 110 passengers on board. Among these passengers were Nicholas and Jane Guy, their daughter Mary, and hired men, Joseph Tayntor and Robert Bayley. Of the few settlements around Boston they chose Watertown, and it is most likely they had friends there, as most of the passengers went to Newbury and Sudbury.

Were we to indulge a little in romance, we might say that Joseph Tayntor, *enamored with the charms of Mary Guy*, came over with the family to this country, as it appears that they were married soon after their arrival. It might be further imagined that, pleased with the prospects of the New World, young Tayntor wrote home for his parents to follow, which may account for the appearance, a few years after, in Connecticut, of Charles Tayntor and his family. It is very probable that *they* first arrived in Boston, and from thence went with Cambridge and Watertown people (who were the first settlers of Connecticut) to Branford. How early this may have been, it is useless to conjecture, the early records of Connecticut being very incomplete. But the name of one of the sons* is found in Windsor as early as 1643.

The account of a number of the early forefathers of our family, is in the following pages brief. They perhaps are deserving of more extended biography, but we have been unable to prepare them from the scanty materials which have accumulated in the silent lapse of time; but from such as there are, extracts have been given, partially as illustrative of their standing in society, and partially as items of curiosity and interest. That our fathers acted well their part in the stirring scenes of the past, in the wars and privations of the land, these pages amply testify. As a whole, humble but highly respectable, they appear to have been actively interested in all matters pertaining to the civil and religious affairs of the community in which they lived, supporters of the gospel, and peaceful members of society.

Several of their family letters, clothed with the moral and religious sentiments peculiar to the early settlers of New England, we have found preserved in unexpected quarters. Having been the companion of the pioneer in his log cabin with smoky chimney and weather-inviting roof, they bear the evidences of both antiquity and exposure; aside from their words of eloquent piety, their very appearance impresses the mind with a kind of involuntary veneration, which more modern productions fail to produce, and though presented to the reader in the handsome print of the present day, they cannot fail to inspire

* The two sons were about the same age as Joseph Tayntor, and our *presumption* is that he was an older *brother*.

and excite the imagination. We forget the present in the retrospect of one or two centuries, and imagine we see the forms of those grave and faithful puritans, as they came on a sabbath morning from their lowly dwellings, accompanied by their wives in " matronly decency," and their children in " well-ordered sobriety," their garb plain and their countenances stern, saluting each other as they met, with stiff but friendly greetings, and directing their steps with pious joy to the place of their solemnities. The simplicity of ancient days is not to be expected amidst the refinement, the bustling enterprise, and the improvements of the present; but may we not wish that we had retained more of the devoted sincerity, the sentiment of reverence, which warmed and hallowed the hearts of those men *and women* of the olden time?

A curiosity no doubt is generally entertained to know the origin and history of the name prior to the settlement of this country, and we have made attempts to satisfy ourselves in this particular, as far as the facilities of this country admit; but it remains for some interested person in England to present in a tangible shape this part of our family history, though the writer has not been without a little success in this quarter.

About the year 1800, the British Parliament appointed Commissioners to compile and print some of the earlier Norman Latin Records of England. In their works we find the following names:

> Robert Le Teynturer and wife Beatrix.
> William Teynturer.
> Stephen Le Tainturer and wife Johanna.
> Agnes, who was the wife of Warren Le Teyntur.
> Henry Le Teynturer and wife Agnes.
> William, son of Richard Le Teynturer and Matilda his wife.
> Roger Le Teynturer.
> Alen Le Teynturer and wife Matilda.
> Hugo Le Teynturer " " Ada.
> John, son of Elias Le Teynturer.

The paragraphs in which these names appear, translated all read about as the following, being probably records of church tithes.

County Essex, A.D. 1222. John de Albro of the Monastry of the Royal Court near Chelmeresford, should recover of Robert Le Teynturer and Beatrix his wife, fifteen of the rents in Halstead.

County Wilts, A.D. 1237. William Teynterer, of New Saxony, senior, gives twelve marques to be given to the deacon and to the chapter of the Blessed Marie.

No doubt is entertained that the above was our name seven hundred years ago, and that in the course of ages the superfluous syllables of the name have from time to time been dropped, the same as during the past two hundred years the long letter *y* has been substituted for the more easily written letter *i*, by the greater part of the family in this country.

The above gives us a clue to the national origin and derivation of our name — *Le Taint* being the French for *The dyer*, and *er* or *eror* for *man*; i. e., Stephen Le Tainturer — *Stephen the dyer man.* Thus the inference is that our ancestor, at the remote period when our name was adopted, was a dyer by occupation, Norman French, and that some of the name went, in the eleventh century, with William the Conqueror into England.

The name of Tainturier is a French one at the present time, and the following appears in the Paris Directory:

> *Tainturier freres, Chapeaux, Simon le Franc* 5.
> *Tainturier (Mme), Lingerie Confect, St. Denis* 229.

Translated — Tainter Brothers, Hatters, No. 5 Simon le Franc.
Tainter Madam, Fancy Confectionery, No. 229 St. Denis.

There are in the French Directories to manufacturing towns, lists of Teinturiers (dyers). Teynturetto was an early Italian painter, and history says that he received his name from the occupation of his father, who was a dyer.

Books on Heraldry, Surnames, County Histories, &c., have been searched in vain for later mention of the name. English Directories contain none, and none appear incorporated into the pedigrees of other families; still we cannot doubt that the name may be found in other quarters. (See Simms's Manual for the Genealogist.)

We are informed that Amherst College Library contains "Statutes of the Realm" (4th William and Mary, Vol. 6, A.D. 1692), in which the name of Thomas Tainter is several times mentioned as a Commissioner for the County of Wilts. We have the date of marriage of Margaret Tentor to Thomas Estay, in Co. Berks, A.D. 1613.

From the ill success of the author in searching for the name in the above-mentioned works, he is inclined to the conclusion that our family descended from the yeomanry rather than gentry of the old world, and though he has what purports to be a Pedigree and Coat of Arms of the Tayntor family, of Pershore, England, he has as yet been unable to find any proof to warrant the belief that there ever was such a family.

But it does not concern American citizens, as it does the subjects of European Princes, to trace a line of descent from ancestors who wore crowns or coronets, or who were adorned with garters, stars, and other badges of eminence. It is rather a subject of self-congratulation on our part, that a remote forefather was one of a band of untitled voluntary exiles, who fled from persecution, to the rock-bound shores of New England.

Yet it is, in all cases, a legitimate object of inquiry with us, to ascertain the origin and standing of our family. No man can repel an honorable pride in the virtues or patriotism of his ancestors, and it should be indulged rather than discarded. What nobler examples can there be held up to the young, and what nobler ambition can be possessed by youth, than to make as respectable men as their fathers before them.

The writer has not advanced in the compilation of this work, without a deep sense of his incapacity for the task; and if the following pages lack scholarly exactness, or historic dignity, he trusts that they may not be scanned with a critic's eye. Were they written by a person of leisure, they might claim more credit in these respects than they do; but written as they have been by one whose only leisure consists of evening and midnight hours, he trusts that he shall receive the charitable consideration of the reader.

Our family, though one of the oldest of New England, is yet one of the smallest, and we have thought that all desired to know as much about each other as possible. Consequently we have given, in an off-hand informal manner, whatever particulars of the family, past and present, we have been able to collect, we trust, correctly; but there will, no doubt, be mistakes discovered. It is impossible, in a book of this kind, to get *all* of the dates correct, and it is hoped that whatever errors may be found, will be divided between *the printer*, the author, and his pen and ink acquaintances.

We have had to adjust a great many conflicting dates sent by different correspondents, sometimes repeatedly.

We will cite one instance. The name of a person born in 1818, was given us as having married in 1831. After remaining on our pages several months, it occurred to us that it was not probable that any of the Tainter family had been quite so precocious as to marry at the age of 13, but looking over our letters we found it so returned three times. Still we changed the date to 1841, which proved correct, our correspondent having received the date wrong from one of his correspondents.

But it is not our intention to make light of the labors of our correspondents. On the contrary, we tender our heartfelt thanks to those who have kindly and patiently answered our many inquiries, and who have encouraged us by prompt attention thereto.

With grateful acknowledgments to those who have answered our circular, with their subscription, these pages (with words by an ancient author) are hurried on their mission.

Nov. 25, 1859.

" Farewell my little booke, and tell thy friends
The deluge of the deepe confusion ebs ;
Then shew thy leafe to all, but haile the best,
And safely leave it in their holy hands,
That will uproot thy language, cleere thy sense
As matter but of mere pre-eminence.
Yet as the starre that onward bringes the sunne,
Thou hast perfection where thy light begunne :
This tell thy friendes, and little booke farewell."   A.D. 1603.

Persons desiring to trace their lineage through the following pages, should first find their own name, and then by means of the numbers trace back. For instance, the last name in the book is Sarah S., number 534. She is a daughter of number 397. On turning to that number in the body of the book, it is found that he is son of number 202; number 202, the son of 102; and so on.

There were early settlers of Massachusetts bearing the name of Taint and Painter, and some historians have confounded the name with Taynter. The name of Painter is a common one in Pennsylvania and some of the other Middle States, at the present time.

A number of copies of this book, over the number subscribed for, have been printed. They may be had by any person who forwards the price (per copy $1.25) to D. W. Tainter, Boston, Mass.

ERRATA.

Page 20, at the middle of the page, for 183 Dollars, read Pounds.
Page 36, over the word Family, read Ephraim for Ezekiel.
Page 44, Stephen (154) died æ. 67, not 69.
Page 51, for Rev. Orasamus Tayntor, read Orsamus.
Page 55, Henry C. (224), date of marriage is wrong.
Page 61, Caroline M. (628), b. July 14, not 17. Thomas P. (631), b. in 1825, not 1823.
Page 73, for Charles S. (484), read Sumner.
Page 75, several names at the bottom were omitted. See pages 84 and 85.

Pages 1-6 do not exist in this book.

It is paginated i-viii and 7-100

JOSEPH TAYNTER. (1)

THE pilgrim forefather of the Watertown Tainters, and their descendants, embarked at the age of 25 years, for New England, at Southampton, England, April 24, 1638, in "*y* goode shipp y* Confidence of 200 tonnes belonging to London.*"

OLD TAINTER HOUSE, WATERTOWN.*

From what part of England he originated, or whether he came from Wales, we know not. Whether he was of near or distant kin to Charles Taintor, who with two sons and a daughter is said to have emigrated from Wales, and who appeared soon after the same date in Connecticut, is likewise unknown. The writer is inclined to think that they were related to each other, though there is but one circumstance on which to ground a presumption that they were, which is, that Col. David Wells (great-grandfather of Charles M. Taintor, Esq.), whose wife was Mary Taintor, a descendant of Charles, the Connecticut emigrant, did upon attending the meetings of the Continental Congress at Watertown, make it his home at Eaires Tainter's. This fact betokens a probability that there was a tie of consanguinity existing between them.

JOSEPH TAYNTER came to this country in the service of Nicholas Guy, a carpenter, whose daughter he married soon after their arrival and settlement at Watertown. Of him and his immediate descendants we have received nothing by family tradition. All that we are at this time able to present of their history, is what has been gathered from the time-worn records of the past. What they afford, though meagre indeed, is of the highest interest.

From the old records of Watertown, we learn that he was an active and prominent man among the early settlers of the town, and that he was for many years, between 1640 and 1680, one of the Selectmen, Constables, Tything-men, &c.

In the following pages will be found interesting extracts from these records, being mostly paragraphs wherein his name appears. From them the reader will infer that he was an educated man, a man of standing in the Church, and one possessed of the good will and respect of his fellow-townsmen.

His name appears on the Watertown records as early as 1639, it being on a list of those who shared in the division of Sudbury meadows in that year.

The homestead and lot, of which the foregoing is an illustration, was occupied by successive generations of the family for one hundred and fifty years, and until sold by Eaires Tainter, who removed to Leominster, at which time the house had received an addition, which is not included in the engraving. The house was demolished about thirty years ago.

The "home lotte," comprising about twenty acres of as fine land as there is in Watertown, still retains its original size and shape. It is situated at the corner of Main Street and Lexington road, and has on the Main Street side a walk of twenty feet in width shaded by a double row of noble elms, of some sixty trees. Within the lot, there is still to be seen a part of the old pear orchard, represented in the engraving.

The farm, at the time of his death, consisted of 317 acres, stocked by three horses, one yoke of oxen, seven steers, and five swine, which was that of a "well-to-do" farmer in those times.

He died Feb. 20, 1689-90 (old style), at the age of 77 years. His wife died in 1705, aged 86.

1657.

---

* The house was built by Dr. Simon Eire, the first physician of Watertown, who removed to Boston about the time that Joseph Taynter married. (The greater part of the lands that belonged to Joseph Taynter at his death, had been purchased from Dr. Eire or his heirs.) The windows were of the old fashioned diamond-shaped panes of glass, "brought from England," with sash of lead, which was quite common about Boston up to the time of the Revolution, when they were substituted by wood, and the lead moulded into bullets.

Joseph Taynter's youngest son, Simon, was probably named for Dr. Simon Eire, who had recently died.

1647. Wher as there is a difference between Joseph Taynter and widow Barnard abought a piece of land lying at y⁰ end of widow Barnard's swampe behynd Joseph Tayntor's house (hee purchased of Ould Peirce) it is determined at present, that y° land is y° towns.

1651. Ordered That Joseph Taynter shall be warned unto y° next meeting of y° Selectmen to answer for taking in of a piece of y° Towns land.

1653. Samuel Thatcher and Joseph Taynter are chosen survayers for this year.

1654. Leiftenant Beeres hath received of Joseph Tayntor 10s. being a fine for felling treese upon y° Townes land also a bushel of wheet towards his pay for perambulation.

1654. A rate of 71£. 15s. 5d. is delivered into y° hands of John Livermore and Joseph Taynter, Cunstables.*

1655. Delivered into y° hands of Joseph Tainter and John Livermore cunstables, a rate for the county and the colledg, the sum of 52£. 7s. 10d.

1656. Chosen this 8th of Decem to order y° Towne affaires Capt. Mason, Ephraim Child, Ensign Shearman, Left. Beeres, Brother Bearsto, Will Bond, Joseph Tainter.

1656. Ordered that Goodman Tayntor, warn Jonathan Phillips if he see cause, to come before y° 7 men and there give acompt of y° spending of his time.

1656. Ordered that Joseph Tainter doe warne Richard Beech to y° next meeting of y° 7 men and thereto give acompt of y° improvement of y° time of hisself and family.

Richard Beech apearing acording to order it is further ordered y° there shall be an acompt taken by Joseph Tainter every weeke of y° improving of y° time of y° family of y° s' Beech y° for y° te'me of three months and to make a returne thereof to y° Towne.

1659. * * * * * * bounds to be marked by Joseph Taynter and Richard Bloyse.

1659. A road laid out from Watertown to Boston by y° townes of Boston, Watertowne & Cambrig.

For Boston.	For Watertown.	For Cambrig.
WILL COLBRON,	JOSEPH TAINTER.	JOHN JACKSON.
WILL PADDY.		

1660. Joseph Tainter and Henry Freeman are chosen to look to y° order concerning y° hogs and fences.

1663. Joseph Tainter being complaned of for taking in of 5 or 6 foote of y° highway, both of y° South and east side of his home lotte, it being confessed by himself, wee (y° selectmen) doe leave it to y° consideration of y° whole towne.

1663. At a generall Towne meeting it is ordered that Joseph Tainter shall enjoy that land which he hath taken in and that it is y° trew boundary of his home lotte.

Ordered for to order y° Towne affaires for this year, Ensigne Sherman, Myhell Berstow, Serjant Bright, Nathaniel Treadaway, Joseph Tainter, John Bisco, John Haman, John Coolidge senior, John Sawin.

1663. Joseph Tainter and Nathaniel Treadaway are appointed to make y° Towne rate.

1663. M'. Whitney making some mistakes in casting y° invoyce whearby sum wrong is done in severall rates, it is ordered that Joseph Tainter and Nath' Treadaway shall view y° invoyce and what thay find not to be right cast up, they are to cast it right and amend it on y° rates.

1664. Att a meeting of y° Select men at John Bisco's, y° 30th of y° 1st, 1664.

It appearing that John Trayne had taken into his hands, one barrell of y° Powder, that was provided for store, by order of y° Generall Court, it is ordered that John Trayne shall forthwith provide one barrell of good powder, for y° supply of y° said store, and goodman Tayntor is to search y° barrell of powder in Charles Chadwickes hands to try what condition it is in, and make report to y° select men at their next meeting.

1664. Joseph Tayntor is chosen to prize goods that com in for Towne debts or rates.

Joseph Tayntor having searched y° barrell of powder in Charles Chadwicks hand, informed y° Towne that y° said barrell of powder is in good condition, and is farr better than y° barrell that John Trayne hath provided, for what y° said Trayne took away.

---

* A Constable, in early days, served sometimes as a magistrate, and was usually a man of dignity and judgment. On official occasions, they carried a black staff six feet long, tipped with brass. They collected the taxes, put forth "pursuites, or hue and cryes," &c. &c.

1664. Ordered that for y* future Nath'. Treadaway and Joseph Taynter with y* Deakons are chosen and empowered to act in all imergent occasions and to place people in the meeting house as need do require. And Thomas Whitney is chose to take care that no dogs come into y* meeting-house upon y* sabbath days, by whipping them out of y* house, or any y* be near to y* house at such times, and to have for his pains and care, thirty shillings y* yeare.

1664. Deacon Bright and Joseph Tayntor being apoynted by y* selectmen to take care to lodge y* ammunition, provided by order of y* general court, in y* chest provided in y* meeting house,—made their returne that they had done it and y* store of ammunition there lodged by them was, two barrells of Powder containing five score & 14 pounds per barrell ne(a)tt & thite, and five rundletts, and one bag containing bulletts to y* amount of three hundred and two pounds, with y* cash gross hundredds, and sixty-four pounds of mach.

Captⁿ. Mason, John Sherman, Joseph Tayntor, Nath'. Treadaway, John Cooledge, senior, Goodman Barstow, John Bigulah, are chosen to order y* affaires of y* Town for y* yeare insuinge.

Att a meeting of y* selectmen att Joseph Tayntors 11th of y* 8th 1664, goodman Bisco, goodman Treadaway and goodman Tayntor are apoynted to viewe y* wateringe before Charles Stearnes house adjoyning to Thomas Underwoods ground, Also y* water course at y* end of y* lane above goodman Springes which useth to pass through y* corner of y* lott that was William Palmers, and order what shall be done and make return to y* towne.

1664. Goodman Barstow, goodman Cooledge, and goodman Tayntor, appointed to detain two men from going to Cape fear without making suitable provision for their wives and children who may be in want in their absence

1664 Goodman Bairstow. goodman Coolidge, and goodman Tayntor, chosen and empowered to sell a farm. "Y* time appoynted for y* attending of y* said sale is next Monday by 9 of y* clock in y* morning at goodman Tayntors house."

Y* invoyce of y* Towne taken for towne rates being perfected by addition of housinge stock and trades, Joseph Tayntor, Nath'. Treadaway, with Nathan Fiske, weare apoynted to make y* Rates for y* Pastor and Towne charges.

Joseph Tayntor and Nath' Treadaway, with Nath Fiske, having made y* Pastors and Towne Rates, y* Rates weare entered in to y* Towne Book of accounts and affirmed according to y* agreement of y* Selectmen.

1665. Att a Generall Towne Meeting, Capt. Mason, John Sherman, Joseph Tayntor, John Cooledge Nath Treadaway, Corporall Bond, John Livermore, John Shearman, was chosen to keep y* Booke.

1665. Ordered that goodman Tayntor and goodman Treadaway shall warne Ould Goodman Page and his wife, goody Gearfield, goodwife Stuart, John Ball & goodwife Sawtell, to y* next meeting of y* Select men at John Bigulah's (y* last Tuesday of June next) to answer for not attending their seats in y* meeting house apoynted them by y* Towne.

Ordered that Capt Mason, Joseph Taynter and John Sherman, shall viewe y* two acres of land granted to Isaack Mixer in patch medow and consider y* grant with y* respective bounds and determine whether there be not land left for a highway for y* use of y* Towne.

Att a meetinge of y* Select men at Joseph Tayntors 5th of y* 7th 1665

Y* Comittee above seyd made their return upon y* viewinge of Isaack Mixers grant in patch medow, that there is left for y* Towns use fower rods for a highway notwithstanding Isaack Mixers grant, And thearfor doe determine that y* proprietors of that land shall have a highway from South to North of fower rods wide with this provise, that it be att which end y* proprietors please, either East or West.

1668. Chosen to perambulate for this year goodman Tayntor, Corporall Bond, Stephen Cooledge.

1670. Paid to Joseph Tainter for perambulation 1£.

1670. At a meeting of the Selectmen Jan. 17, It was agreed that whereas there have been a grievance in the towne for a long time y* there are soe many catle in the towne that are let goe at liberty from under the hand of a keeper in common and high wayes, whearby many men are much damnyfied &c. &c.

It was ordered that there should be kept in Watertown four heardes of Cowes and working oxen and that they shall be ordered as followeth. Ordered that the first heard shall begin at Richᵈ. Sangers and shall drive alonge to Joseph Tainters and to Wedow Waights &c. &c.

1670. Upon a review of a former judgment of what Joseph Tainter was fined for swine and cattle defective, y⁰ said fines of 1£ 6s. 6d. is abated 4s and soe y⁰ fines are made 1£. 2s. 6d.

1671. At a meeting of y⁰ select men March 29 It was voted whether y⁰ goods that were taken by y⁰ constables from Joseph Taintor for his fines, for hogs and cattle, should be set at liberty, and ther was non of y⁰ selectmen of y⁰ mind that they should be set at liberty.

1671. Oct. 16, Joseph Tainters fine again abated 4s. 3d.

1671. Nov. 6, At a generall Towne meeting Chosen to order y⁰ Prudential Affaires of y⁰ Towne, Capt. Mason, Charles Chadwick, Nathaniel Treadaway, Simon Stone, Joseph Tainter, John Sawin, Joseph Beamis.

Y⁰ Towne being desirous to settle thear diffarences about stinting thear feeding land and y⁰ walkes of thear heardes have chosen 7 men amongst themselves to agree abought that matter, and if they cannot agree to y⁰ satisfaction of y⁰ Towne then they have chosen three others out of town, altogether unconsarned in that bisnis who shall have full power to determine the same and all in refarance to prevent a sute now depending in Charlestowne courte.

1671. At a meeting of y⁰ Select men y⁰ 27 of Nov⁰. it was agreed that Cha⁰. Chadwick, Joseph Tainter and Simon Stone, should agree with Widow Bartlit for y⁰ dieting of Ould Bright, and with goodman Bisko for to suply him with wood, and Martin Townsend to make his fyar, and cut his wood and help him up and to bed as he needeth. Also that 2 Shurts should be provided for goodman Thorp.

1671. Dec. 27. Agreed that Joseph Tainter and Nath'. Treadaway shall make y⁰ Towne and Pasturs rate. Agreed by y⁰ Select men that thay with y⁰ cunstabelles will teak thear turns Each man his day, to looke to y⁰ boyse uppon y⁰ Lords day.

At a meeting at Leift. Beers, March 3, 1671. There coming a complaint to us y⁰ Select men concerning y⁰ poverty of Edward Sandersons family y' that they had not wherewith to maintaine themselves and children either with suply of provisions or employment to earne any—And considering y' it would be y⁰ charge of y⁰ Towne, to provide for y⁰ wholl family which will be hard to doe this year, and not knoweing how to supply them with provisions, we considering if we shoulde suply them, and could doe it, yet it would not tend to y⁰ good of y⁰ children for their good eaducation and bringing up, soe as they may be useful in y⁰ common weal, and themselves to live comfortable and usefully in time to come, We have therefore agreed to put out two of his children into some honest fameleys where they may be eaducated and brought up in y⁰ knowledge of God & sum honest calling or labor, And therefore we doe order that Thomas Fleg and John Bigulah shall have power to binde them prentises, with sum honest people with y⁰ consent of their parents, if it may be hade, and if y⁰ parents shall refuse then to use y⁰ help of a magistrate.

1673. A road laid out between Watertown and Concord.

For Watturtown.	For Cambrig.	For Concord.
JOSEPH TAINTER,	JOSEPH COOKE.	JOHN FLINT,
SIMON STONE.		CALEB BROOKS.

1673. 14thᵈ of y⁰ 8th m. Paid to Joseph Tainter for perambulation, he and his son, and carying a load of wood to Richard Beech 2£ 3s. 0d.

1674. At a jenerall Towne Meeting y⁰ 12ᵗʰ d. 8ᵗʰ m. Y⁰ Towne being called together to confer about y⁰ 2 thousand acres of land, due to them from y⁰ cuntry, it was voted that y⁰ Towne would improove Captin Mason, and goodman Taintur to treat with Mr. Paine and in case they finde by him incurridgment, then to endevur that there may be wav made for petishionning y⁰ jenerall courte for a plantation, if we can find convenient place for it.

1677. Chosen Cunstabell, Joseph Taintur and Sam'. Livermore.

1677. Chosen to joyne with Decon Hastings and goodman Taintur as a committy to seate men in y⁰ Meeting house, Cap'. Mason, Left. Shearman and Father Coolidge.

1677. Voated that these parsons foloing, shall be y⁰ men to inspect y⁰ severall inhabytance of this towne according as y⁰ laws injoynes, to witt, John Coolidge senyer, Deacon Heastings, Left. Shearman, John Stratton, Mr. Goddard, Corp' Bond, Antony Pearce and Mihill Eines, Joseph Taintur, Insine Warren, Geo. Parks, John Levermore jun., and that Cap'. Mason shall send a note to each of them to signify to them y⁰ severall families that ear committed to each mans ceare.

1678. Goodman Taintur cuming to y[e] Select men & requesting liberty to set up an addition to his barn, it standing joyned to y[e] highway, y[e] select men granted him a liburty to teak in to y[e] vallue of 14 foot in length at y[e] end of his barne, and also for a cow house at y[e] side of it to y[e] same extent.

1678. Y[e] Selectmen, Tythingmen and cunstabells meeting together after lectur do agree to goe too tithingmen and a selectman togethur, for to see that each person that have not teaken y[e] Oath of fidelity and alegiance, to take it as y[e] law requireth, to wit.——Father Coolidg, Deacon Heastings, Corporall Willington together, John Stratton, Mr. Goddard and Simon Stone together, Left. Shearman, Corporall Bond and Gregory Cooke together, Joseph Tainter, Mihill Eines and John Whitney together, &c. &c. &c.

1679. At a generall Towne Meetinge y[e] 3[d] d. 8th mo. Chosen Select men, Father Coolidge, Decon Hastings, Decon Bright, Left. Shearman, Corp[l]. Bond, Joseph Taintur, Mr. Bisco.

In reference to y[e] law concerninge y[e] excessive apparrell, y[e] select men being by y[e] said law, enjoyned to use y[e] best means for y[e] reforming of Such enormities, as are thearin specified, and taking notice of Sundry persons in this Towne, who are in their habitts contrary to y[e] said law, Wee doe therefore declare y[t] from hence forth none of our inhabitants except such as y[e] Law doth allow doe either weare silke goods or silke scarfes, gould or siluer lace or buttons, Ribonds at knees, or trossed handkerchers, upon y[e] forfeiture of what penalty y[e] law doth apoynt, which is that they shall be rated in y[e] Country rate after 200£ in y[e] same.

1679. Joseph Tainter senyer requesting of y[e] Town a little corner of land to straiten his fence of y[t] land neere goodman Hagars house, y[e] Towne appoynt Sam[l]. Stearns and W[m] Bond to view y[e] said corner of land, and make report of y[e] matter at y[e] next Town meeting.

1679. Dec. 23, it is agreed uppon y[t] Lieut. Shearman, Joseph Tainter senior, and W[m] Bond shall make and perfict y[e] County, Towne and Pasturs rates.

1679. At a meeting of y[e] select men at y[e] house of John Bisco, y[e] 30th of December, It was agreed upon that there should be publike notis given, for to call y[e] Town together y[e] next Monday, that so y[e] Town may come to forme a loveing agreemeut and conclusion about a schoole master. John Bisco is to warn y[e] Town together, and Joseph Tainter senior is chosen to cary on y[e] worke of y[e] day as moderator.

1679. Joseph Tainter senior, Lieut. Sherman and William Bond senior, are appointed to lay out a road to Sudbury.

1680. At a meeting of y[e] select men, April 5, Joseph Tainter requesting a small parcell of trees y[t] were secured y[e] last yeere for y[e] Towns use, y[e] said Joseph pleading y[t] y[e] Towne had formerly had some trees off from his ground for their use, for which he have had no satisfaction y[e] select men considering y[e] justnes and equitie of his plea, grant him y[e] said trees for his satisfaction.

1680. At a meeting of y[e] Selectmen at y[e] house of Joseph Tainter, y[e] 21 of Aprill, Joseph Bemiss being warned into said meeting for fencing in part of y[e] highway, upon y[e] report of Joseph Tainter. who hath viewed y[e] same, and found it was no prejudis to y[e] highway as to carting, y[e] selectmen were willing y[e] said fence should stand as it doth.

1680. Chosen to order y[e] prudential affair's for this year as followeth——John Coolidge sen[r]., Decon Hastings, Decon Bright, Cap[t]. Sherman, Joseph Tainter senior, William Bond senior, John Bisco.

1680. Chosen to preambulate y[e] bounds of Watertown as y[e] Law directs——Joseph Tainter senior, Sam[l]. Jenison, &c. &c. . . . . and Joseph Tainter is to give notise to our bordering townes of time and place of meeting.

1681. Voated, a liberty to Jonathan Browne to straighten his fence against Sudbury roade, at that joynte of it said to be formerly against y[e] Pine stumpe, and goodman Tainter to oversee to y[e] doeing of it—y[t] y[e] Town be not thereby prejudised.

1682. Voated that a committy shall be chosen to place persons in y[e] Meeting house. The persons chosen are Cap[t]. Shearman, Decon Hastings, goodman Tainter senyer, Corporall Bond and Simon Stone.

1682. Joseph Taintur senyer, cuming unto y[e] Select men to inform them y[t]. in y[e] year 77 himself and Samuel Livermore being Cunstabells and having received of y[e] selectmen warrant to gather of severall persons y[t]. were behind in the paying y[e] Pastur y[e] sum of 13 pounds 7 shillings, and have cleared said thirteen pounds and seven shillings save only twelve shillings, he requests of y[e] select men that they would discharge y[e] said constabells of y[e] sum above said and pay to themselves six shillings four pence, Because of Sam[l]. Pages rates which were in all one pound three shillings thay could not obtain any thing of it by reson of his poverty, y[e] Select men do grant naybur Taintur his request.

WILL.

IN THE NAME OF GOD AMEN. I Joseph Tainter of Watertown In New-england being at this present of perfect understanding & memory tho weak In body, comiting my Soul unto the hands of Almighty God & my body to decent burial, In hope of a resurection unto Eternal Life by ye Merits and Power of Jesus Christ my most mercyfull Saviour & Redemer, Doe thus dispose of my temporal Estate, which God hath graciously given me.

Imprimis. My Just depts being payed and Funeral charges defrayed I give & bequeath unto my beloved wife Mary Tainter the sole use and benefit of my estate, during her natural life, and to be managed for her benefit by my Executour afterwards mentioned.

Item. I give & bequeath to my Son Joseph, al my lott lying near to ye Meeting hous which was my Father Gyes, together with two Acres of Medow lying in broad meadow bounded by Capt. John Sherman on ye North and nor== west & M^r. Samuel on the South, to be delivered to him after his Mothers deceas to him and to His Heirs forever.

Item. I give and bequeath to Joseph abovesaid a sute of arms for a foot-Soldier to be delivered at my deceas.

Item. I give and bequeath to my Son Benjamin 20£. after my wives deceas.

Item. I give and bequeath to my Son Jonathan, beside what of mine he hath now in his hands 20£. after my wives deceas.

Item. I give and bequeath to my Daughter Mary Pollard ten pounds, to be paid to her by my Executour within 5 years after my wives deceas.

Item. I give and bequeath to my Son in Law Elnathan Beers, my part of meadow on ye back side of John Cutings hous, ye plain meadow, and also my black Colt horse to be delivered to him Soon after my deceas.

Item. I give and bequeath to my Son in Law John Taylor 5£. to be payed him after my wives deceas.

Item. I give and bequeath to my Grand Child John Taylor one sute of arms for a foot-Soldier to be delivered soon after my deceas, also 20s. to be paid by my Executour when he shall acccomplish the age of 21 yeais.

Item. I give and bequeath to each of my Grand-children, which shal be found living at my deceas, 20s. a piece to be paid to them by my Executour as they shall accomplish the age of 21 years, & if any of each or any family shall happen to die before they be of full age, then the remaining of that family to receive the Legacy of ye Brother or Sister deceased.

And I doe appoint my loving friends Simon and John Stone of Watertown overseers of this my last Will & Testament, & doe herby give them power to determine any difference y^t. may arise between my Executour & y_e Legates above said about ye premises aforesaid.

Lastly. I ordain and appoint my Son Simon Tainter the sole Executour of this my last Will and Testament, to whome I give and bequeath all the rest of my estate, both houses, Lands, Chattles, depts from whomsoever due and to his Heirs forever.

In confirmation wherof I have herunto set my hand & seall this 18 of February Anno Dom. 16$\frac{89}{93}$.

JOSEPH TAYNTER.

Witnessed by us
JOHN STONE
NATHANIEL STONE

INVENTORY.

"This is an Inventory of the whole Estate of Joseph Tainter senior of Watertown, who dyed the 20th of February Anno Dom 16⅜⅜, taken this 11th of March of the beforenamed date.

	£.	s.	0.
In CASH	34	01	00
wearing Apparrell of all sorts	05	01	0d

In the Lodging Roome.

A feather bed with all belonging to it, with bedsted, curtains & vallance, as it stands	07	00	00
A trundle bed-stid with a feather bed & what belongs to it as it stands	03	00	00
A Fine pair of sheets : seven pillow coates	01	00	00
Three tables cloathes, Eighteen napkins, six towels	02	08	00
One Chest, two boxes, two chairs, two cushions	00	12	00
A warming pann, A glas case with a parcel of glas bottles	00	07	00
A wodden mortar, A parcel of trenchers	00	05	00
A parcel of Books	01	10	00
A piece of black cloath	00	10	00

In the Fire Roome.

Twenty pewter platters, Six pewter porringers, one pewter flagon, one pewter drinking pott, four pewter drinking cups, two cups of tin, two basins of pewter, three pewter platters, one candle stick, one saltseller, one little bottle all of pewter, & a pewter chamber-pot, four saucers	03	00	00
Two brasse kettles, two brasse poles, two skillits of brasse, a little brasse mortar & pestle, a brasse candlestick, a brasse skimer & baleing ladle	02	10	00
Two iron pots, one iron kittle, an iron mortar & pestle, an Iron candlestick, an Iron skillit, two paire of pott hooks, a spit, a paire of coh irons, two tramels fire pan & tongs, a grid iron	02	05	00
Two small tables, fower chairs, a smoathing box, Eleven vessels of chiny ware, a dosen of trenchers, A fowling piece, two muskets, a case of pistals with holsters, fower swords with scabbardes and belts, two pair of bandolers* with ammunition	05	04	00

In the Chamber.

A feather bedd with the bedstead and apertanances to it, as it stands	03	10	00
A flock bedd with the beddstead and the appertinances to it, as it stands	02	00	00
Several small remnants of new cloath	01	05	00
Two moos-skins ready dressed, and a parcel of small skins	03	00	00
One chest, two trunks & a parcel of buttons In one of the trunks	02	10	00

Furniture for a hors, as bridles, saddles, pannels and a wodden bason, and a small lot of waiters	01	10	00
A parcel of ground malt and rie	01	15	00

In the Cellar.

Two powdring tubs with in them	03	00	00
A quantity of tryed suet, a parcel of butter, A parcell of Cheeses, Nine barrels of Sider, Six empty barrels and other lumber	04	10	00

All utencels for housbandry as carts, yoakes, chains, wheels, axes, krows, beetles, wedges, sickels, saws and old iron	6	08	00
Hay and corn in the barn	4	00	00
Three horses, two about three years old, one sucking colt	12	00	00
Two oxen, seven cowes, two steers of three years old, three coming three years old, two of a year old	32	00	00
Five young swine	02	00	00

A Dweling house and barn with two small orchards & about eighteen Acres of land adjoyning to it	100	00	00
Six acres of land comonly cailed Benjamins lott & part of Bakers	20	00	00
Six Acres of land lying near to the land of John Knop	20	00	00
Ten acres of land lying near by the Meetinghous with an Orchard to it	30	00	00
Sixteen acres of land near the fresh pond	30	00	00
Eight acres of land lying between the County highway and the Widow Hagers	16	00	00
A farm of about an hundred and sixty acres lying remote	10	00	00
Another farm of about fifty acres	03	00	00
Two acres of meadow at Bever Brook	05	00	00
Five acres of meadow near the great plain	05	00	00
Twelve acres of meadow near to Samuel Saltinstals meadow	04	00	00
Seven acres of meadow lying on a branch of Stones brooke	14	00	00
Five acres of meadow lying near to Thomas Wilsons	10	00	00
Six acres of meadow lying in the great meadow			
	£444	06	00

Apprized the day & year above named by us   WILLIAM BOND senior
HENRY SPRING senior
SIMON STONE senior
JOHN STONE senior

* Ancient cartridge boxes, being a belt of raw hide filled with wooden bottles, each containing a charge of powder.

MISCELLANEOUS ITEMS.

THE summer of 1638 was marked by an unusual number of arrivals from England. Winthrop says as many as 20 ships.

9th of the 7th mo. 1641, Nicholas Guye and Joseph Tainter witnessed the will of Richard Carver of Watertown, and testified before the Governor, JOHN WINTHROP.

10th of 12th mo., 1654. Writ agst. Thomas Arnold & Jno. Warren sen., for neglect of worship.   JOSEPH TAYNTER, Const.

(Copy of a paper in the hand-writing of Joseph Taynter.)

The 26th 9 mo. 1657.

Rec of * Ensigne John Sherman, John Livermore & hanah Hamond, executors to Tho: Hamonds estate in the yeare 1653, the som of twenty-five pound, wch estate Thomas Hamond Rec^d, of me hanah Crose in his life time, of wch som of twenty five pounds I doe acquite & discharg the aforesaid debtors & ther heires & assignes of the aforesaid som of twenty five pound I say

Recⁿ.

Witness,   by me, Anna Crose
    Ric. Beeres   my × marke
    John Coollidge
        Joseph Taynter.

30 of 9th mo., 1659. At Charlestown, Before three jurors, Thomas Underwood, Joseph Tainter and Richard Satle, one Waite was indicted for drunkenness on Election day at Boston.

Oct. 1660, Mr. William Paine of Boston, made his will, in which he makes bequests to several friends, among others unto Mr. Joseph Tainter, 10£.
The will concludes—" I doe request M^r. Christopher Clark, M^r. Joseph Tainter, and M^r. Oliver Purches, to bee my overseers, in trust of this my will."

Sept. 1675. " In the meantime a few Praying and other Indians had been captured, and were in prison at Boston, and the following named gentlemen were chose by the Town to sit as jurors at their trial, namely, Capt Ja^s. Oliver, M^r. Thomas Deane, Ens. Richard Woody and M^r. John Fairweather——M^r. David Anderson and M^r. Thomas Tucker were chosen by Charlestown, John Bowles Senr. and M^r. Thomas Gore by Roxbury—M^r. William Sumner and M^c. Richard Baker for Dorchester, and M^r. Joseph Tantor and Corp. William Bond for Watertown."—Drake's Antiquities of Boston.

1681. Dec. 20, William Bond, Joseph Tainter and Simon Stone sen^r., were appointed by the Court to divide Mr. Phillips estate, they reported April 3, 1682, and the next day, Ap. 4, Capt. John Sherman, W^m. Bond and Simon Stone were appointed to divide the estate of Mistress Phillips, among her children. They reported that nothing could be done.—Bond.

1682. Zorobabel Phillips lived at Long Island in Ap. 1682, and Joseph Tainter of Watertown was his Attorney in regard to his right in his parents estate, &c.—Bond.

A few years ago an old stone was re-cut and placed in the old burying-ground at Watertown, to the memory of Joseph Taynter. But a few, if any, of the original stones dating back to 1691, are to be found there at the present time.

In Memory of
Mr. JOSEPH
TAYNTER, an early
settler of Watertown,
who sailed from
England April, 1638,
departed this life
February 20 1689–90
Æ. 77 Years.
" Each in his narrow cell forever laid,
The rude forefathers of the hamlet sleep."

---

* Killed at the Swamp fight, in 1675.

FIRST GENERATION,

FROM ENGLAND.

(1) **Joseph Taynter,** born 1613 } married about 1640, { died 1690, æ. 77.
    Mary Guy, born 1619 } { died 1705, æ. 86.

THEIR CHILDREN WERE THE

SECOND GENERATION.

(2) **Mary,**   b. ———; m. [William?] Pollard [of Boston?].
(3) **Ann,**   b. yᵉ 2ᵈ day 7th month, 1644.
(4) **Joseph,**   b. yᵉ 2ᵈ day 7th month, 1645 ; lived a bachelor ; d. Aug. 7, 1728, æ. 83.
(5) **Rebecca,**   b. yᵉ 18th day 6th month, 1647.
(6) **Benjamin,** b. yᵉ 22ᵈ day 11th month, 1650 ; m. Mary ———.
(7) **Jonathan,** b. yᵉ 10th day 7th month, 1654 ; m. Elizabeth, daughter of Daniel Warren,
                   of Watertown, Dec. 6, 1681. She died June 14, 1692. He m. 2d, Mary
                   Randall, of Watertown, March 5, 1702 [3?], d. 1712, æ. 58.
(8) **Sarah,**   b. yᵉ 20th day 11th month, 1657 ; m. Elnathan, son of Capt. Richard Beers,
                   who was killed in the Philip's war. They lived in Watertown, and had
                   five children.
(9) **Simon,**   b. yᵉ 30th day 7th month, 1660 ; m. Joanna, daughter of Deacon John Stone,
                   of Watertown, May 9, 1693 ; d. Jan. 19, 1738-9, æ. 67.
(10) **Dorothy,** b. yᵉ 13th day 7th month, 1663 ; m. John Taylor [son of Rev. John Taylor,
                   of Concord?].

(3 & 5) **Ann** and **Rebecca,** daus. of Joseph Taynter, were living in 1666, as appears by the will of their grandmother Guy ; but as they were not mentioned in their father's will, and as we have found no further trace of them, it may be presumed that they had died in the meantime, probably unmarried.

(6) **Benjamin Taynter,** says Ward, "lived in Sudbury with his wife Mary in 1691." But I have been unable to learn much concerning him ; the Sudbury Records make no mention of his name. His name appears with his brother's, on the list of those mustered to serve in the Philip's war, 1675, and by his father's will it appears that he was living at the time of his death in 1690. Mr. Charles M. Tainter has in his possession a book, printed in 1661, entitled "*An Explanation of the Grounds of Religion.*" On the inside is written This probably belonged to him, though it may have belonged to his nephew, Benjamin (12), who is supposed to have sailed in one of the

HIS BOOK, ANNO DOMINY 1705.

King's ships. On the same cover is also written, three years after, "WILLIAM PATTEN, His Book. In 1708." He (Patten) was of Cambridge and Billerica,* and a search in Billerica might result in our learning more of Benjamin Tainter, but it is not probable that he left male descendants.

---

* Here lyes buried yᵉ body of Deacᵃ William Pattin, of Billerica, who died Octobʳ 5th Anno Domi 1730, in yᵉ 60 year of his age.—*Cambridge Epitaph.*

Joseph Tainter, Jr., who lived a bachelor, refused to serve in the Philip's war. Capt. Mason complained of him to the Council in Boston, and he was summoned to appear.

From the papers on the subject, it appears that three of the four sons were put on the muster roll, who thought it unjust that but one, and he the youngest, aged only 15, should be left at home to manage the farm; their father and "many of the neighbors" maintained that it was unjust.

As the want of men was great,* it is probable that the Council sustained Capt. Mason, and Joseph Tainter, senr., agreed to go himself, instead, or send a substitute. He sent a substitute named Clarke.

"February 1, 1714–15. Received of Joseph Tayntor of Marlboro', administrator to Jonathan Tayntor's estate in Watertown, the sum of eight pounds four shillings, i say received by me

Joseph Taynsor

OF WATERTOWN.

He died in 1728, æt. 83, his inventory amounting to £231 14s. 3d.

"Administration on the Estate of Joseph Taynter (4), late of Watertown, in the County of Middlesex, who died intestate, is committed unto Simon Tainter [his brother], of sᵈ Watertown, Yeoman, and he hath given Bond in Six hundred pound, William Morse of Cambridge in sᵈ County, Blacksmith, Surety. Done at Cambridge 26 of Aug. 1728. Jonᴺ Remington, Jᵈ. prob."

"An Inventory of all and singular the Goods & Credits, Lands and Tenements of Mr. Joseph Tayntor, late of Watertown, in the County of Middlesex, Deceased, Intestate, Taken by us the subscribers the 2d of September, 1728, as followeth, Viz.

Ten ounces of Silver	£		Benjamin Hastings	9	00	0
In Copper mony 7s. 3d. In			Simon Taintor, Jr.	4	00	0
bills of Credit 2s.	9	3	John Taintor	7	04	0
Due by Bond to said Estate,			Nathan Ball	5	00	0
Principle Debt not allow-			Samuel Barnard (in silver			
ing the interest, as follows,			money)	3	00	0
from			Due from Mr. Caleb Churches			
Edward Saunderson	3 8 6		Estate Book Debt	1	09	6
John Chadwick	3 10 0		In Wearing Apparel	13	00	0
George Cutting	10 00 0		A Sword, Rasour, &c.		13	0
Rebekah Livermore	5 00 0					
Simon Tainter, senr.	11 00 0		Personal Estate	£79	14	3
Ephraim Cutter, senr.	3 00 0					

In Real Estate as follows

A Lott called Guyes Lott, nine Acres	140	00	0
A Lott of Meadow Land two Acres	12	00	0

ABRAHAM BROWN, }
NATHAN FISK,   } Appraisers.
JOHN COOLIDGE, }

£231 14 3

SIMON TAYNTER, Administrator.†

---

* In the Philip's war, when all the Indian tribes had conspired together to exterminate the white men, every able-bodied man in New England was called upon to defend their homes and families from the savage foe.

† Simon Tainter signed the Administrator's Bond at Cambridge by making his mark, but signed the above Inventory by writing his name. This is the only instance, where one of the name signed thus, excepting Joseph Taynter, senior, who signed his will two days before his death, probably in bed, with a mark, and in the case of Capt. John Tainter, who signed the codicil to his will, probably under like circumstances, by a mark, having previously signed the Will with his name.

In early times, as a great many were unable to write, persons making out papers would often make them out in full, with a "His mark" attached, leaving a space to be filled with a mark, by the signing party, who would insert a cross, even though they were able to write their names. In some instances, it appears that the signing parties, instead of making a mark, have indignantly struck out the "His mark," and in a bold hand wrote their name beneath.

Jonathan Taynter, [7]

Of Watertown, born 1654, was out in the King Philip's war, and was at the "great swamp fight" in 1675.* He married Elizabeth, daughter of Daniel Warrin, of Watertown, in 1681, and held several of the minor offices in town. His wife died in 1692, leaving four children. He married, second, Mary Randall, who survived him and married John Tucker, of Boston. ' Jonathan Taynter died in 1712, æ. 58. His estate consisted of "one Mansion House, eight acres of land, 1 mare, 1 cow, etc." From the inventory of his effects we should judge that he was a carpenter.

FAMILY.

(11) **Jonathan,** b. July 12, 1682; m. Mary Butcher, in Boston, Dec. 12, 1711.
(12) **Benjamin,** b. June 20, 1685, fate unknown. (*I think I have heard my father say that he had an uncle named Benjamin, and who was a seaman, had sailed on board a hundred and twenty gun ship, had been in great battles, &c.*" [J. T. 1847.]
(13) **Joseph, (Deacon)** b. May 25, 1688, m. Thankful Barrett, of Marlboro', April 20, 1715 ; d. Feb. 19, 1764, æ. 76.
(14) **Elizabeth,** b. ——; m. Hezekiah How, of Marlboro', 1715.
(15) **Randall,** b. Jan. 21, 1703–4; d. July 15, 1705.
(16) **Susanna,** b. May 30, 1705.
All born in Watertown.

Simon Taynter, [9]

Of Watertown, farmer, youngest son of Joseph and Mary, inherited the homestead and greater part of his father's property, and was executor to the will. He married Johanna, dau. of Dea. John Stone of Watertown, Aug. 9, 1693.

In 1713 he made as a free gift to the children of his deceased brother, a house, or £60 in lieu thereof, if they preferred it.

He was a man of means, and was pious and charitable. He made no will, but deeded his property to his heirs a few years before his death, having previously converted a part of it into personal property.

He was chosen at various times, Tythingman, Constable, Surveyor, &c., and did considerable public business in town. There are copies of deeds in the Middlesex Registry of Deeds Office signed by him, he being on a committee ten years for laying out and making sale of the common or undivided lands in Weston.

He died Jan. 19, 1738–9, aged 68.   *Simon Taynter*

FAMILY.

(17) **Simon, (Deacon)(Lieut.)** b. Feb. 28, 1693–4; m. Rebecca Harrington, of Watertown, May 25, 1714; went to Westboro', d. 1767, æ. 73.
(18) **Mary,** b. Jan. 24, 1695–6; d. Jan. 13, 1697–8.
(19) **John, (Deacon) (Captain)** b. March 13, 1698–9; m. Johanna Harrington, May 25, 1720; d. [Oct.?] 1768, æ. 69.
(20) **Rebecca,** b. May 26, 1701; d. Dec. 14, 1715, æ. 14.
(21) **Mary,** b. Nov. 27, 1703; m. Benjamin Hastings, of Watertown, April 14, 1726; had five children; she d. Feb. 18, 1765, æ. 62.
(22) **Dorathy,** b. May, 1706; m. Daniel Whitney, of Watertown, in 1722; d. Aug. 7, 1788, aged 82. They had fourteen children. One of her sons, Elisha, a graduate at Harvard College in 1766, was a surgeon in the Revolutionary Army, physician in Hamilton and Beverly, and died in 1807.

* The swamp fight happened on a severe cold night in December, in which about 50 English were killed in the action and died of their wounds or of the severity of the storm and cold. Three hundred or 350 Indians, men women and children, were killed, and as many more captivated. It is said 500 wigwams were burned with the Indian Fort, and 200 more in other parts of Narraganset.

The place of the Fort was on an elevated ground, or piece of upland, of perhaps 3 or 4 acres, situated in the middle of a hideous swamp, about 7 miles nearly due west from Narraganset south ferry (now Warwick, R. I.).

See Drake's History of the Philip's War, which concludes thus :

"The sufferings of the English after the fight are almost without parallel in history. The horrors of Moscow, with the myriads of modern Europe assembled there, bear but small proportion to the number of their countrymen, compared with that of the army of New England and theirs, at the fight in Narraganset."

Agreement of 63 of the Inhabitants of Watertown to Rev. Mr. Sturgeon, 11 Jan., 1721-2.

WE the subscribers, Inhabitants of Watertown, in the County of Middlesex, in the Province of the Massachusetts Bay in New England, being sensible of the DUTY we owe to our SUPERIORS, would be always ready to testifie the same by giving unto their PUBLICK DIRECTIONS and to many of us: as were then of Capacity did with a Christian unanimity and Cheerfulness come into that Order of Superiour authority that appointed the Meeting and House for the publick WORSHIP OF GOD in a Central place in Watertown, where the whole town, (Weston now so called excepted) might meet for public worship.——

The House was accordingly Erected at the place appointed, and the Rev. Mr. Samuel Angier was called to the Church of Christ in Watertown and there settled in the work of the ministry, and did abide therein till he could no longer by Reason of Death.

It is well known that the charge of building that House and supporting the Ministry at the Place afores^d. did lye principally upon some of us the subscribers; and furthermore for the accommodation of ye ministry to the s^d place, We have purchased an house and land & devoted it to a ministerial use. We have been carried on in this great work, we hope with a Just Regard unto the glory of GOD, the SPIRITUAL BENEFIT AND EDIFICATION of our selves, and our DEAR POSTERITY.——

After many years of enjoyment the great and General Court or Assembly did in the year past order the removing of both Meeting houses or building of new ones, which Direct the Removal of ye PUBLICK WORSHIP into other places, and we would not be thought to offer anything that should look contemptious or Rebellious thereunto, nor carry any Reflections in it upon the wisdom and authority of ye Court, and pray that which we here bind our selves unto may not be Interpreted that way by any publick or private person whatsoever. Nevertheless we being desirous of having the CONVENIENCE of GODS WORSHIP continued unto us, as we have enjoyed for many years by the favour of GOD and of the GOVERNMENT, We who have hereunto subscribed our Names do now most cheerfully and peaceably with all possible DEFERENCE unto PUBLICK AUTHORITY enter into the most Solemn and Strongest Obligations, one with another by these present and Declare Our Selves and our Estates to be holden and firmly bound by these present, unto the REV. MR. ROBERT STURGEON, in the Sum of ONE THOUSAND POUNDS Current money of New England, to the payment whereof unto him the s^d Rev. Mr. Robert Spirgeon his heirs, assigns or lawful Attorney, We bind Our Selves and our Estates firmly by these present, signed in Watertown this Eleventh day of January, 172½ in the Eighth Year of his Majesty's Reign.

Thomas Straight, Simon Tainter, Richd Sawtell, Joshua Warrin, Edwd. Harrington, Saml Pearce, Joseph Harrington, Thos Willington, George Harrington, Saml Barnard, Jno. Pierce, Phillip Shattuck, Sen., John Parkest, Thos. Hastings, George Lawrence, Junr., Jno. King, Benj^a. Shattuck, Saml. Hastings, Isaac Church, Eben^r Wellington, Jon^a. Harrington, John Dix, And^w White, Nathl. Bowman, John Stearnes, Jno Ormes (?) Willm. Hastings, Joshua Warrin, Junr., Nathaniel Stearnes, Daniel Whitney, Saml. Stearnes, Joseph Willington, Daniel Far(?), Jno Smith, Phillip Shattuck, Jun., Amos Shattuck, James Barnard, John Bemis, Joshua Biglo, Joseph Shattuck, Saml, Hagar, Simon Taynter, Junr., Zachariah Cutting, John Parker, Daniel Harrington, Joseph Taintor, John Taintor, John Phillips, Caleb Church, James Barnard, Junr., Isaac Stearnes, John Barnard, John Hastings, Richard Clark, Saml. Parkhurst, Benj^a Whitney, Junr, And^w White, Jun., Nathl Clark, John Fisk, John Fisk, Jun., Saml. Whitney, David Whitney, Benja. Whitney.

"STURGEON.—Rev. Robert Sturgeon was one of those who officiated some time in the church gathered by Rev. Mr. Angier. He had some strenuous opposers in the town, but was sustained by the church, or a large part of it, embracing many of the most respectable persons in the town. Jan. 11, 1721--2, sixty-three of the substantial citizens signed an obligation to pay him a salary of £84 per annum. Aug. 28, 1722, caution by the selectmen of Watertown against (the settlement of) "Robert Sturgeon," who came from Woburn, Dec. 1721.—Jan. 9, 1722--3, information was lodged against him, and he was obliged to give bonds for his appearance at Court. At the Court, Mar. 12, 1722--3, the Grand Jury found an indictment against him, charging him with "preaching and administering the Holy Ordinances, and acting as a pastor to the pretended Church in Watertown," and "continuing his wicked and malacious inclinations to overthrow, ruin, and subvert, as well the Churches of said Watertown as the other Churches of this province, here hapily and religiously established," &c. &c. He was found guilty, and fined £20 and costs, appealed and gave as security Ebenezer and Thomas Wellington.*—Bond.*

[See Note, opposite page.]

FOURTH GENERATION.

1716 — 1748.

BEING THE CHILDREN OF

Deacon JOSEPH TAYNTER, of MARLBOROUGH.

Deacon SIMON TAINTER, of WESTBOROUGH.

Deacon JOHN TAINTER, of WATERTOWN.

Soon after the decease of Mr. Angier, a controversy arose about a division of the town into two precincts, and about the location of the two meeting houses. These subjects were referred to the General Court, who appointed a committee of 3 of the Council, and 4 of the House of Representatives; and they reported, Dec. 3, 1720, the boundary between the two precincts (which was surveyed Dec. 13) ; and that the New or Western [Mr. Angier's] meeting-house, shall be removed within two years to the rising ground 20 rods west of Nathaniel Livermore, or a new one built, and that within ten years, the old or East meeting house to be removed, or a new one built on School House Hill. Ap. 29, 1721, at a town meeting, it was voted to remove the meeting houses. Many of those best accommodated with the Angiers meeting house where it was, were not disposed to accept or comply with the report of the committee, and determined to maintain worship, where it had been done for about 25 years.

For this purpose, they employed Mr. Sturgeon, as their pastor, and his concurrence in their purpose appears to have been the only ground of the heinous charges brought against him.—*Bond*.

𝕯𝖊𝖆𝖈𝖔𝖓 𝕹𝖎𝖈𝖍𝖔𝖑𝖆𝖘 𝕲𝖚𝖞, was from Upton-Gray, Southamptonshire, England (and it is probable that Joseph Tayntor was from the same locality, though it may not have been his native place). He was 50 years of age at the time of his embarkation, consequently was 61 years of age at the date of his death, July 1, 1649. His wife, Jane, was 30 years of age, and was doubtless his second wife. Their daughter, Mary, who became Joseph Taynter's wife, was aged 19. This is all the family that appears to have come over in the Confidence, though there appears to have been another daughter, Maria, or *Mary*, who married Henry Cuttriss [Curtis], of Sudbury, and with whom Mrs. Guy spent the last years of her life (died 1666). She might have been *her* daughter by a *former* husband, while J. T.'s wife was Deacon Guy's daughter by a former wife. There is a probability that both of their names were Mary.

Administration on the Estate of Jonathan Taynter, (7) late of Watertown, in the County of Middlesex, Dec^d. intestate, was committed unto his son Joseph Taynter of Marlboro', in ye s^d County, and Bonds taken for his fidelity in £200 at Camb. Feb. 2^d, 1713.   DAN FOXCROFT, *Reg^r*.

An Inventory of the Estate of Jonathan Taynter of Watertowne, apprized 30 January, 1713.

Arms, £1; his wearing apparrel, woollen & linen & some books, £5,	6 00 0
Sundry Furniture*	3 00 0
Tuter, bras tramel, fire hooks, tongs, iron pot, skillet & warming pan	2 10 0
Coop tools £1—3 old chairs, 2 chests, 2 boxes and some old Lumber, £1	2 00 0
3 bls of Syder, 30s.; 1 Cow, 50s.; 1 mare, £3; 4 young swine, 30s.	8 10 0
One small Mansion House and about 8 acres of Land, part arrable, part wood and feeding Land	160 00 0
Abt. 500 of new and old Boards, 20s.; 500 of board and Shingle Nails 5s.	1 05 0
Appprized by	$183 05 0

Benj. Gearfeld, Jno. Fisk, Maning Sawing.
Some small debts Due to the Estate and some fro it.

"Joseph Taynter now admitted to Adm^r. on his late father's Estate, does exhibit this as a full Inventory of his Estate, Except such movables as came by his mother in Law Mary, w'ch she hath agreed wth this Adm^r. and his sister Elizabeth of full age to accept, that is, so much as are now left, and ten pounds besides in a years time, hence, in lieu of her thirds or dower in the said Dec^d real & personal Estate, and hereby quit her claim in full of her right of Dowry and now declares the same before me, and also promises to provide at her owne cost for Susanne her only Child by her deceased husband Taynter, and that his Estate shall be at no charge for her bringing up, her share in his Estate is hereby saved to divide with the rest, and the Land and house being the free gift of their Unckle Simon Taynter, and no deed or legal conveiance yet having been made, he promises to make and execute a deed but gives it to the Deceased's four children equally to be divided, and this he does now declare before me Maning Sawin and W^m. Shattuck. Simon Taynter moreover now sayes he will pay Sixty pound in money to the said Administrator for him to account for in his father's Estate but still sayes it shall be equaly divided as afores^d. Done at Cambridge 2 Feb 1713.
        FRA. FOXCROFT, *J. probate.*
        Note, the £60 aboves^d. is in lieu of the afore s^d. house & land
                                        F. F.—J. Prob.

Guardianship to Susannah, a daughter of Jonathan Tayntor, late of Watertowne in ye County of Middlesex, A minor in her ninth year of age is committed to Mary Tayntor ye s^d deceasd's widow, bond is taken in £50, Cambridge first of February 1714.   Att   F. FOXCROFT — J. prob.

Deacon Joseph Tainter, (13)

Of Marlboro', was born in Watertown. He went, when a lad, to Marlboro', with a Mr. Morse, who had bought one of the Marlboro' farms, then a new plantation. In 1715, he married Thankful Barrett, of M.

A story of him has been handed down through his descendants, which is somewhat remarkable, and perhaps as difficult for the present generation to believe as stories of the Salem witchcraft. "A number of young ladies went out to make an afternoon visit, and he knowing the time in the evening and the path by which they were to return, took a sheet, went out into the woods beside the path, and wrapped himself up in it, in order to scare them, but did not succeed ; for when he had the sheet around him, he could not stir a step until he had taken the sheet off ; he could give no reason why, but supposed that an Almighty power prevented. Under the influence of this, he was converted, and afterwards became a deacon of the Church."

A notable mortality occurred in his family ; four of his children are recorded to have died within three weeks, two of which on the same day.

He died Feb. 19, 1764, in the 77th year of his age. Just before his death, he writes to his son Benjamin, under date of Marlboro', Jan. 2, 1764. It is an excellent production, and breathes the spirit of a kind and affectionate father, and its orthography, style and penmanship are worthy the effort of a modern scholar.

Marlboro', Jan. 2d, 1764.

DEAR CHILD,—Such is my Age and such my bodily state, That its probable this may be the last Epistle that you will have opportunity of receiving from me, and therefore hope you will regard it accordingly.

Believe it, tis the tenderest regard of a fathers heart for your real comfort and Eternal happiness, which dictate every sentiment and word in it, and my request and even charge to you is, That in all things and thro' out your whole Life you give the preference to Religion, and shew it by attending on all Branches of it, PUBLICK, PRIVATE & SECRET ; To GOD, your neighbor and yourself—as this was the main end of your existence, let it be the main concern of your life. Converse frequently and Seriously wth. the word of Life which is able and was Given to Save your undying Soul. Talk of them when you lie down and when you set up, in the House and by the Way, and teach them to your Children. —— In particular let not yours be a prayerless house. I am jealous over you on this account, but perswade myself you will not continue thus to depart from the way of the Lord, but endeavor to walk in this and all other God's Commandments and ordinances blameless. Do this as you would not greave me, but what is far more, as you would not displease your Heavenly Father, whose favour is life. Do it, for then it shall be well with you and your Children forever and ever.

From y^r Decaying, concerned Father

Inscription on Grave Stone at Marlboro'.

In Memory of Deacon
JOSEPH TAYNTER, who
(*served Twenty two Years in*
ye Church) died February
ye 19th A.D. 1764, in ye
77th year of his age.

The stroke of *Death* hath laid my head
Down in this *dark* and *silent* bed.
The *Trump* shall *sound*, I hope to rise,
And meet my SAVIOUR in the skies.

Joseph Tainter

For Mr. Benjn: Tainter, in Princeton. These.

FAMILY.

(23) **John,**   b. Nov. 1, 1716 ; m. Hannah Goodell, of M., Jan. 6, 1739-40, and Sarah Ward, of Shrewsbury, May 20, 1741 ; d. 1805, æ. 88.

(24) **Elizabeth,** b. April 8, 1719 ; m. a Mr. Smith, of Boylston, Mass.

(25) **Hannah,**   b. Feb. 19, 1721-2 ; unmarried.

(26) **Jonathan,** b. Jan. 7, 1724 ; m. Sarah, daughter of Benj. Woods, of M., Nov. 18, 1755 ; d. June 9, 1803, æ. 84.

(27) **Joseph,**   b. April 4, 1726 ; d. Feb. 28, 1739-40, æ. 13.

(28) **Zerviah,**   b. Feb. 4, 1728 ; unmarried.

(29) **Miriam,**   b. Nov. 21, 1729 ; d. Feb. 11, 1739-40.

(30) **Benjamin,** (**Deacon**) b. Jan. 3, 1733 ; m. Sarah Brigham, of M., June 4, 1755 ; died 1798, æ. 65.

(31) **David,**   b. Jan. 3, 1735 ; d. Feb. 15, 1739-40, æ. 4.

(32) **Mary,**   b. Feb. 15, 1737 ; d. Feb. 11, 1739-40, æ. 2.

All born in Marlboro'.

WILL OF DEACON JOSEPH TAYNTER, OF MARLBORO'.

In the name of God Amen. The Twelfth day of December, 1763, I Joseph
Taynter of Marlboro', in the County of Middlesex in the Province of the Massachusetts Bay in New England, Tailour, being weak in Body but of perfect mind
& memory, thanks be to God. Therefore calling to mind the mortallity of my
Body & knowing it is appointed for man once to die, Do make & ordain this
my last Will & Testament. That is to say. Principally and first of all I give
& Recommend my Soul into the hands of God that gave it, & my Body I Recommend to the Earth to be *Buried* in Decent Christian Manner at the discretion of my Executor, hoping at the Ressurrection to Receive it again by the
Mighty Power of God, & as touching such Worldly Estate wherewith it hath
pleased God to Bless me in this life, I give, demise and dispose of the same in
the following manner & form.

Imprimis. I give to my well beloved wife Thankful Tainter the use of the
Eastern or new part of my Dwelling house, so long as she Remains my Widow,
& all my household stuff to be at her dispose forever. It is my Will that my
wife have Two Cows, & that they be well kept for her on the place, Winter &
Summer, by my Executor hereafter mentioned, & it is my Will that my Executor Provide for her & bring into the house fifteen bushels of Indian Corn,
four bushels of Rye, three Bushels of Malt, Two Bushels of Salt, one bushel
of Wheat, Six Barrils of Cyder, & Apples what she needs thro' the year.
Further it is my will that my wife have Provided for her & brought to the
house by my Executor One hundred & sixty pound of Pork, Two hundred &
forty pound of Beaf & Twenty loads of Wood, & that he pay her annually
Eight Shillings to procure her such small Sundries, & all this I mean she should
have so long as she Remains my Widow, & if she dies so, my Executor shal
bury her Decently.

Item. I give to my Eldest Son John Tainter my wearing apparrel & the
Silver Buttons I lent him, besides what he has already Received.

Item. I give to my youngest son Benjamin Tainter one heiffer & my Silver
Buttons on my leather Breeches, besides what he has already Received, & it is
my Will that upon giving his Brother Jonathan Tainter a Note or Bond for
forty pounds, whatever Notes or Debts lye against him should be Cancelled.

Item. I give to my Daughter Elizabeth Smith forty pounds, besides what
she has already Received, to be paid four years after my Decease.

Item. I give to my Daughter Hannah Tainter fifty three pounds six shillings and eight pence, to be paid her three years after my Decease.

Item. I give to my Daughter Zerviah Tainter fifty three pounds six shillings and eight pence,
to be paid her by my Executor three years after my Decease.

Tis my Will that my Two youngest Daughters Hannah & Zerviah, upon their mothers
Decease or Marriage, have the use of one Convenient Room in my house both to keep fire & lodge
in, & to have provided for them sufficient Cellar Room & Ten load of Wood brought to the door
for them by my Executor annually so long as they Remain Single.

Item. I give to my Grand Child Hannah Tainter Six pounds, to be paid her by my Executor
four years after my Decease.

Item. I give to my Grand Child Jedediah Tainter Ten Shillings, to be paid him by my Executor three years after my Decease.

Item. I give to my Son Jonathan Tainter, whom I appoint my sole Executor, all my Real
Estate, Upland & Meadow, Bonds, Notes & Money, with my Dwelling house & Barn, Cyder
Mill, Stock, husbandry utensils, I mean what ever I have in possession Excepting only what I
have already disposed of in this my last Will, he performing & Executing what I have ordered
above & below.

For Lastly, I Will that all my just Debts be paid by my Executor, and do hereby disallow,
Revoke, Disannul all & Every former Testament, Wills, Legacy's, or Bequests, by me any ways
before named, Willed & Bequeathed, Ratifying this & no other to be my last Will & Testament.

In Witness whereof, I have hereunto set my hand & Seal the day & year above written.

Witnessed by THOMAS HOW,   JOSEPH TAINTER [*Seal.*]
            SAMUEL STEVENS,
            ALPHEUS WOOD.

Deacon Simon Tainter, (17)

Of Westboro'*, was born, and lived in Watertown until the year 1726, when he removed to Westboro'. He was admitted to the Church there, April 3d of that year, was chosen deacon in 1757, and died in 1767, æ. 73. Rebecca, his wife, was admitted to the church by letter from Watertown, Jan. 27, 1731 : she survived him, and spent her last days in the family of her grand-son, Joel Tainter, of Millbury.

From the town records of Westboro' it appears that he was chosen a School Committee man, Moderator of town meetings, Assessor, Surveyor of highways, Tythingman, &c.

He was a town officer in Watertown before he removed to Westboro'.

April, 1763, Simon Tainter, gentleman, of Westboro', made his will, in which he bequeathed his "silver cup" to his grand-son Simon,

From Rev. Mr. Parkman's Journal, 1767.

April 2. MY DEAR FRIEND AND BRᴿ, DEACON SIMON TAINTER DYD ! He expired about 11 o'clock a.m. — May G— Sanctify this death in a peculiar manner to me and mine. Tho my good Deacon is gone, yet *GOD* who is all sufficient lives and is unchangeable forever.

April 4. The sorrowful Day of the Funeral of Deacon Tainter ! I prayed among a grt. Concourse of people. Read the Will there to the heirs and some of their Friends,—and delivered it to yᵉ Exʳ Capt Baker of Bolton. O that the impressions by yᵉ Providence may be deep & abiding.

April 5. I read Isai. 51. Preached a. m. on the occasion of the Sorrowful Death, on 1 Thess. 4-18, read also 14, but could not handle that. Capt Tainter of Watertown and his sisters Hastings and Whitney dined here.—P.M. read John 16 and gathered up from divers parts of Sermon on Isa. 57-1-2 a Discourse on the same mournful Occasion and subjoined some character of yᵉ Deacon, and wish it may be without offence and profitable !

April 6. Drew up some *account of Deacon Tainter* and Delivered it to Mr. Danl. Whitney of Watertown to carry it to a printer.

OBITUARY.

Westborough, April 4th, 1767.

This day was interr'd the Remains of Deacon *Simon Tainter,* who expired on the 2d instant, in the 74th year of his age, having been a member of the church in this place nigh one and forty years.

A man of that excellent spirit which ever disposed him to Piety, Charity and universal Usefulness.

His *Piety* was manifested by his high regard to the house of God, his constant attendance there, his esteem of the ordinance and ministers thereof.

His deeds of *Charity* were unstinted, his heart and hands being ever open, to relieve and help, and to supply the necessitous, who now deplore the loss of such a friend and father.

But his *Usefulness* and *Serviceableness* was very noticeable and memorable ; he was of a generous temper, of a public spirit, and was ever ready to all acts of benevolence ; promoting to his utmost, the great interest of true religion, the glory of God, and the kingdom of the glorious Redeemer, in the souls of men.—*Boston Evening Post, Apr.* 13, 1767.

FAMILY.

(33) **Simon,**   b. April 8, 1715 ; m. Mary Bruce, of Westboro', Nov. 20, 1740 ; d. July 17, 1787, æ. 72. She d. Nov. 30, 1781, æ. 62.

(34) **Rebecca,**   b. Jan. 1, 1716-17 ; m. Timothy Warren, of Westboro'.

(35) **Johanna,**   b. Feb. 16, 1717-18 ; m. Joshua Kendall, of Suffield.

(36) **Susanna,**   b. Dec. 18, 1720 ; m. Samuel Baker, of Bolton, Nov. 24, 1747.

(38) **Benjamin,**   b. May 25, 1725 ; m. Hannah Wood, of Somers, Ct. [1748?] ; d. Aug. 1810, æ. 85.

(37) **Jonathan,**   b. Aug. 5, 1723 ; d. July 31, 1744, æ. 21.

The above born in Watertown.

(39) **Sarah,**   b. Aug. 1, 1727 ; m. Joseph Bowker.

(40) **Elizabeth,**   b. Jan. 8, 1729 ; m. Stephen Sadler, of Upton, Nov. 19, 1750.

(41) **Joshua,**   b. Feb., 1733 ; died young.

(42) **Samuel,**   b. May 9, 1736 ; died young.

Born in Westboro'.   * Westboro' was set off from Marlboro' in 1707.

WILL OF DEACON SIMON TAINTER, OF WESTBORO'.

In the name of God Amen. I Simon Tainter of Westboro', in the County of Worcester, in the Province of Masachusetts Bay in New England, Gentleman, although sound in mind yet apprehensive of my bodily Frailty, have made this my Last Will & Testament: In which In the first and main place I give and recomend my immortal Soul into the Hands of God that gave it, and my Body I committ to the Earth, out of which it was formed, to be buryed in such decent manner as my Executor shall see fit; hoping for a Resurrection to Eternal Life thro Jesus Christ our Lord. And as touching such worldly Estate as it hath pleased God to bless me with, I give & dispose of the same in this following manner.

Imprimis. My will is that all my just Debts be truly and fully paid.

Item. I give to my well beloved Wife Rebecca her just Thirds according to Law : That is, of moneys or Debts owing to me, (we having disposed of our real Estate to our Son Benjamin, as appears by a Deed of the same Date with this Instrument,) and the whole of the Household Goods during her Life.

Item. I give unto my son Simon or heir's or Assignes the Sum of Twenty Six pounds, thirteen Shillings & four pence Lawfull money of this Province, to be delivered to him at my Decease — also all my wearing Apparell.

Item. I give unto my Son Benjamin, his Heirs or Assignes, All my Husbandry Tools : having given to him already in other respects what I have thought sufficient.

Item. I give to my Five Daughters, namely Rebecca wife of Timothy Warren, Joanna wife of Joshua Kendall, Susanna wife of Samuel Baker, Sarah wife of Joseph Bowker, & Elizabeth wife of Stephen Sadler, to each of them or their Heirs or Assigns, whatever of Money's I shall leave, or Debts due to me at my Decease (my own Debts to others, being first paid, and such Legacy's or Bequests as are mentioned in this Will, first fulfilled and discharged) to be in equall Proportions to them, and Likewise Half the Neat Cattle which my Son Benjamin shall be in possession of, or the just value thereof, at the Time of my and my Wifes Decease, shall be my said Dauters or their Heirs, in equal Division one with another.

Item. I give unto my Grandson Simon Tainter, the son of my forementioned son Simon, my Silver Cup.

Item. I give and bequeath unto the First Church of Christ in Westboro' aforesaid, of which I am a member, the sum of Six pounds, thirteen shillings & four pence.

Furthermore I do hereby constitute & appoint my son in Law Samuel Baker aforesaid, of Bolton in the County & Province aforesaid, Gentleman, Executor of this my last Will & Testament —— revoking and disannulling all other Wills or Testaments whatsoever, but ratifying and establishing This.

In Witness whereof, & every part of the foregoing Testament, I have hereunto set my Hand & Seal this Seventh Day of April, in the Third year of the Reign of our Sovereign Lord George the Third of Great Britain, *France* and Ireland, King, Defender of the Faith, &c., and in the Year of our Lord one Thousand, Seven hundred & sixty three.

Signed, sealed & declared to be my Last Will & Testament

in presence of DANIEL FORBES,   SIMON TAINTER.
                ELISHA FORBES,
                Eb[r] PARKMAN.

INVENTORY OF SIMON TAINTER, OF WESTBORO', GENTLEMAN, APRIL 16, 1767.

His apparel	£05 18 0
Debts due to the Estate	335 09 9
Household Goods	14 01 5
His stock of Cattle	25 8 0
His husbandry tools	3 7 4
His Horse furniture and Gun	1 15 4
His books	2 9 4
A Silver Cup	1 6 8
Disperate Debts	9 6 8
Sum total,	399 2 6
I add money recd of Benj[n] Tainter	3 2½
A Book	1 4
	£399 7 0½

Westboro', April 21, 1761.   NATH[l] WHITNEY,
                                                      DANIEL FORBES,
                                                      JONA. BOND.

EXTRACTS FROM THE JOURNAL

OF REV. MR. PARKMAN, OF WESTBORO'.

1757.

Jan. 27. Lieut. Tainter came from Boston, and brought wool and cotton for Lucy—he dined with us.

Jan. 27. P. M. Ordered a Church meeting to chose a Deacon instead of Dea. Jon. Forbush, Jr. deceased,—after prayer & acquainting the Church what the Design of the meeting was, I read what the Platform says of Deacons' Business: Votes were brot in,—There appeared 12 out of 25 for Lt. Tainter, six were for Br. Whitney,—five for Danl Forbush,—one for Br. Francis Whipple, & one for Br. Moses Warren. We tryed again, and there were 17 for Br. Tainter. whereupon he was declared Chosen.

May G—. be with his Servt. who has been elected! I cant but look upon him as being, all things considered, the suitablest Person among us for said Office, and hope G— will graciously accept and reward him for his readiness to serve, he having in a distinguished manner a manifest Disposition, and is very helpful to the poor and afflicted.

Jan. 30. Mrs. Hastings & Mrs. Whitney of Watertown (sisters of Lt. Tainter) dined here.

Feb. 14. It was so dark & slippery, that being afoot I called at Lieut. Tainters, supped there, and he accommodated me with horse and lad to wait upon me home.

March 13. I administered the Sact. of the Supper. Deac. Tainter waited (with Deac. Bond). Deac. Tainter and Mr. How dined here.

April 13. My wife rode to Boston to Day, & Lt. Tainter waited on her.

April 15. My wife with Deac. Tainter returns from Boston, and safely, D. G. (*Dei Gracia*, Glory to God.)

May 29. At Dinner were Mrs. Tainter and her daughter Forb.

June 5. The Deacons Tainter & Bond, & Mr. Moses Twitchell, with their wives, dined with us.

July 1. I visited old Mr. Rice, Mr. Joseph Bruce, Le Blane, Deacon Tainter & Bond, but got home to dine with my wife.

July 11. Dined at Mr. Moses Brighams, where I borrowed 25£ old Tenr. This I carryed 22£ 10, of, to Deacon Tainter, hereby returning wt he kindly lent me last Thursday.

Sept. 11. N. B.—Mr. Benjamin Tainters wife dined with us.

Sept. 26. Mr. Winter & his wife P. M. ride to Deacon Tainters. I went with them,—But my wife confined with her lameness which increases.

Sept. 28. Mrs. Tainter yesterday brot and applied a tobacco ointment to my wifes Legg.

Oct. 4. N. B.—Mr. Kendall from Suffield & Mrs. Bowker, heretofore Sarah Tainter, lodged at Mr. Forb. last night.

Oct. 25. Widow Forbush, Deac. Tainter, Bond, & Ensign Harrington bring me 140 feet of boards & some Slabbs for floor of my kitchen chamber.

Oct. 29. Deacon Tainter dines with me.

Oct. 30. At eve. Mr. Tim. Warrin undertook to provide my wood for 35£ old tenr. N. B. Deacon Tainter & Mr. Jonas Twitchell were here & heard wt was agreed to—as did Capt. Wood also.

Nov. 29. Deacon Tainter came & with him Peter Blane, & kill for me a Steer we was wont to be called ye Stagg.

Dec. 1. My wife rode with me to Deacon Tainters, where I preached, text, Psalms 51—11.

Dec. 11. (Sabbath) P. M. Mr. Benjamin Tainter, tything-man, as soon as the Blessing was given, spake aloud to two young women for laughing, &c. in ye time of Divine Sirvice—yy were Abigail Whipple, & Lydia, daughter of James Maynard. Tis matter of great grief yt persons from wm I ought to hope so well shd. behave so ill!

Dec. 22. Deacon Tainter and his son came & kindly killed an hog for me—wt 239¼, and the Deacon came at night, cut it out and salted it.

1758, Jan. 20. This important day for studying was greatly interrupted by both Mrs. Tainters, wo came to make cake & biskitt for my wife. Deacon Tainter & his Daughter Warren here at Evng. Their kindness & service verry acceptable had this been at anor Time.

Jan. 30, P.M. Mr. Ebenezr Whitney comes with a Whirry & carries me to Deacon Tainters whr a No. of ye Brethrn meet with Robt. Cook to confer with him about his confession.

Feb. 10. Deacon Tainter goes to Boston & carrys the Genealogist acct of or Family, (containing ye acct. of my fifteenth child Hannah) to my eldest Brother.

Feb. 28. Deacon Tainter puts my mare into his team to teach her to draw.

March 1. Deacon Tainter having kept my mare, comes with her & another in a sleigh or whirrey, to accompany me to Southboro. We called at Dr. Chase's, but he was not at home, and to see ye French pp at Southboro,—I cant but take special notice of the Deacon's readiness to serve & waite upon me, in a very respectful manner, and in the mean time is doing me the Grt. Kindness to Subdue my new mare to drawing. I hope he does all sincerely, & as to ye L (ord), for I am utterly unworthy,—but this conduct must quicken me to endeavor to deserve it. May G. reward him with abundt Spl. Blessings!

March

1758.

March 2, P.M. Deacon Tainter comes again with my mare in his whirry, and we go to ye Private meeting at Mr. Bradock's. At eve Dea. takes my mare home still to keep and tutor.

March 10, Mr. Sol. Woods here & tells me he is going over to Mr. Whipples with Benj. Tainter to endeavor a reconcilement.

June 11. Deacon Tainter & his wife (and others) Dined here.

June 21. Dea. Tainter came & invited me and my wife to dinner, we accgly. dined there. N. B. yy had dressed a very large Pigg to entertain us.

Sept 11. Deacon Tainter Dines here.

Sept. 13. Deac. Tainter observably careful to have me supplyed with fresh meat, &c.

Oct. 22. Deacon Tainter & his wife, Mrs. Bond, Mrs. Steward & the Widow Patience Forbush dined here. O, y^t G— w^d be gracly Pleased to bless such Opportunitys for or saving advantage.

Oct. 30. N. B. Capt. Wood here at Eveng,—also Capt Tainter from Watertown.

Nov. 6. Deacon Tainter Brought me a second load of Wood.

Nov. 7. It rained, yet I rode to Sutton, Deacon Tainter with me (to attend a Council.) Mr. Cushing & I Lodged at Mr. Simon Tainters.

Fine Spring like weather,—Deacon Tainter & Judge Ward Dined here.

Dec. 3. After meeting Lt. Whitney of Watertown & his son were here, & Deacon Tainter and his son Warren came in with y^m.

Dec. 14. I rode home, had Deacon Tainters, his Wifes, & Dauter Forbs, company.

Dec. 20. Deacon Tainter goes to Boston & carrys divers sorts of edibles for my wife to markett, Butter, fowls, &c.

Mr. Benjamin Tainter and his wife came after dinner, Drank tea, and tarried till supper—she being much recovered.

Dec. 23. Deacon Tainter returns and brings Sundries from Boston.

1759, Jan. 2. Deacon Tainter kills my fat Heifer, Gamel helps him, and they dine here.

Jan. 4 Mr. Joseph Bowman keeps School at D^a Tainters.

Jan. 12. Deacon Tainter comes & kills a Pig for me, weighs 126 Pound, he comes also kindly at night, & cuts, & salts, & supps.

Feb. 15. Mr. Jon^a Fay returned from Boston,—did not go to Mrs. Hill, but carried the letter to Capt. Tainter, of Watertown, & says he delivered the money to him w^o. said he w^d go to Mrs. Hill, & w^d write me a line of his doings,—at night reckoned with Deacon Tainter, and gave him a note to Mr. Jonn Fay.

Feb. 28. Received, I suppose P. favour of Capt. Tainter of Watert. a letter from Mrs. Providence Hill of Cambridge.

March 6. At eve Deacon Tainter here, tells me he has been to Sutton, & to see Mr. Wellman, who remains very stiff, vindicates himself, & says he has done no evil,—W^c fills me with much grief.

March 13. Deacon Tainter, Mrs. Bond, and Mrs. Burnap dined here.

March 20. Deacon Tainter and Mr. Samuel Grow dined w^h us.

March 29. Deacon Tainter goes to market to Boston, & carrys some things for my wife.

April 13. Deacon Tainter from Boston,—Brot my wife a Bottle of Maderia.

May 2. ——— But Deacon Tainter came and invited me and my wife to dine at his house. Though it was a warm pleasant day, & tho my wife went to the door, yet she did not venture to go so far. I went and dined there.

May 8. I rode to ye Council at Sutton, Deacon Tainter also accompanying me.

May 13. Deacon Tainter, with leave of ye Modr, goes home, but N. B. we voted by Opps. (opposition.) Mr. Fessendon dined here, as did Mrs. Tainter and her sister Harrington of Framingham.

June 12. N. B. Much perplexed and Disapointed in the article of an horse to plough among my corn,—till I ride to Deac. Tainters, who presently told me he had purposed to come to my house upon the very affair. He takes his horse from his own plough, & rides with me, and goes to ploughing in my field.

June 13. Deacon Tainter ploughed in my Island Field.

July 30. Was at Deacon Tainters—at his request I rode with him to Mr. Joseph Rices, to talk with him & his wife on account of their Jerry. He made some acknowledgments—Promised reformat^n & hoped for amendment.

Aug. 1759. Deacon Tainter came & ploughed with my mare, not without turbulent opposition, he worked till middle of afternoon.

Aug. 3. Deacon Tainter came in ye morning and ploughed & sowed awhile, and then went home, his son being not well, and his affairs pressing and urgent.

Sept. 14, P.M. Am sent for to go to Mr. Benja. Tainters wife, w^o is very ill, went and conversed and prayed with her.

Oct. 3. Deacon Tainters Sisters, Hastings & Whitney, call here. Send by ye Deacon a letter to Mr. Draper, printer, an acc. of ye Death of Rev. Mr. Rice of Sturbridge !

Oct. 8. Sarah rides in ye Chair whever ye weather allows. Deacon Tainter brot to her from Boston a few oysters in the shells.   Nov. 2.

1759.

Nov. 2. Mr. Zeb. Rice and after him Deacon Tainter, came here to see whether I thot it probable y^t I should preach next Sabbath, for otherw it was proposed to send for young Mr. Dorr again.

Nov. 6. Mr. Benja. Tainter dined here.

Nov. 14. At eve Mr. Benj. Tainter and his wife w^o have come up from Boston where she has been for a while for her health.

December 13. At eve Deacon Tainter came to see me to discourse about the still Sorrowful Conda of ye PP (people) at North Sutton, he having been lately at Mr. Wellmans and at his sons. The Deacon wants me to write him y^t he maynt be stiff with his antagonists, nor make such sharp remarks upon their letters to him. But I fear my engaging in it will make the matter worse.

Dec. 25. Deacon Tainter, agble to his kind offer, came with his sleigh or whirrey, with two horses, to wait on me and my Daughter Sarah to Marlb. but he had the frenchman, Le Blanc with him to carry him to Marlb. likewise.

1760, Jan. 8. Deacon Tainter brings me an horse to waite on me to Lt. Holloways funeral.

Jan. 16. Deacon Tainter came with his whirrey and two horses to wait on my wife and me in visiting ye west neighbrhood and part of Shrewsbury.

Jan. 21. Deacon Tainter brings Artemas Bruce, and we had sent for Mr. Hez. Pratt to help us kill an Hog—weighed 11 score & 7 pounds; at Eve Mrs. Prudence Hardy and her sister Rice of Sutton and her son Asahel, supped here, as did Deacon Tainter, who not only killed, but cut and salted up my pork.

Feb. 2. Deacon Tainter brings me from Boston. The Deacons neice Miss Molly Whitney comes up with him.

Feb. 21. Mr. Simon Tainter and Mr. Benjamin Carter of Sutton here and acquaint me with their present state, of their parish, &c. Deacon Tainter returns from Boston with a team. His Horses took a start in Framingham and he is wounded sorely in both his leggs, by the Horses kicking him with y^r Corks.

Feb. 25. Visited Deacon Tainter and saw his wounds dressed by Dr. Crosby, dined there.

March 11. My wife and I rode in my sleigh to see Deacon Tainter, who, tis hoped, is in a healing way. Dr. Crosby and Dr. Ball were there, and we saw both leggs dressed.

April 1. Deacon Tainter dines here. N. B. He kindly serves me by putting a new handle to my spade.

April 25. At eve reconed with Deacon Tainter and paid all,—And for 4 load of wood wh are not yet brot.

May 1. Deacon Tainter receives of me ye Contribution money for Boston, £60—2—2 Old tenor.

May 5. Mr. Tainter Brings a team P. M. to harrow my field at the Island—he leaves his boy with Elex. to do it and y^r do it accordly. Mr. Tainter went to a Kenebuk meeting at Capt. Wood.

May 15. My sons go about in vain to get an horse to furrow out or remaining ground, till Mrs. Tainter (Benjs. wife) rode here for this end y^t their horse might plough for me. She dines here and my sons plough, furrowing out and finishing or planting of Indian corn, a few beans, peas, &c.

May 13. Deacon Tainter informs me from Mr. James Fay, that his wife lately dyd of bilious Cholick, and that she dyd gloriously.

July 23. At Deacon Tainters motion a No. of hands came and cut down my Field of rye back of the Meeting-house.

Aug. 1. N. B. Messrs. Kidder and Tainter here from Sutton, and acquaint me how their parish affairs go.

Aug. 22. Deacon Tainter returns from Brookfield.

Sept. 12. My Rowing mowed by Deacon Tainters young man.

Oct. 20. It was my design to have got in my corn last Thursday, but Deacon Tainter and Capt. Wood advised me to let it alone till this day, I therefore did so. To day Mr. Tainter brot a load of wood, and brot in the corn from the Island, being 4 load.

Nov. 1. Deacon Tainter Brings wood and a barrel of Cyder.

Nov. 5. Walked to Deacon Tainters. Breakfast there. N. B. Young Mrs. Tainter shows me a Dream w^c so impressed her y^t she had writ it out, and wanted my judgment of it.

Nov. 21. N.B. I now take Deacon Tainter's Stallion.

Nov. 24. P.M. Mr. Benj. Tainter bears me a Message from Mr. Elijah Rice, who waits upon ye corps & the procession are moving along, requesting I w^d. pray wh. y^m, somewhere — I directed y^m. into the meetinghouse & prayed there.

Dec. 10. Deacon Tainter & Capt. Wood came to kill the Baker Pig, but first weigh it, and tho he had had a good breakfast, yet he weighed but 130. I sent for Mr. Baker w^o. came & on his part tells me he had weighd at home ye pigs he had of me, and tho last night when he weighd them yy. fell short but half a Pound apiece, yet this morning he weighd them, and they fell Short 16 pound. But we left ye affair in ye hands of ye two neighbrs here with us w^o proceeded to kill the Baker Pig.

Dec. 11. Deacon Tainter came and tells me the affair of the Piggs is settled y^t the weight shall be allowd accdg. to w^t. they were at each of their homes, viz., mine 150 and Mr. Baker's 136

wh

1760.

w^h gives 14 lbs overplus for Baker to pay me for at 16d. p^r pound, as we at first agreed. Deacon weighs the dead pig & finds it (as he says) 96. He cuts & salts it up for me.

Dec. 24. I rode in Deacon Tainters Sleigh with him, his son & Daughter to Southboro'-Fast, we was on acct. of the Small Pox there.

1761, Feb. 10. Deacon Tainter kindly came and weighed my hoggs. N.B. This day Mr. Bowmans School, at Deacon Tainters finishes.

Feb. 16. N.B. Dispute with Deacon Tainter about the beginning of the sabbath.

Feb. 26. Deacon Tainter brot in Mr. Jonah Warren & Mr. Danl Hardy, those latter being disquieted with an expression in my Sermon last Lords Day.

Feb. 28. Deacon Tainter dined here, and gave me an account of ye occasion and manner of his coming with Mr. Warren & Hardy on ye 26. For altho they were so disturbed, y^t they would not have come here (that he knows of) except he had insisted upon it and come with them — yet they *would* talk at the Smith's shop, — ye custom of many persons, I am greatly troubled for.

March 28. Mr. Simon Tainter of Sutton, here.

April 8. Deacon Tainter killed a calf for me, — and carryd 3 Quarters of itt to Boston.

March 21. Deacon Tainter sets up the Dial by my shop.

Lieut Tainter with his team & Ensign Harrington with his, plough my field behind ye meeting house.

1764, July 4. Deacon Tainter came with a Horse and ploughed my field and dined with us. —P.M. Capt. Wood,—Messrs. Zeb. Rice, Kendall & B. Tainter hoed for me.

Aug. 13. Deacon Tainter wth Boy & horse comes to plough among my corn.

Oct. 16. N.B. Had been a great deal concerned about Deacon Tainter, — how he would bear ye journey, being old and under so grt indisposition.—But behold he was got to Mad^m Dennis's before me, & there were also Col. Brigham & Capt. Ward from Southboro'.—N.B. Deacon Tainter was directed to call at Mr. Adams' at Roxbury for my Breeches, but none came. — I was obliged to borrow,—for my own were become unfit.—besides Mr. Greens Gss who lent me a pair of velvet. Young Mr. Stone lent me a pair of black leather to wear home.

1765, March 11. Capt. Brigham & Mr. Tainter come from the Precinct Meeting to desire me to go & pray w^h y^m—w^e I did.

March 26. P.M. Came Mr. Tainter & brot his wife's uncle Mr. Danl. Wood of Somers, who informs me of a wood newly discovered in a tract of land in New York Gov^t called the nine partners which wood will not consume.

April 6. Deacon Tainter Brot from Boston Magazines for Sept. Oct. Nov. & brings a vine, a Mulberry tree, Goosebury bushes &c. from Mr. Holbrook wt^h a letter, Letters from brother Park^m, Saml, & for Dr. Robie, wt^h Scudders Daily walk.

June 12. Made a visit to Mr. Tainter's under their bereavement, y^y having lately lost their little Daughter, and may G^d please to sanctify it to them !

Aug. 30. My mind has been in gt agitⁿ abt ye present times, & peculiarly at the Capital, Boston.—The L— himself direct his people and help us Suitably to humble ourselves under ye very awful Dispensation !*

Deacon Tainter here in ye evening Lamenting &c.

1766, Jan. 3. Deacon Tainter going to Boston, dines with us.

Jan. 8. Deacon Tainter with his father & his wife come with their Sleigh again and waited on us to ye Funeral of Mr. Seth Rice Junr.

Dec. 23. Deacon Tainter returns from Boston—brings ye sad news of Elder Halsey's & Mr. Nathl Proctor's Sudden Deaths. May I be ever ready.

1767, Feb. 4. Mr. Tainter with five teams and a number of cutters, Sleds 20 Loads of wood from Mr. Bradish's.

Feb. 5. Deacon Tainter brings sad news of a fire in Boston night before last, we broke out at a bakers near mill Bridge and run down each side of mill Stream.

March 12. Deacon Tainter as he goes to Boston comes in and tells me y^t ye Brⁿ y^t were so disturbed, went to Capt. Woods last eve and y^t there is great warmth.—May G. himself guard, direct and fortify me against such unreasonable plottings and attempts.

March 14. Deacon Tainter returning from Boston, brings a letter from Saml w^c informs me y^t my aged Brother is so feeble y^t he chiefly lies on his bed. May ye Grt God be his support, and prepare him—and me ! for Dissolution !

March 26. Deacon Tainter very bad. I visited and prayed with him. He tells me y^t Mr. D. Forbes and Mr. Z. Rice were at their house last night and very full of Disquietment &c. and that his son was with them in it.

March 29. Deacon Tainter remains bad.—His Son Simon dines here. Before night Mr. Benjamin Tainter brings a Sorrowful letter from Mr. Morse of Shrewsbury.

March 30. P.M. Rode to see Deacon Tainter w^o remains bad yet.

April 1. Capt. Baker of Boston comes with an horse for me to go to see the Deacon—find him very Low,—Dr. Darling and Dr. Ball are there, and do all that in them lies. Prayed with him. Mr. Andrews being there, I gave the Deacon an hint to exhort him to peace, w^c he did and both of us, was much in exhortation to all. Parted with him very Solemnly.

* Stamp Act trouble, meetings of Sons of Liberty, &c.

Deacon John Tainter, (19)

Of Watertown, was chosen deacon of the church in 1761, was one of the Selectmen, Captain of the militia company, and one of the leading men of the town at the time.

He married Johanna Harrington, May 25, 1720, and occupied the old homestead which he received by settlement from his father. He died in 1768, æ. 69.

John Tainter

1767.

"1741, May 15. Voted by the town that Oliver Livermore, John Tainter, Jonathan Church, John Bright and Henry Bond, be a committee to new seat ye meetinghouse and to make report at ye adjournment."

"Voted that the committee in seating ye meeting house have regarde to Age, Honour and usefulness, and to Real and Personal Estate, as it stands in the last Invoice."

"June 16, 1746, Nathan[l] Harris, John Taynter and Josiah Convers, Gentlemen of Watertown as a Committee empowered by the town, deeded lands in Watertown to Nath[l] Bright & John Kimball.— *Vol.* 45, f. 434 *M. R.*

"1749, July 14. Voted and chose Capt. John Tainter to be of the church committee to let out on Interest the Legacy left to this Church by Mrs. Ann Mills."

"1761, July 10. At a meeting of the Church of Christ in Watertown, in order to make choice of some suitable Person to be a Deacon in said Church, the Brothers voted and chose Capt John Tainter to said office, and he declared his acceptance thereof."—*C. Records.*

FAMILY.

(43) **Mary,** b. June, 1721 ; d. Feb., 1745, æ., 24.
(44) **Hannah,** b. Feb. 14, 1723 ; m. Moses Stone, of W., Nov. 25, 1746.
(45) **Rebecca,** b. Aug. 18, 1725 ; m. —— Watson.
(46) **Susanna,** b. July 29, 1727 ; m. Aaron Hill, of Cambridge, Nov. 13, 1753.
(47) **Johanna,** b. Dec. 10, 1730 ; m. Ebenezer Shedd, of Charlestown, Nov. 1, 1750.
(48) **John,** b. Aug. 12, 1732 ; m. Mary Shedd, of Charlestown, May 31, 1754 ; death not recorded in Watertown.
(49) **Ann,** b. Aug. 12, 1734 ; m. Daniel Watson, of Cambridge, Nov. 24, 1757.
(50) **Samuel,** b. March 25, 1737 ; A soldier at Lake George, 1758 ; d. Jan. 4, 1759, æ. 22.
(51) **Eires,** b. July 20, 1741 ; m. Elizabeth Coolidge, of Waltham, Dec. 15, 1767 ; died July 24, 1824, æ. 83.
(52) **William,** b. June 1, 1746 ; d. March 6. 1759, æ. 13.
(53) **Elizabeth,** b. Jan., 1748 ; m. Nathaniel Jarvis, of Cambridge, Dec. 18, 1766.
All born in Watertown.

" Our ancestors lived on bread and broth,
And woed their healthy wives in homespun cloth.
Our Grand 'ma's nurtured to the nodding reel,
Gave our good mothers lessons on the wheel.
Though spinning did not much reduce — the waist,
It made the food much sweeter to the taste.—
They never once complained, as some do now,
Our Irish girl can't cook, or milk the cow.
Each mother taught her red-cheeked, buxom daughter,
To bake and milk and draw a pail of water.
No damsel shunned the wash-tub, broom or pail,
To keep unharmed a long-grown finger nail.
They sought no gaudy dress, no hooped out form,
But ate to live, and worked to keep them warm."

WILL OF DEACON JOHN TAINTER, OF WATERTOWN.

In the name of God Amen. The twenty second Day of February in the year of our Lord one thousand seven hundred & sixty eight, I John Tainter of Watertown, in the County of Middlesex & Province of Massachusetts Bay in New England, Gentleman, being at this time of perfect mind & memory for which I Desire to bless God, And calling to mind the Mortality of my Body, & knowing that it is appointed for all men once to die, Do make and ordain this my last Will and Testament. That is to say, Principally and first of all I Give and Recommend my Soul into the Hands of God that gave it, And for my Body I recommend it to the Earth to be Buried in a Christian like and decent manner at the Discretion of my Executor hereafter named, nothing doubting but that at the General Resurrection I shall receive the same again by the mighty Power of God, And as Touching such Worldly Estate wherewith it hath pleased God to bless me with in this life, I Give, Devise and Dispose of in manner following, That is to say, in the first Place my Will is that all my just Debts and funeral Charges be paid by my Executor, with all other sums of money hereafter willed and Bequeathed.

Item. I give & Bequeath to Johanna my Dearly beloved Wife, the Use & Improvement of the South lower Room in my Dwelling House & one half the Cellar under the same, and one half the Use of the Kitchen, & one half of the Chamber over the same, & what Priviledge in the Garret is necessary for her. Also one third part of the Barn with the Priviledge of the Yard around the same & the Priviledge of the Well to git Water at. I also give unto my said Wife the Use and improvement of all my household furniture during her natural life or while she remains my Widow. I likewise give unto her my Riding Chair with the use of a Horse when necessary, & the Improvement of two milch Cows with one third part of the produce of that part of my Real Estate hereafter willed to my Executor. Also my will is that my Executor provide the necessary fireing ready at the Door fitt for use, & if she dies my Widow my Will is that she be Buried in a decent manner at the Charge and Discretion of my Executor. But if my Wife should marry again, my Will is that she should be provided for as the law directs, & no otherwise, at the charge of my Executor.

Item. I give & Bequeath to my well beloved son John & to his Heirs & Assigns forever, the Dwelling house where he now lives, with about half an Acre of land adjoining, Bounded East on a Town Road, North on Land of Daniel Bond, West on the old Highway line, & south as the Fence now stands. Also I give unto him one other piece of Land lying East of said Town Road, Bounded as follows, beginning at a Stake and heap of Stones at said Road, & to run a strait line Eastward on the South Side of the Causeway till it comes to a Stake & heap of Stones at the middle Wall, then turning with said Wall till it comes to land of John Whitney, thence Easterly with said Whitney's land till it comes to land of Lieut Daniel Whitney, & thence with his land till it comes to Land of Daniel Bond, & with his Land till it comes to the aforesaid Town road, & with said Road till it comes to the first mentioned Stake & Heap of stones. I likewise give unto him one third part of my Wood lott lying in Waltham on Prospect Hill (so called). Provided never the less my Will is that if my Son shall think fitt to sell said House & Land he shall first offer them to the owner of my other House & Lands before he makes Sale of them to any other person. Further I give unto my said Son John all my wearing apparell, of every Sort, & two Cows, and one sixth part of my Household furniture when my wife has done with it.

Item. I give & Bequeath unto my well Beloved Daughter Hannah Stone, the Sum of Four Pounds Lawfull money, to be paid by my Executor within three Years after my Decease, also one sixth part of my Household furniture, at the time before mentioned.

Item. I Give & bequeath unto my well beloved Daughter Rebecca Watson, the sum of four Pounds for her Improvement till her Son John arrives to twenty one years of age, & then to go to him, said Sum to be paid by my Executor within four years after my Decease. Also, I give unto my said Daughter Rebecca, one sixth part of my Household Furniture at the Time above mentioned.

Item. I give unto my well beloved Daughter Susanna Hill the sum of forty Pounds to be paid by my Executor within five years after my Decease, And I give unto her one sixth part of my House hold Furniture at the Time the others receive theirs.

Item. I give & Bequeath to my well Beloved Daughter Ann Watson the sum of four Pounds, to be paid by my Executor within six years after my Decease, also one sixth part of my Household Furniture at the time the others receive theirs.

Item. I Give & Bequeath to my well beloved Daughter Elizabeth Jarvis one sixth part of my Household Furniture when her sisters receive their parts, which with what I gave her at the time of her marriage will be full *Equall* with her Sisters.

FIFTH GENERATION.

1742 — 1816.

BEING THE CHILDREN OF

JOHN TAYNTOR, of Shrewsbury and Boston. (23)

JONATHAN TAYNTOR, of Marlborough. (26)

Deacon BENJAMIN TAYNTOR, of Marlborough. (30)

SIMON TAINTER, of Sutton (now Millbury). (33)

BENJAMIN TAINTER, of Westborough. (38)

JOHN TAINTER, of Watertown. (48)

EAIRES TAINTER, of Watertown and Leominster. (51)

Families, 7.

---

* Guardianship of Jedediah (at his own Election), a minor upwards of fourteen years of age, Son of John Tayntor, late of Marlboro', in the County of Middlesex, is on this Twelfth Day of March, A.D. 1764, granted (by the Judge of Probate for said County) To Thomas How, of Marlboro', aforesaid County, Gentleman, who gives bond in the Sum of five hundred Pounds with Jonathan Tayntor in said Marlboro' in said County, Yeoman, surety for the faithful discharge of sd trusts.

Attest, ANDW BORDMAN, Regr.

Item. I Give & Bequeath unto the three Children of my well beloved Daughter Johanna Shedd, Deceased, the sum of four Pounds, to be paid by my Executor with in seven years after my Decease, said sum to be equally divided amongst them.

Item. I Give unto my well beloved Son *Eirs Tainter*, whom I likewise Constitute, make & Ordain my only & sole Executor of this my last Will & Testament, all & singular my Housing & Lands, with all my Stock & Utensils, with all my Estate both Real & personal, of what ever name or nature were ever lying or being, to be his & his Heirs & Assigns forever. Provided he shall have any lawfull Heirs, but if otherwise, my Will is that at his Decease the said Real Estate shall return to my other Heirs as the Law directs. All the Aforesaid Estate not before willed & bequeathed, to be by him freely possessed & enjoyed. And I do here by utterly Disallow, Revoke & Disannul all & every other & former Testaments & Wills & Legacies, & Bequests, by me in any way before this time named, Willed & Bequeathed, Ratifying & Confirming this & no other to be my last Will & Testament. In Witness whereof, I have hereunto set my Hand & Seal the Day & Year aforewritten.

JOHN TAINTER. [*Seal.*]

Witnessed by WILLIAM HARRINGTON,
   ESTHER BROWN,
   JONᴬ. BROWN.

CODICIL. TO ALL PEOPLE to whom these Present shall Come be it known that whereas I, John Tainter of Watertown, in the County of Middlesex & State of the Massachusetts Bay, Gentleman, have made and declared my last Will & Testament, in Writing under my hand & seal bearing date the twenty seventh Day of February in the year of our Lord Christ one thousand seven hundred and sixty eight, I the said John Tainter by this present Codicil do Ratify & Confirm my said last Will & Testament, And whereas by my said last Will & Testament I have given my land East of the Town Way to my two Sons *Ayres* Tainter & John Tainter, my meaning is that the lines between them be as follows, Viz. Beginning at said way north of the draw barrs at the Crank in the fence running on a straight line Easterly to the South side of the Causeway, thence Easterly to the Cross Fence. And whereas in my said last Will & Testament I ordered that the line at the said Cross Fence should turn & run southerly on said Fence till it comes to the land of John Whitney, I now Order that the said line at the said Cross fence should not turn southerly but extend Easterly to the land belonging to the Heirs of Lieut Daniel Whitney, Deceased, the said line to run between two swamp White oak Trees growing in the same Land. And also Whereas in my said last Will & Testament I gave all my wearing Apparell to my Son John, I now Order that all my wearing Apparell be divided equally between my two Sons John & Ayres, and my Will & meaning is that this Codicil be, and be adjudged to be part & parcel of my said last Will & Testament, & that all things here in mentioned & contained be faithfully & truly performed as fully & amply in every respect as if the same were so declared & sett down in my said last Will & Testament.

Witness my Hand & Seal this twenty fourth Day of October, Anno Dominix One thousand seven hundred & sixty eight.

his
JOHN × TAINTER.
* mark & seal.

Witnessed by JOHN REMINGTON,
   ABRAHAM WHITNEY,
   MARY WHITNEY.

(Continuation of opp. page.)

A LETTER TO HIS SON JEDEDIAH.

DEAR CHILD,   *Yarmouth, Nov.* 16*th day,* 1773.

  I rejoice to have one more opportunity to write To you. I am now in a good State of health and Have Injoyed a great measure of health Eversince I Traviled abroad. I now dwell att the head of the Cape in the (then) government of Novascotia. My Situation is mean and bad as to the things of this world. I should be glad with all my heart to see you. Since I Cannot, Let me Beseech you in the name of God, Shun all Vices, all bad Companions, Set up the practice of piety and keep up the fear of God in your house, Which Will be The only means to Build you up in this life and prepare you for Eternal Hapiness.

  May Allmighty God bless you in all your Ways. No more at Present.

I am your Loving Father, JOHN TAYNTOR.

* See Note at foot of page 16.

John Tainter, (23)

Of Shrewsbury, was born in Marlboro', 1716 ; admitted to the Church in Shrewsbury, May, 1742 ; dismissed to the Church in Woodstock, Conn., in 1751. He lived in Woodstock several years, likewise in Boston, and Halifax, New Hampshire.

He married *Hannah Goodell, of Marlboro', Jan. 1, 1739–40 ; second, Sarah, daughter of Obadiah Ward, May 20, 1741. By the latter he had five children. She died in Woodstock soon after his removal to that place.

He appears to have been a very pious man. He writes from Boston July 1, 1758, to his brother Benjamin, living in Woodstock, expressing his deep sympathy for him and his family in their sickness, and addressing them in the following admonitory words :

" I understand that you have not had one of your children baptized. O do not neglect it. If they should not live you might repent when it was too late, therefore hear the advice of a brother. I myself am an afflicted man. I therefore think I am the more able to give you advice. I have in my day borne the chastisement of God, which might have been better improved by me, but I pray God to sanctify all that I have yet to meet with. . . .

I wrote to you to take care of Joseph, but understand that when Mr. Wallis came down you were to get a lad. If you do not need him I would have Mr. Wallis take him, for I have agreed with him already.

This from your Loveing Brother

Boston, Dec. the 1st, 1757.

Brother and Sister, after giving Love to you, I would inform you that I and my family are in good health, and likewise am sorry to hear that you are still sick. My wife returned last Monday Evening without any harm Except once or twice Falling from off her horse without receiving much hurt. This from your loveing Brother, JOHN TAYNTOR.

Boston, May the 10, 1758.

Loveing Brother and Sister, after love to you and yours and my Son, I would inform you that I and my family are in a measure of health, hoping these lines will find you and yours in the same good circumstances.

I understand you have removed from the famous sitty of Woodstock to Shrewsbury. I hope you will find peace in your mind. A discontented mind is like rottenness in the Bones. I desire your Prosperity. I understand my Son wants Clothes, which I will send by the first opportunity. These from your
Loveing Brother,

To Mr. Benj. Tayntor
In Shrewsbury
with care and speed.

It will be seen, by the above autographs, that he spelt his name in both of the now prevailing ways, within the space of three months.

John Tayntor spent the latter part of his life with his son Jedediah, in Marlboro', N. H., where he died in 1805, æ. 88.

FAMILY.

(54) **Miriam,** b. March, 1742.
(55) **Albovin,** b. July, 1743.
(56) **Joseph,** b. Jan., 1745 ; m. Dorcas Post, of Norwich, Conn.
(57) **William,** b. Sept., 1746 ; died young.
(58) **Jedediah,** (Lieut.) b. July 25, 1748 ; m. Mary Maynard, May 22, 1770 ; died March 26, 1817, æ. 69.

All born in Shrewsbury.

* John Tainter and Hannah Goodell, both of Marlboro', were married in *Sudbury*, by Rev. Israel Loring, Jan. 1,1739–40.

Jonathan Taynter, (26)

Son of Deacon Joseph, of Marlboro', was a farmer, member of the Church, and one of the Selectmen of the Town, lived and died in Marlboro'. He married Sarah Woods, Nov. 17, 1755, and died June 9, 1808, æ. 84. His widow died in 1820, æ. 89.

FAMILY.

(59) **Catherine,** b. May 6, 1756; m. Antipas Howe, of M., Nov. 23, 1774.
(60) **Daniel,**   b. April 5, 1759; probably died young.
(61) **Anne,**   b. Aug. 31, 1761; m. Aaron Howe, of M., Oct. 19, 1791; 2d, John Nurse, of Framingham.
(62) **Lydia,**   b. Nov. 23, 1762; d. Jan. 4, 1835, æ. 70.
(63) **John,**   b. Oct. 14, 1764; m. Esther Goodnow, March 30, 1786; d. March 17, 1807, æ. 43.
(64) **Joseph,**   b. Feb. 12, 1766; m. Nancy Gould, June 24, 1800; d. Sept 13, 1845, æ. 79.
(65) **Sarah,**   b. Nov. 11, 1767; m. David Wilkins, March 30, 1786.
(66) **Lucy,**   b. March 25, 1770; m. Stephen Bush, Nov. 26, 1787.
(67) **Elizabeth,** b. Nov. 18, 1775; m. Levi Bailey, March 2, 1803.
      All born in Marlboro'.

Deacon Benjamin Taynter (30)

Was born in Marlboro'. He married Sarah Brigham, of M., June 4, 1755, and settled in Woodstock, Conn., but soon returned to Massachusetts. After living a short while in Shrewsbury, he with others settled the town of Princeton; but he remained there only 10 or 15 years, as at the time of the Revolution we find him again of Shrewsbury. It is thought that he lived awhile in Hubbardston or Holden. He possessed property, but sold it for Continental money, which eventually became worthless, and he was reduced almost to poverty. He served in the Revolutionary war.

In 1791, his wife being dead, he with his two sons migrated to New York State, and settled in Worcester, Otsego County. He was a deacon in the Presbyterian Church of that place, and died in 1798, instantly, supposed to be a fit of apoplexy, æ. 65.

His descendants are numerous in the state of New York.

FAMILY.

(68) **Sarah,**   b. March, 1756; m. Ebenezer Rice, of Holden. Their children, Rollin, Ebenezer and Sarah, are settled in Illinois.
(69) **Miriam,**   b. April 28, 1758; m. Stephen Potter, of Marlboro', May 2, 1787.
(70) **Annis S.,** b. June 19, 1760; m. Cyrus Kingsbury, of Worcester; had a son Cyrus K., jr.
(71) **Lucy,**   b. Oct. 30, 1761; m. Abel Hubbard, of Holden, removed to Putney, Vt., where they lived and died, having had a family of nine children.
(72) **Lucretia,** b. Oct. 30, 1763; died young.
(73) **Joseph,**   b. Nov. 2, 1765; died young.
(74) **Electa,**   b. July 28, 1767; died young.
(75) **Patty,**   b.   ; m. John Perry, of Holden.
(76) **Benjamin,** b. about 1768; m. Dinah Houghton, of Worcester, N. Y., in 1790; died in 1835.
(77) **Joseph,**   b. July 6, 1775; m. Abigail Fuller, of Lanesboro'; d. Dec. 22, 1847, æ. 72.

(68) and (69) born in Woodstock, Ct., (70) in Shrewsbury, (71) (72) (73) (74) in Princeton, (75) (76) (77) ?.

Simon Tainter, (33)

Son of Deacon Simon, of Westboro', was born in Watertown. His parents removed to Westboro' when he was ten years of age. He married Mary Bruce, of that town, in 1740, bought a farm and settled in Grafton, where he lived until 1748-9, at which time he returned to Westboro' and remained until 1754. He then bought a farm in Sutton, North Parish (now Millbury), where he died July 17, 1787, æ. 72. His wife died in 1781, æ. 62.

He was admitted to the Church in Grafton, Aug., 1741 ; dismissed to the second Church in Sutton, Sept., 1754.

He was Constable in Sutton in 1764-5—was chosen one of a committee to take care of, and provide for the families of such persons as were in the Continental service, Dec., 1776, also one of a committee to inspect and prosecute all breaches of the law, agreeably to a late Act of the General Assembly of March 8, 1779—in 1756 was chosen one of a committee to treat with the Rev. Mr. Wellman, about his salary—in 1763 was chosen one of the parish committee. Four of his sons served in the Revolution.

FAMILY.

(78) **Simon,** b. July 22, 1741 ; d. March 17, 1769, æ. 28.
(79) **Abijah,** b. June 7, 1744 ; m. Sarah Small, of Sutton, Oct. 22, 1772 ; d. April 1, 1828, æ. 84. She died May 26, 1831, æ. 87.
(80) **Mary,** b. Nov. 14, 1746 ; d. March 10, 1762, æ. 15.
(81) **Joel,** b. March 19, 1748-9 ; m. Abigail Goddard, Sept. 28, 1786, and Elizabeth Bancroft, Dec. 13, 1798. He died Oct. 7, 1822, æ. 73.
(82) **Nahum,** b. Feb. 23, 1750-51 ; m. Huldah Sibley, of Sutton, May 3, 1781 ; died July 6, 1816, æ. 65.
(83) **Eleanor,** b. Nov. 11, 1753 ; d. March 10, 1762, æ. 8.
(84) **Hannah,** b. March 20, 1758 ; m. Joseph Bancroft, Sept. 14, 1780 ; died 1791, æ. 33.
(85) **Anna,** b. July 16, 1760 ; m. Robert Goddard, April 30, 1780 ; died 1792, æ. 32.
(86) **David, (Dr.)** ⎫ ⎧ m. Catherine Houghton, of Sterling, 1785 (?), died
             ⎬ b. April 6, 1762 ; ⎨   Aug. 20, 1791, æ. 29.
(87) **Daniel,** ⎭ ⎩ m. Rebecca Jacobs, of Ward, Jan. 31, 1792 ; died June 16, 1795, æ. 33.

(78) (79) (80) (81) were born in Grafton, (82) (83) in Westboro', the remainder in Sutton.

John Tainter, (48)

Son of Deacon John, of Watertown, was a mason, and occupied a house built by his father on the homestead lot, a few rods west of the old house, which with a number of acres of land he received by his father's will.

He and his brother Samuel were soldiers in the Indian and French war, at Lake George, in 1758 ; belonged to Capt. Jonathan Brown's company. He was also in service in the Revolutionary war, at Dorchester Heights, under Washington, and as guard to the powder magazine at Watertown.

He married Mary Shedd, of Charlestown, May 31, 1754, and raised a large family of children, all of whom lived to maturity and married.

"March 1779. Paid to John Tainter for repairs for the Ministerial place, £1. 15s. dito Great Bridge, £4."—*T. Rec.*

Names (88) to (94) on next page. ### FAMILY.

(95) **Mary,** bap. Jan. 4, 1756 ; m. Wm. Popenbury, of Lexington, Sept. 20, 1784.
(96) **Susanna,** bap. Jan. 1, 1758 ; m. Henry Gibson, Aug. 20, 1776.
(97) **Sarah,** bap. March 9, 1760 ; m. Matthew Pierce, of Ashburnham, Oct. 5, 1777.
(98) **Johanna,** bap. April 4, 1762 ; m. —— Sawyer, a Hessian.
(99) **Samuel, (Rev,)** bap. June 2, 1765 ; left for the Mohawk River as a Missionary to the Indians ; m. Hepzibah Eaton, of —, N. Y., June 19, 1799 ; d. in 1836, æ. 71.
(100) **Elizabeth,** bap. Oct. 12, 1766 ; m. —— (?)
(101) **Hannah,** bap. Dec. 13, 1767 ; m. Ezra Wyman, of Pelham, N. H.
(102) **John,** bap. April 20, 1770 ; m. Olive Lewis, of Roxbury, Mass., June 16, 1797 ;
(103)   died June 7, 1821, æ. 51.
(104) **Nathaniel,** bap. Aug. 14, 1774 ; m. Lois Howard, of Malden ; d. Feb. 20, 1852, æ. 77
(105) **Dolly,** bap. Nov. 25, 1775 ; m. William Gammon, of Boston.
    All baptized in Watertown.

Benjamin Tainter (38)

Was born in Watertown, in 1725, and in the following year his parents removed to Westboro'. He was admitted to the Church there in 1743.

When a young man, he was taken a captive by the Indians (at Adams, Mass.), remaining in captivity one year.

"June 11, 1746. The Indians attack Fort Massachusetts, but are repulsed—wounding only two men, Gershom Hawkes and Elisha Nims, but they took prisoner Benjamin Tainter. One of the Indians was killed. Tainter was son of Dea. Simon Tainter of Westboro'."

Drake.

Two years after his captivity he married Hannah Wood, of Somers, Conn. She was received into the Church at Westboro', by letter from Somers, April 3, 1755.

He lived in Westboro' until about 60 years of age, and held various town offices ; is frequently mentioned in the Parkman journal. He owned a good farm, but sold it for Continental money which proved of little value. He then migrated to Vermont. After living a short time in Newfane, Vt., Amherst, Mass., and Somers, Conn., he returned to Vermont and lived with his son Samuel (92), and Ezekiel and Hannah Rice until his death, Aug., 1810, in his 86th year.

FAMILY.

(88) **Benjamin,** b. May 27, 1753 ; m. Margaret Hinds, of Newton, May 16, 1776 ; d. June 24, 1844, æ. 91.

(89) **Jonathan,** (Deacon) b. June 26, 1755 ; m. Jemima Root, of Somers, Conn., Sept. 21, 1776 ; d. July 30, 1801, æ. 46.

(90) **Josiah W.,** b. July 24, 1757 ; d. June 16, 1759, æ. 2.

(91) **Stephen,** (Dr.) b. Oct. 13, 1760 ; m. Elizabeth Gorham, Dec. 18, 1791, and Mercy Winslow, Feb. 11, 1802 ; died July 11, 1847, æ. 87.

(92) **Samuel,** b. May 3, 1763 ; unmarried ; d. Oct. 22, 1846, æ. 83.

(93) **Hannah,** b. March 9, 1765 ; died young.

(94) **Hannah,** b. May 2, 1769 ; m. Ephraim Rice, in 1796 ; d. July 12, 1843, æ. 74. He died Sept. 5, 1847, æ. 76.

All born in Westboro'.

Mr. Samuel Tainter Rice, in answer to inquiries respecting his grandfather's captivity, writes as follows :

. . . . "When he became advanced in years and near the close of his mortal journey, and while bordering on his second childhood, his mind went back to the days of his captivity with a great deal of interest, and it became a habit with him to relate the history of it to persons that called at our house. Uncle Samuel at that time was carrying on the pottery business, and many were the persons that daily called to buy wares, and hearing his story so often, many particulars of it became pretty well established in my mind, but it being nearly fifty years since I listened to those recitals many parts of less interest I have forgotten, but I will follow the thread of the history as well as I can. About the time of his captivity the Colonies were much troubled by the Indians, and for their safety they had prepared garrisons of protection, and when there was a prospect of danger the inhabitants in a given locality would all repair to their place of safety and there continue until the danger was over, and when the men went out to their labor one of their number would with gun in hand go out with them as a sentinel, to watch the approaches of danger. It had been the custom of the sentinels when stationed on the mountain to wile away the time by starting rocks, and watching them tumble to the plain below. The day before his capture it was difficult to make one roll. The smallest bush or crag would impede their descent. Fatigued they had amusement but with their thoughts, and forebodings of danger was the result. On returning to the fort at night, the story of the rocks was considered a divine warning of the presence of danger, and precautions taken accordingly. The next day sentinels were sent only as far as the fields. Perhaps Benjamin Tainter was more superstitious than the others, for that morning he had his head shaved. (If the Indians catch me now, remarked he to his comrades, 'they will be bothered to get my scalp.'

It was his lot to go as guard to the ploughing field, and the workmen were ploughing with a strong team, while he with his gun over his shoulder would follow a rod behind. Soon after they commenced, they killed a large rattlesnake and hung it on a bush, and as Benjamin had heard it remarked that a snake would live until the sun went down, he thought that he would see if the saying was true, and as they would come around to that side of the field, he would linger for a moment to look at the snake; once he lingered longer than usual, until the team got some distance ahead. At this moment his attention was arrested by the report of a gun. He looked towards the place from whence the sound came, and to his astonishment, just over the fence in the edge of the woods he saw some Indians that had fired upon them. As quick as thought he levelled his piece and returned the fire. At the moment a ball from one of their guns passed through his hat and cut the skin on his head as it passed along. Whether it was the shock from the ball or at the instant he stubbed his toe which caused him to fall, he never could tell, but he fell, and as he arose he was closed in the arms of a sturdy Indian. A thought occurred to him—One Indian alone shall never carry me off. He grappled in with the Indian for the mastery. At the moment he received a heavy blow on the back of his head, and turning he saw that he was surrounded. He was secured and taken into the woods, where he soon found himself among a large company of Indians. When they had led him to a safe distance, they lashed him to a tree. The Indians then formed into a line, and as each passed him, he would receive a heavy blow. One of their number, rather a rough-looking Indian, as he came up placed one hand on his head, turned it back and struck him a hard blow under the nose and the blood ran freely. It was told him that this was to be his master, and he thought if this was true, he would have a merciless one, but this was the only act of severity that he ever exercised towards him. After being unbound, his master stated to him that when he fired upon the Indians he killed one of them, which was his own dear brother, and for that cause he should claim him as an adopted brother, in place of the one he had killed, and he ever after treated him with all the kindness of a brother, and when they were out on their hunting excursions and became short of provisions his master would go without and give to him, saying as he drew his belt tighter about him, 'Indian can go without better than white man.' They soon after started for Canada, where they resided. On their way they struck the head waters of Lake Champlain, followed down the lake, where all was a dense wilderness, now changed into large towns, cities and a rich farming country. They continued their journey until they reached St. John's, La Prairie, Three Rivers and Montreal, and other places. He went with his master on their hunting excursions, bearing all kinds of hardships as readily as any of the Indians. Sometimes he would lie down at night wrapt in his blanket, and when he awoke in the morning he would find himself under a deep snow. He used to tell of some of his hunting exploits, but they have long since been forgotten. After a while he was sold to the French, and carried from Montreal to Quebec,* where he was confined in prison six months, suffering much for want of food and clothing, and with the yellow fever (which took the hair off of his head save a lock behind each ear, and he never had any more while he lived). At the end of that time he was exchanged or redeemed, and returned to Boston. In appearance my grandfather was stern, but was very pleasant and even in his ways, and a devoted christian.

In person he was tall, straight and robust, and was 'rough with the Indians,' who liked him the more for it—and during his captivity he became a great favorite with them."

* "Feb. 15, 1747. To day my nephew Daniel How and six more prisoners were brought down from Montreal (to Quebec), viz., John Sunderland, John Smith, Richard Smith, William Scott, William Scoffil and Benjamin Tainter, son to Lieut. Tainter, of Westborough, in New England." —*Nehemiah How's Captivity among the Indians.*

Eaires Tainter, (51)

Son of Deacon John, of Watertown, was born July 20, 1741. He was Executor to his father's will, and inherited the old homestead farm. He married Elizabeth, daughter of Capt. Coolidge, of Waltham, Dec. 15, 1767.

In Revolutionary times he was one of the minute men of Watertown, and on the morning of the 19th of April, 1775, meeting others at sunrise on the church green, hastened to Lexington. He was on the Heights of Dorchester under General Washington during the siege of Boston, and afterwards on guard at the Magazine and Stores in Watertown.

In 1789, he sold the farm which had continued in the Tainter family a century and a half, and removed his family to Leominster.* He had lived there but a few years when his house was burned.

"The girls had gone out to spend the afternoon with a neighbor, and before joining them, Sally arranged the kitchen in order, and lastly swept the fire from the hearth into the chimney corner. It was supposed that a coal remained in the broom, as but a short while after she left the house it was discovered to be in flames."

As was the custom in those days, on the occasion of such a calamity, the neighbors turned out bringing with them boards, shingles, nails, &c., each with something, intent on bearing a part of their neighbor's misfortune. They then had one of those events of by-gone days, "a raising," and ere long the house was rebuilt.

An old inhabitant of Leominster, who was a young lad at the time, relates the following anecdote, which we repeat in his own words.

"I remember Mr. Tainter well, as a very tender hearted and conscientious man. He had lived here but few years when his house was burnt down, and as was the custom in those times, and in this town, the neighbors proceeded to help make their neighbor's loss good. One man, Thomas Hale, who was quite eccentric, came up to the house with a quarter of veal concealed inside of his frock. After a few remarks, he said seriously and in an under-tone, siding up against Mr. Tainter—

"'Grandfer' Tainter, I've got a little something agin' you.'

"'Against me!' replied Mr. Tainter seriously.

"'Yes,' returned Hale.

"'I am very sorry, sir; I did not know that I had wronged you.'

"'Well, I *have* got something against you,' again said Hale.

"'I am very sorry, Mr. Hale, if I have done you any injury. Can I make you satisfaction?'

"Mr. Hale's serious tone had begun to tell on the feelings of Mr. Tainter, and a tear glistened in his eye.

"'O, tis nothing but a quarter of veal, which I had *against* you, Grandfer' Tainter,' said Hale, as he drew it forth."

Besides the usual products of a farm, he gave considerable attention to the raising of herbs. His garden was a model of neatness and order. In the fall he would label and take the herbs to his son's, in Watertown, where he would spend a part of the winter, proceeding on market days to Boston on horseback, with panniers on each side filled with them. After a few years his son William took the farm and carried it on, while he returned to Watertown, where he lived with his son Daniel until his death, in 1824, at the age of 83 years. He died of a cancer which had appeared on his left temple seven years previous. His wife died of the same disease, previous to his removal to Leominster.

Eaires Tainter

1769.

FAMILY.

(106) **Elizabeth**, bap. Dec. 4, 1768; m. Edward Follansbee, of Leominster.

(107) **Lucy,**   bap. Sept. 2, 1770; m. Elijah Fairbanks, of Leominster.

(108) **William, (Capt.)** bap. July 19, 1772; m. Betsey Kilburne, of Lunenburg, Nov. 21, 1799; d. 1824, æ. 52.

(109) **Rebecca,**   bap. Nov. 26, 1774; m. Lemuel Jenkins, of Townsend; d. 1856, æ. 82.

(110) **Daniel A.,** b. July 24, 1779; m. Elizabeth Barnard, of Watertown, Dec., 1808; died June 22, 1839, in his 60th year.

(111) **Sally,**   bap. July 11, 1784; unm.; d. of lockjaw occasioned by stepping upon a All born in Watertown.   needle which penetrated her foot, in 1817.

"1774, Mch 4. Ordered that there be paid to Eirs Tainter, for his wifes keeping ye school two weeks at their house, £0--10s.--4d."—*Wat. Rec's.*

"1776. Voted by the town that there be paid to the following persons the respective sums affixed against their names, being money expended by them for the benefit of the present war, viz.," among others, "Eires Tainter, £14--13--4."—*Wat. Rec's.*

* After the Revolution, thousands of families who had before been in affluent circumstances, but had become reduced by an active participation in the struggle, or by the distracted state of the country and the depreciation of the Continental currency, were obliged to sell their property (generally at a sacrifice) and remove further into the interior, where land was cheap and the country new. Among these was Eaires Tainter, who removed to Leominster, Deacon Benjamin Tainter, who removed to New York State, Jedediah Tainter, who removed to New Hampshire, and Benjamin Tainter, who removed to Vermont.

SIXTH GENERATION.

1781 — 1822.

BEING THE CHILDREN OF

JOSEPH TAINTER, OF NORWICH, CONN. (56)

LIEUT. JEDEDIAH TAINTER, OF MARLBORO', N. H. (58)

JOHN TAYNTOR, OF MARLBORO', MASS. (63)

JOSEPH TAYNTOR, OF MARLBORO', MASS. (64)

BENJAMIN TAYNTOR, OF RUSSIA, N. Y. (76)

JOSEPH TAYNTOR, OF LEBANON, N. Y. (77)

ABIJAH TAINTER, OF SUTTON, MASS. (79)

LIEUT. JOEL TAINTER, OF SUTTON, MASS. (81)

NAHUM TAINTER, OF LEICESTER, MASS. (82)

DR. DAVID TAINTER, OF WESTBORO', MASS. (86)

DANIEL TAINTER, OF SUTTON, MASS. (87)

BENJAMIN TAINTER, OF JAY, MAINE. (88)

DEACON JONATHAN TAINTER, OF SOMERS, CONN. (89)

DR. STEPHEN TAINTER, OF WHITINGHAM, VT. (91)

REV. SAMUEL TAINTER, OF MOHAWK VALLEY, N. Y. (99)

JOHN TAINTER, OF BOSTON. (102)

NATHANIEL TAINTER, OF MALDEN. (104)

CAPT. WILLIAM TAINTER, OF LEOMINSTER. (108)

DANIEL A. TAINTER, OF WATERTOWN. (110)

FAMILIES, 19.

6

A Muster Roll of the Company under the Command of Capt. Samuel Barnard, which marched from Watertown to Lexington, on the alarm, April 19th, 1775.

Samuel Barnard, Capt.
John Stratten
Phineas Stearns
Edwd Harrington
Saml Sanger
Christopher Grant
Josiah Capen
Stephen Whitney
Isaac Sanderson
Moses Stone
Nathl Bright
Willm Harrington
Nathan Coolidge
Willm Leathe
Nathl Bemis
Thos Learnard
Stephen Cook
Danl Collidge
Josiah Saunderson
Moses Collidge
Sith Sanderson
Francis Brown
John Sanger
Isaac Prentice
Tillay Mead
Thos Hastings
Abram Whitney
Aires Tainter
John Whitney
Josiah Norcross
David Whitney
Danl Whitney
John Villa
Zechariah Shead
Danl Mason
Jonathan Whitney
Spencer Gooding
David Stone
Jona Coolidge Gooding
Willm Chenery
Thos Stafford
Richard Everitt
Edwd Harrington, Sen.
Thos Coollidge
Saml Sodin

John Fowle
David Capen
Peter Harrington
Saml White, Junr.
Saml Barnard, Junr.
Jona Bright
Danl Sawin, Junr.
Phineas Childs
Joshua Stratten
Jonas Bond, Jnr.
Thos Clark
Richard Clark
Saml White
John Remmington
John Chennery
Simon Coollidge
Danl Cook
Jona Stone
Phineas Childs, Jnr.
Benja Capen
John Hunt, Jnr.
Bezaleel Larnard
Amos Bond
John Bullman
Elias Tuffts
Penuel Parks
James Austin
Phinehas Jenneson
Henry Bradshaw
David Beamis, Jnr.
Elkanah Wales
Jedediah Learnard
Benja Learnard
Saml Bond
Jonas White
Joel White
Ebenr Everitt
Thos Prentice
Jas Mallard
Elnathan Whitney
Zechariah Hicks
John Cook
Nathl Harris, Jnr.
John Randall
Saml Benjamin, Jun.

Elisha Tolman
Jonas Barnard, Jnr.
John Crane
Willm White
Willn Jennison
Leonard Bond
Daniel Learnard
Peter Richardson
Jacob Sanderson
Oliver Learnard
Jonas Learnard
Jona Benjamin
Moses Souler
Saml Warrin, Junr.
Willm Learnard
Elijah Feizee
Oliver Munroe
Willm McCurtain
Phinehas Harrington
Moses Hagar
Willm Watson
Elisha Brewer
Jonas Coolidge (killed)
Jona Childs
Edmond Fowle
Thos Hunt
Stephen Harris
Simon Hastings
Henry Gypson
Danl Jackson
Ephraim Jones
Richard Leathe
Willm Parks
James Tufts
John Willington
Ezekiel Whitney
Cornelius Stone
Cornelius Parks
Jedediah Leathe
Willm Sanger
David Parker
Thos Wellington
Converse Spring   133

---

* The manner in which intelligence of the landing of the British at Cambridge, was communicated to Watertown, has probably never appeared in print.

The night before the battle at Lexington, Abraham Whitney started off for Lynn, on horseback, at about midnight, with panniers filled with shoes, wh ch his brother desired to have delivered in Lynn early in the morning. Abraham Whitney had got about to Charlestown, when he was startled by a voice in the dark, wh ch stealthily asked him—" if he knew that the Regulars were landing." He replied that he did not; whereupon he was informed of the particulars. Relieving his horse of the load of shoes, he galloped him back to Watertown, where arousing a few of his neighbors, it was not long ere the words, " The Regulars have landed, be on the church green at sunrise," had resounded on the still night air, from each man's door-way, and soon lights began to gleam from house to house, an index of life and bustle within.

Prompt to the summons, the sun arose on a line of men ranged on the green in front of the old meeting-house. We can imagine the anxious countenances of the wives and children, the compressed lips and stern faces of the men, as they listened to a few words from their leader, and their strong and measured tread, as at the roll of the drum they hastened away, in answer to the first call of Liberty.

Joseph Tainter, (56)

Son of John Tainter, of Shrewsbury, was born in 1745, and at an early age went from home to learn the tanner's trade. He settled in Norwich, Conn., and married Dorcas Post, of that place. They had three children. But little else is known of him. He went to Fayetteville, N. C., about the year 1790, and soon after died there. His widow resided in Norwich, where she died about the year 1798.

FAMILY.

(112) **William**,   b. —— 1781 ; m. Elizabeth Jordan, of Albany, N. Y. ; "d. a few years ago."

(113) **Fanny**,   b. March 22, 1783 ; m. James Levaughn, of Lebanon, Conn., and lived in Genesee, N. Y.; had two sons, James and Wm. ; m. second, Lory Smith, and lived in Hartford, where they had four children, Frances Ann, Joseph Tainter, Charles Loren and Sarah Corning Smith. She died Nov. 27, 1851. Joseph Tainter Smith resides in Jacksonville, Illinois.

(114) **Sarah**,   b. Feb. 27, 1785 ; m. Elisha P. Corning, of Hartford. (His second wife, a widow, resides in Hartford.) Died March 2, 1818.

Born in Norwich.

Lieut. Jedediah Tainter (58)

Was born in Shrewsbury, in 1748, married Mary Maynard, May 22, 1770, and settled in Marlboro', Mass. In June, 1776, he removed with his wife and two children to Marlboro', N. H., then a new settlement, the journey to which was performed on horseback.* He was a carpenter by trade, for which he served seven years, was a man of limited education, but of very superior native talent. It was his custom to sit up late at night to read after the rest of his family had retired, and it is said that when reading Rollin's Ancient History, which was kept in the social library, about three miles from his house, taking but one volume at a time, he would read and return three volumes a week besides doing a full week's work at farming.

He was Corporal in a company of minute men of Marlboro', who marched to Lexington at the alarm, April 19, 1775, was at the battle of Bunker Hill, and in the army at Cambridge at the time Washington took command. After removing to New Hampshire he again joined the Continental Army, and was Orderly Sergeant in one of the companies under Col. Graton. He was afterwards a Lieut. in the State Militia, was a delegate to the Convention that adopted the Federal Constitution, and a Representative from Marlboro', N. H., in the State Legislature several years. He also filled other offices of trust and responsibility.

He died March 26, 1817, in his 69th year. His widow died June 29, 1842, æ. 91.

Jedediah Taynter

1764.

FAMILY.

(115) **Darius**,   b. March 7, 1772 ; left home when about 20 years of age, and was never heard from.

(116) **Mary**,   b. April 6, 1775 ; m. Maj. John Wiswall, of Marlboro', Jan. 17, 1799 ; is still living in Marlboro', N. H.

(117) **Jedediah**,   b. Aug. 7, 1781 ; died April 2, 1786, æ. 4 years.

(118) **Daniel**,   b. June 6, 1790 ; died Aug. 9, 1793, æ. 3 years.

(119) **William**,   b. July 19, 1793 ; died Aug. 4, 1793, æ. 1 month.

(120) **Betsey**,   b. April 7, 1795 ; died Oct. 5, 1805, æ. 10 years.

The two first were born in Marlboro', Mass., the others in Marlboro', N. H.

The Wiswall family, of Marlboro', N. H., are the only living descendants of this branch of our family, consequently we give their record on p. 53.

* One hundred years ago, commodities were transported almost entirely in panniers, on horseback ; wheel carriages were very rarely, if ever, used.

John Taintor, (63)

Of Marlboro', farmer, lived and died on the place where he was born in that town. There were two houses on the farm, one occupied by his family, and the other by that of his brother Joseph (64). He married Esther Goodnow, March 30, 1786, and died March 17, 1807, æ. 43. His widow married William Loring, Oct. 5, 1815, and died in 1833, æ. 67.

FAMILY.

(121) **Sarah,**   b. May 5, 1787; m. Aaron Arnold, of Marlboro', Sept. 9, 1802.
(122) **Nancy,**   b. Oct. 31, 1789; m. Apollos Pond, of Sherburne, afterwards of Sangerville, Me.
(123) **Luther G.,** b. March 21, 1792; m. Marion Hill, of Charleston, S. C., Aug. 1, 1824; died at Philadelphia, Pa., March 13, 1836, æ. 42.
(124) **Joel,**   b. Nov. 13, 1796; m. Lydia Leland, of Sherburne, April 18, 1821; resides in Framingham.
(125) **Calvin,**   b. ——; died young.
(126) **Aaron,**   b. April 19, 1798; d. Oct., 1818, æ. 19, at Alexandria, D. C.
(127) **Lucy,**   b. Sept. 30, 1801; m. Dana Warren, of Framingham.
(128) **Asa,**   b. May 27, 1804; m. Almira Trowbridge, of Marlboro', Nov. 1, 1825; resides in New York City.
(129) **John,**   b. Oct. 5, 1806; died June 7, 1807, æ. 8 months.
All born in Marlboro'.

Joseph Tayntor, (64)

Of Marlboro', was a farmer, and lived and died on the farm where he was born. He married Nancy Gould, June 24, 1800, who is still living with her son in Marlboro'. He died Sept. 13, 1845, æ. 85 years. Both were members of the Congregational Church.

Joseph Tayntor

FAMILY.

(130) **Eliza,**   b. June 19, 1801; m. William Symmes, of Dorchester, Nov. 28, 1834; died Aug 26, 1835, æ. 34.
(131) **Henry,**   b. Jan. 14, 1803; resides in Marlboro'.
(132) **Hollis W.,** b. April 1, 1804; m. Olive W. Wiley, of Medway, June 12, 1855.
(133) **Sophia,**   b. April 18, 1806; m. Dea. Rufus Howe, of Marlboro'; d. July 1, 1855, æ. 49.
(134) **Abigail B.,** b. Dec. 1, 1808; died April 12, 1810.
(135) **Abigail B.,** 2d, b. July 6, 1811; died Feb. 5, 1812.
(136) **Jonathan,**   b. July 24, 1814; died March 24, 1843, æ. 29.
(137) **Ann Maria,** b. July 6, 1817; died Feb. 5, 1843, æ. 26.
(138) **Sarah B.,**   b. Aug. 11, 1819; m. Dr. William Knight, of Atkinson, N. H.
All born in Marlboro'.

Benjamin Tayntor (76)

Migrated with his father and brother (77), to New York State in 1791, at which time he was about 23 years of age. He married Dinah Houghton, of Worcester, N. Y., in 1790?–92. They lived in Worcester, afterwards in Russia, N. Y., where he died in 1835.

FAMILY.

(139) **Benjamin,**   b. ——; m. Eliza Foster, of Sharon, N. Y.; died in Eaton, N. Y., Jan., 1855.
(140) **Sarah,**   b. ——; m. Elisha (or Russell?) Treat, of Decatur, N. Y.
(141) **Olive,**   b. ——; m. Charles Root; died, leaving one son, who was adopted by his grandfather, taking the name of Lorenzo Tayntor.
(142) **Cyrus,**   b. ——; died May, 1856.
(143) **Lavina,**   b. ——; m. ——, now a widow, lives in Decatur, N. Y.
(144) **Mary,**   b. ——.
(145) **Jonah,**   b. Dec. 4, 1805; m. Roby Luther, of Thuxton, N. Y., Jan. 3, 1835.
(146) **Philetta,**   b. July 17, 1808; m. John Popple, of Russia, N. Y.; resides in Trenton, N. Y.

All born in Worcester, N. Y., except Cyrus, who was born at Bowman's Creek, N. Y.

Joseph Taynton (77)

Of Lebanon, N. Y., left New England in the 16th year of his age (A.D. 1791), in company with his father and brother, for New York State. The following beautiful notice, from the N. Y. Baptist Register of February 17, 1848, makes further lines from our pen unnecessary.

"DIED,—In Lebanon, Madison Co., Dec. 22, 1847, Mr. Joseph Taynter, æ. about 73 years. He was born in Worcester Co., Mass., in 1775, married Abigail Fuller, of Berkshire County, and removed* to Lebanon in 1808, then almost an entire wilderness. Here in the dreariness of winter, and in the solitude of an extended forest, he gathered his little family around the parental fireside, sheltered from the bleak winds by a rudely constructed log cabin, built of the materials that grew on the ground where it stood; and on this very spot, endeared by a thousand interesting considerations, he lived full forty years. Here he spent the vigor of manhood, here he experienced the infirmities of age, here he consecrated himself to Christ, and reared the altar of prayer, which was not neglected to the day of his death. Father Taynter became a member of the second Baptist Church in Eaton, in 1834. Since that time he has been a faithful, devoted follower of the Lamb. His religion was not of a transient, intermitting character, but warm and ardent, like the gushing of an overflowing stream. He loved the prayer and conference meeting; he loved the Bible and appreciated its claims and promises; he loved the church and prayed for the peace of Zion, and would often sing—

> 'There my best friends, my kindred dwell,
> There God, my Saviour reigns.'

"His daily deportment corresponded with his profession. He was faithful to God, persevering in his efforts to do good, and diligent in his calling as a disciple of Christ. He possessed a firm unyielding integrity, and had no fellowship or sympathy with covetousness, in any of its forms, but his alms and his prayers were offered a willing sacrifice to relieve the needy and distressed, and mitigate the wants and woes of his race. Father Taynter had, as usual, invited his family connections to reciprocate a social family visit, under the paternal roof, which proved to be on the very day of his burial; so that his family were convened in accordance with his own invitation, though not to a house of feasting, but to a house of mourning, and to pay the last sad office of kindness and respect to a departed friend and father. He left five sons and a daughter, the church and a large circle of friends to mourn his loss. His funeral was attended by a large assembly, on the 24th, and was improved by the pastor of the church, Elder Daniel Putnam, from 1 Cor. 15 : 57; 'but thanks be to God who giveth us the victory through our Lord Jesus Christ.'"

FAMILY.

(147) **Abigail,** b. Oct. 30, 1799; d. June 27, 1843, æ. 44.
(148) **Joseph,** (Deacon) b. April 3, 1803; m. Ann Bennett, of Eaton, Nov. 19, 1829.
(149) **Patty,** b. June 17, 1805; m. Fisk Wellington, of Nelson, N. Y., Aug. 28, 1822; died (?) 1840.
(150) **Orsamus,** (Rev.) b. Feb. 25, 1808; m. Roxanna M. Daniels, of Eaton, Sept. 19, 1832; 2d, Mrs. Sophia Denman, of Buffalo, March 4, 1857.
(151) **Lucy,** b. Oct. 21, 1812; m. Charles Bond, of Ashford, N. Y., Nov. 12, 1850.
(152) **Ira B.,** b. Sept. 14, 1814; m. Thankful C. Darrow, of Eaton, March, 1837.
(153) **Erastus P.,** b. Sept. 19, 1816; m. Marietta S. Beebe, of Fenner, N. Y., Aug. 14, 1838.
(154) **Cyrus K.,** b. Dec. 25, 1818; m. Ruth A. Beebe, of Fenner, N. Y., March 24, 1843. She d. April 10, 1851. He m. 2d, Abigail Harris, of Thuxton, N. Y., Sept. 8, 1851.
(155) **Rufus H.,** b. Jan. 23, 1821; d. Aug. 20, 1841, æ. 19 years.
(147) (148) (149) were born in Worcester, N. Y.; the others in Lebanon.

* After living a few years in Worcester, N. Y.

Abijah Tainter (79)

Was born at Grafton, in 1744, was a carpenter by trade; married Sarah Small, of Sutton, Oct., 1722; bought a farm and settled in Sutton. They were received into the church in that place, Dec., 1790, and "were pious, honest and respectable."

He served in the Revolution; was at Lexington, a Sergeant in the Sutton Company; their march was one of over forty miles. He died April 1, 1828, æ. 84.

FAMILY.

(155) **Stephen,**   b. 1776; m. Polly Dyke. She d. July 4, 1834. He m. 2d, Lucretia Gates, Oct. 18, 1834, and died in 1843, æ. 69.

(156) **Abijah,**   b. 1778; m. Mercy Shumway, of Oxford; m. 2d, Mrs. Hannah Smith; died in 1830, æ. 52.

(157) **Sally,**   b. April, 1781; d. in Millbury, April 11, 1859, æ. 78.
All born in Sutton.

Lieut. Joel Tainter (81)

Was born in 1749, at Grafton. In 1754, his father bought a farm and removed to a part of Sutton, now Millbury. He succeeded his father on this farm, and lived and died there.

He served his country on several occasions during the Revolution; was at Lexington, at the taking of Burgoyne, &c.

He married Abigail Goddard, Sept 28, 1786. She died May 24, 1790, æ. 29, leaving two children. He married, 2d, Elizabeth Bancroft, Dec. 13, 1798. She died Jan. 27, 1834, æ 74. After the war he was a Lieut. in the Mass. Militia, was a Prudential Committee man of the town, Moderator at Parish meetings, a member of the Church, and a pious, respectable and honest man. He kept a journal during a part of his life, but it has been lost.

He died Oct. 7, 1822, æ. 78.

FAMILY.

(158) **Polly,**   b. July 8, 1787; m. Salma Carter, of Millbury, April 22, 1818.
(159) **Nabby,**   b. May 23, 1790; died Nov. 22, 1813, æ. 23.
(160) **Simon,**   b. Oct. 16, 1799; m. Hannah Rice, Sept. 3, 1822.
All born in Sutton.

Nahum Tainter, (82)

Of Leicester, lived in early life at Sutton, enlisted under Washington, at Roxbury, Dec. 26, 1775, a volunteer in the company of Capt. Andrew Elliott, and was a Sergeant in the campaign to White Plains, in 1776, and also at the taking of Burgoyne, in 1777. He was in the Sutton company that marched to Lexington, April 19, 1775. In April, 1783, he bought a tract of land in Leicester, and the next year began to clear it, and to build a house.

In 1789, he fractured his skull, while felling a tree, and was found soon after, senseless, by the side of the log. It was successfully trepanned, a few days after, by Dr. Waldo, of Connecticut.

He was honest and respected, and died   *Nahum Tainter*
July 6, 1816, æ. 65.

FAMILY.

(161) **Mehettable,** b. Nov. 1, 1781; m. Simon Bancroft, of Sutton, July 28, 1805; died March 20, 1857, æ. 75.

(162) **Harvey,**   b. Jan. 9, 1784; m. Lucy Copeland, of Leicester, Sept. 12, 1816; lives in Leicester.

(163) **Eleanor,**   b. April 27, 1786; m. Col. Prentiss Cushing, of Lowell; died May 29, 1829, æ. 43.

(164) **Nancy,**   b. Sept. 7, 1788; m. Rufus Sibley, of Millbury, April 15, 1817; m. 2d, Otis Morse, of Lebanon, Conn., and d. Feb., 1842, æ. 53.

(165) **Harriet,**   b. June 12, 1791; m. Luke Harrington, of Millbury, Nov. 16, 1814.
(166) **Roxa,**   b. Oct. 29, 1793; m. John Lilley, of Millbury, Nov. 25, 1817.
The two first born in Sutton, the others in Leicester.

Dr. David Tainter (86)

Was a physician in Westboro'. Our knowledge of him is limited. He married Catherine (Sparhawk?) Houghton, of Sterling, in 1785 (?), and died Aug. 20, 1791, æ. 29, leaving a small property for his widow, who soon after his death removed to Leominster. She remained a widow about twenty years, then married William Nichols, Esq., of L.

FAMILY.

(167) **Catherine S.,** b. May 1, 1790; m. Benjamin Rugg, of Leominster; d. Aug., 1845, æ. 55. Their children were Edmund K. Rugg, banker, in Iowa City, Iowa; Catherine D. Rugg, m. Chas. Wilder, of Worcester; Amelia Rugg, m. Joseph E. Hastings, of do.; Harriet Rugg, m. Jas. S. Kettell, of do.

(168) **Thomas S.,** b. March, 1791; d. May, 1792.

Born in Westboro'.

Daniel Tainter, (87)

Of Sutton,* cultivated, with his brother Joel, the farm before owned by their father.

He served in the Revolution, at West Point, at Rutland, Vt., and in the Rhode Island service.

He married Rebecca Jacobs, of Ward, Jan. 31, 1792, and died June 16, 1795, æ. 33. His widow married a Forbes, of Westboro'.

FAMILY.

(169) **Betsey,** b. Jan. 28, 1793; m. Reuben Merriam, Esq., of Leicester.

(170) **Nancy,** b. March 6, 1795; died young.

Born in Sutton.*

Benjamin Tainter, (88)

Son of Benjamin (36), of Westboro', was born in that place, May 27, 1753. He was a soldier of the Revolution, and served a greater part of the time. He was fifer in a company of minute men from Westboro', under Capt. Seth Morse, who marched to Lexington, at the alarm, April 19, 1775. He was also at the battle of Bennington, under Capt. Timothy Brigham, and in the Rhode Island service, in 1779. He married Margaret Hinds, of Newton, in 1776, and after living awhile in Vermont, settled in Watertown. By trade a stone-cutter. He remained in Watertown till 1803, when he removed his family to Jay, Me.,† and there he cultivated the soil until the death of his wife, Oct. 20, 1817. He then went to Carthage, Me., and resided with his son Simon (177), until his death, June 24, 1844, having lived to the age of 91 years, the oldest age yet attained by any of our family. His eyesight was perfect to the last, and for the last twenty years of his life his almost only book was the Bible. He anticipated the time when he should pass from Life unto Death, and conversed on this subject with the utmost calmness and serenity of mind.

FAMILY.

(171) **Elisha L.,** b. Feb. 5, 1777; m. Sally P. Smith, of Lexington, Feb., 1800, and Lydia Fessenden, of Lexington, Aug. 26, 1810; d. Sept. 19, 1851, æ. 74; widow still living in Medford.

(172) **Sophia,** b. May 12, 1779; m. Ephraim Whitney, of Gerry; d. in Jay, Me., July 28, 1847, æ. 68.

(173) **Clarissa,** b. Aug. 28, 1781; m. William Vose, of Portland, Me.; d. May, 1859.

(174) **Hannah,** b. Dec. 18, 1784; m. Samuel Stone, of Brewer, Me.; d. Sept. 26, 1827, æ. 43, leaving four children.

(175) **Samuel,** b. March 14, 1787; m. Sally Davis, 1812; resides in Bradford, Me.

(176) **Susanna,** b. Jan. 11, 1790; m. Jeremiah Eldridge, of Brewer, Me.; d. Dec. 12, 1854.

(177) **Simon,** b. July 10, 1792; m. Asenath Reed, May 6, 1816.

(178) **Benjamin,** b. May 22, 1795; m. Deborah Merritt, about 1820; d. Aug. 6, 1839.

(171) and (172) were born in Westboro', the last two in Watertown.

* Now Millbury.   † Other Watertown families went to Jay, Me., at this time.

Deacon Jonathan Tainter, (89)

Of Somers, Conn., was born in Westboro', in 1755, and married Jemima Root, of Somers, Sept. 21, 1776. A few days after, leaving his young wife in care of his parents, he joined the army under Washington, and served in New York and New Jersey, until the close of the campaign of 1778, when he returned home, his family having become impoverished by the depreciation of the Continental money, for which they had exchanged their property in Westboro'.

After living in Vermont a few years, he settled in Somers, Conn., where he spent the remainder of his life, and was a Deacon in the Baptist Church.

He was a steady, industrious man, and was peculiarly pleasant in his family relations. One look from him was better, and had more effect, than a multitude of words.

He died of typhus fever, July 31, 1801, aged 46. His widow died at her son's, in York, N. Y., Oct. 2, 1847, aged 91.

FAMILY.

(179) **Polly,**   b. April 18, 1778; m. John Cooley, of Rodman, N. Y.
(180) **Jemima,** b. July 24, 1779; m. Joel Shumway, of Whitingham, Vt.; had five children.
(181) **Josiah W.,** b. Jan. 26, 1782; m. Molly Davis, of Somers, Conn., Aug. 26, 1803; she
            died March 22, 1848, æ. 67.
(182) **Rebecca,** b. Jan. 6, 1789; d. March 2, 1803.
(183) **Lois,**   b. Oct. 22, 1788; m. Peters Hunt, of Somers; resides at Depauville, N. Y.
(184) **Lucinda,** b. March 9, 1790; m. Ansel Winslow; resides at Millsburgh, Mich.
(185) **Jonathan, (Dea.)** b. Sept. 2, 1791; m. Eunice Bowman, Dec. 31, 1821.
(186) **Timothy,** b. April 5, 1796; m. Lois Peck, Feb., 1818, and Jemima Allen, Feb., 1821.
(187) **Loren, (Dea.)** b. April 18, 1799; m. Ruth C. Graves, of Watertown, N. Y., Feb. 26,
            1821, and Mrs. Mary Forbes, of Leicester, N. Y., Jan. 29, 1835.

(179) (180) were born in Westboro', (181) in Dummerston, Vt., (182) in Newfane, Vt., the others in Somers, Conn.

Samuel Tainter, (92)

Son of Benjamin, of Westboro', was born May 3, 1763, and lived a bachelor, residing in the family of his sister and brother-in-law, Ephraim and Hannah Rice, in Sheldon, Vt. He was a potter by trade, and died in Leslie, Michigan, Oct. 22, 1846, æ. 83. Further particulars of him and his sister Hannah, are found in a letter continued from page 37, written by her son, Samuel Tainter Rice (aged 62).

Uncle Samuel and father always lived together, since my recollection. He never married. In the fall of 1816, he joined the Methodist Church, and continued a member as long as he lived. He was indeed a worthy man, and one to whom I was very much attached. My father, Ephraim Rice, was born in Brookfield, Mass. His mother's name was Lois Wood, own sister to Grand Mother Tainter. . . . .

I wish now to speak further about my own dear mother. She was mild in her temper, strict in the discipline of her children, and she possessed all the prominent graces of the Christian.

She was deeply pious, and it was the burthen of her anxieties to see her children grow up in the way they should go. She early taught them of Christ, and of the plan of salvation, and I have not a doubt but that she was instrumental in leading them to the Saviour, and as one of them, I expect ever to thank God for the instructions of a pious mother. With great anxiety and care, she attended to the wants of her aged parents, administered to their comfort, and she ever expressed a satisfaction that she had the priviledge of taking care of them.

My Grandfather Tainter had a glass bottle, stamped with a seal, on which is the date 1726. My mother and uncle Samuel said, by this, that they should ever remember the ages of their parents, for it was between the years that they were born, 1725 and 1727.

The Silver Spoons referred to, were made from (twenty-four) silver buttons that my great grand father, the father of Simon Tainter, *wore on his clothes when he came over from England*, and when he had done with them, Grand father Benjamin wore them, and when he had done with them, Mother had them, and they were made into spoons for my sister Cynthia.   With Respect, I am yours,   SAMUEL T. RICE.
Leslie, Mich., Sep. 3, 1859.

Children of Ephraim Rice and Hannah Tainter his wife.

SAMUEL T., b. Oct. 21, 1797, in Granby, Mass.; m. Bathsheba Washburn, in Leslie, Mich.
CYNTHIA,   b. July 14, 1801, in Sheldon, Vt.; m. Martin Du Bois, of Aliedon, Mich.
DENZEL P., b. June 23, 1809, in Sheldon, Vt.; m. Julia A. Freeman, in Leslie; 2d, Catherine Fuller.
The family moved from Sheldon, Vt., to Leslie, Mich., in 1838. Ephraim Rice died Sep. 5, 1847, æ. 76.
Hannah Rice died June 12, 1843, æ. 74.

Dr. Stephen Tainter (91)

Was born in Westboro', Oct. 13, 1760, and died at his son's, in Wisconsin, July 11, 1847, æ. 87. During a long life he lived in several places, though mostly at Whitingham, Vt., and Gainesville, N. Y. In the latter place he practised medicine twenty-three years.

He was a skilful physician, and a man of much ability and usefulness, and was through life a member of the Congregational Church. He served in the Revolution, was a drummer boy at the battle of Bennington, but was not called into action; was also at the taking of Burgoyne, in 1777, likewise as drummer.

He married Elizabeth Gorham, Dec. 18, 1791. She was born in Barnstable, Dec. 20, 1760, and died at Whitingham, Oct. 3, 1801, æ. 40 years. He married, second, Mercy Winslow, Feb. 11, 1802. She was born in Rochester, April 11, 1763, and died March 15, 1822, æ. 59.

FAMILY.

(188) **Stephen G.**, b. Sept. 15, 1792; m. Anna Hurd, of Sandgate, Vt., Oct. 17, 1813; d. Oct. 12, 1846, æ. 54.

(189) **Ezekiel W.**, (Dea.) b. Dec. 29, 1793; m. Ruth Burnham, of Lysander, N. Y., Sept. 29, 1822.

(190) **Fordice**, b. March 7, 1799; d. Oct. 31, 1802, æ. 3.

(191) **Elizabeth**, b. Sept. 29, 1801; m. Milo Richardson, in 1820; d. in Gainesville, N. Y., Nov. 25, 1829, æ. 28.

(192) **Clarissa K. W.**, b. Feb. 1, 1803; m. Sheffield Burdick, of Gainesville, N. Y., March 1, 1822. He d. Oct. 10, 1829. She m., 2d, David Silliman.

(193) **Adelia M.**, b. Feb. 24, 1807; m. Rodolphus W. Hewett, of Hermitage, N. Y.

(188) was born in Amherst, Mass; (189) in Shelburne; (190) in Somers, Ct.; (191) (192) in Whitingham, Vt.; (193) in Bennington.

Dr. Tainter was much given to poetry and music. The following specimens, for fluency and vividness of description, and style, vie even with Dr. Watts's productions, and the prelude to the second poem (verses 5 to 10 inclusive), are not inferior to some of the first poets.

On the Last Judgement.

1 Ye sleeping saints, lift up your heads,
   For the great Day draws near,
   When time itself shall be no more,
   And Jesus will appear.

2 Hark, hear the great Eternal God
   With Lightning round the sky:
   His awful vengeance guards his throne,
   His Charriot sounds on high.

3 He gives commission to his Son,
   And ends his dreadful wrath—
   My Son, go break up every Tomb,
   And every Grave in Earth.

4 Go tell the Angel for to stand
   And blow the Trumpet round,
   That all my saints, living or dead,
   May hear the joyful sound.

5 Go take My bow and conquering Crown,
   Ride in majestic sway,
   And tell poor sinners now is come
   A dreadful Judgement Day.

6 See, Jesus leaves the Mercy Seat,
   To Judgment He descends,
   And the bright Army in the sky
   Upon Him to attend.

7 He walks the middle region down,
   To set the world on fire;
   Old Heaven and Earth will flee away,
   The Sea will then retire.

8 Jesus will send his Angels round,
   To hurry Nations on,
   Both saints and sinners, for to meet
   Around the burning throne.

9 The Human race of all mankind
   Must have a Meeting there,
   And stand before the Tri-une God,
   At the great August Bar.

10 For Jesus will ascend the throne,
   Under God's great command;
   Here He will take the Book of life,
   And hold it in his Hand.

11 Here he'll unfold before our Eyes,
   The deeds which we have done;
   Our heinous crimes will there be read
   By the Eternal Son.

12 There the great judge of Heaven and Earth,
   While we before him stand,
   Will call his saints, his holy ones,
   To dwell at his right hand,

13 On thrones of Everlasting Love,
   With the great sacred three,
   And sing new Anthems to our King
   Through all Eternity.

14 Then the stern Judge from his bright throne
   To those on his left hand,
   A dreadful sentence there will read,
   While sinners trembling stand.

15 Depart, ye cursed, down to Hell,
   Under my Dreadful wrath—
   With Devils you must always dwell,
   And taste the second Death.

16 I left my throne to save your souls,
   But me you Crucified.
   Once and again I call'd to you,
   But you have me denyed.

17 O sinners, you could stand and gaze
   Upon your Bleeding God,
   And laugh to hear my dying groans
   And triumph in my Blood.

18 'Twas then I bore my father's wrath
   Upon the cursed tree,
   And you shall go and bear *my* wrath
   To all Eternity.

19 I rouse my wrath, and thus do swear
   You shall not see my rest,
   Nor shall you have a portion there
   Or dwell among the blest.

20 There the thick crowds of sinners stand
   Before the shining throne,
   Filled with shame, cry out, O Christ,
   Thy justice we do own.

21 O, down to Hell now we must go,
   Under God's wrath to dwell,
   And lye in the dark regions there
   And bid all joys farewell.

22 There the full vials of God's wrath
   In vengeance he will pour,
   And the foul fiends around us stand
   And Hell Hounds on us roar.

23 Tho millions ages roll away,
   Our torments are the same,
   And lye beneath an angry God
   In the eternal flame.

24 Sinners, awake in time, be wise,
   For that day is at hand;
   See that you make your peace with God,
   And be ready for to stand.

25 Great God, cut short these darkest hours,
   Roll on the glorious day,
   Come, holy spirit, from above,
   And bear our souls away,

26 Up to the courts of endless years,
   Where we can sit and sing,
   With all the Holy Angels there,
   To Jesus Christ our King.

"Father Tainter made a tune himself to suit the Meter."

ON THE DEATH OF SIX PERSONS BY DROWNING.

1 God's sovereign word created all
   That moves around this earthly Ball,
   Man while he in the Garden stood
   Receiv'd from him the greatest good.

2 But soon the glorious scene was changed,
   For Man had broke God's great command,
   Sin like a raging tyrant ran,
   Through every faculty of Man.

3 So Man, that's of a woman born,
   His glory in this world is gone;
   Perhaps you'll ask the reason why—
   I say because all Man must die.

4 Man's days are swifter than a post,
   Or the swift ship that runs her course;
   He lieth down and will not rise
   Till the last Trumpet rends the Skies.

5 O sovereign God, grant me thy Grace,
   Nor hide from me thy shining face;
   While I attempt to paint a scene,
   O may my soul dwell on the theme.

6 Come, mourn, thou sun that shone that day,
   And thou O moon with pale array,
   Ye twinkling stars that shone the night,
   O may the darkness hide your light.

7 Ye feathered songsters of the sky,
   Let not your voices sound on high,
   Fly to some distant shades, and there
   Be silent as the midnight air.

8 Ye scaly thousands of the deep,
   Be still and in her bosom sleep;
   Ye bleating flocks that sport and play,
   Be calm and quiet as the day.

9 Ye savage Beasts that range the wood,
   That seek from God your nightly food,
   Flee to your dens and there repine
   While God is chastening all mankind.

10 Ye liquid streams forbear to flow;
   Ye flaming fires that upward go,
   Each in your course now testify
   That there's a God who reigns on high.

11 Let all the whole creation see
   God's sovereign majesty,
   He reigns o'er all the earth and seas,
   And deals with mortals as he please.

12 Behold he shakes his awful hand
   Over the Town of Wilbraham,
   And there he lets stern justice fly
   On winged vengeance from on high.

(Continued on a future page.)

Reb. Samuel Tainter, (99)

Of Mohawk Valley, N. Y., was a son of John Tainter, of Watertown, and was born June 2, 1765. He studied for the ministry, and when about 23 years of age, left for the Mohawk Valley as a missionary to the Indians.

Nothing in addition to the above was known to the writer concerning the history of Rev. Samuel Tainter until a few months since, when he was informed by Deacon Tainter, of Eaton, N. Y., that there was an aged lady by the name of Tainter in a distant part of the county in which he resided. He subsequently visited her, and communicated the result as follows :—

"I visited the widow Tainter in June last, and found her quite superannuated, both physically and mentally, though still retaining the lineaments of intelligence and beauty. The history she gave of her husband was in the language following :

His name was Samuel, son of John Tainter, of Watertown. He had preached in Boston to large Congregations, and came to Ballston Springs for health. He was a Baptist clergyman, and finding friends at Ballston Springs, he went with them to Florida (N. Y.), about 16 miles from Schenectady, on the Mohawk River. She did not know him as a missionary, though he preached in that region some eight or nine years, making it his home at her father's, who was a Presbyterian clergyman, by the name of Eaton. It was thus that she first became acquainted with him, and subsequently married him, June 19, 1799.

After their marriage, he removed to Saugerfield, Oneida County, and preached there about two years. From Saugerfield he went to Cedarville, where he spent some three years. Besides these places, the old lady mentioned Dennistown, Stockbridge, Oneida and Lenox, Madison Co., where he died suddenly, in 1836, aged about 70 years. His mortal remains rest in the churchyard in the little village of Durhamville."

FAMILY.

(194) **John,**   b. Sept. 3, 1801 ; died March 3, 1802, æ. 5 months.
(195) **Mary,**   b. Jan. 9, 1803 ; died Sept., 1819, æ. 16 years.
(196) **Sally,**   b. May 6, 1807 ; died Sept., 1807, æ. 4 months.
(197) **Betsey,**   b. Feb. 11, 1812 ; died July, 1832, æ. 20 years.
(198) **Clarinda,** b. Oct. 19, 1814 ; m. John Clark, of [Lebanon ?], in 1851.
(199) **Lucinda,**   b. Nov. 11, 1818.
(200) **Anna,**   b. May 9, 1820 ; died June, 1821, æ. 1 year.

John Tainter, (102)

Of Boston, was born of pious parents in Watertown, April 20, 1770. He married Olive Lewis, of Roxbury, October 19, 1796, and settled in Boston, working at his trade, that of saddle and harness maker. It appears by his letters and other papers that he remained in Boston until about the year 1809, when he removed to Pembroke, N. H., to oversee in the paper-mill of his brother-in-law, John Lewis. During his residence here he sent his son John, with Timothy Lewis, to Plattsburg, N. Y., where he remained until the close of the war.

In 1812, he left Pembroke, and returned to Boston, where he again resumed his trade, in the building opposite the Old South Church, one of the *three* which now bears the appellation of "*the oldest house in Boston.*" In 1817 or 1818 he removed to the neighboring town of Charlestown, where he resided until his death, June 7, 1821, æ. 51.

In person he was of medium size, affable in manner, kind and charitable to all. He aspired to no station, but lived a peaceable, quiet and godly life, zealously watching over the moral and religious instruction of his children. Being sensible of his approaching end, and fortified with faith in Christ, the rock of his salvation, his days were closed with a calm resignation to the will of God.

His widow died in 1835 (?), aged 65 years. She was a fine old lady, and was greatly beloved by all who knew her. At her death, her only relatives near were three grandchildren ; Maria, the oldest, but 9 years of age, followed her remains to the grave, her sole mourner.

FAMILY.

(201) **John L.,** (Rev.) b. Dec. 8, 1798 (?) ; m. Judith Ann Dean, of Hudson, N. Y. She died Nov. 9, 1859.
(202) **William L.,** b. Nov. 27, 1800 (?) ; m. Sophia Bachellor, of Billerica, 1825 ; d.—(?), 1833.
(203) **Sarah L.,** b. Feb. 21, 1808 ; died about 1827.
(204) **Charles L.,** b. March 20, 1810 ; died Feb. 13, 1811.

Born in Boston, and baptized at the Brattle Square Church.

Nathaniel Tainter, (104)

Of Malden, was born in Watertown, in 1774. His parents dying while he was quite young, he went to live with the minister in Watertown until old enough to learn a trade. When about 14, he was bound to a saddle-tree maker in Malden, where he staid until 21. About this time chaises came into fashion and saddles fell into disuse, so he quit the trade; and having strained his stomach while doing some work on the farm, which unfitted him for very active toil thereafter, he learned gaiter-boot making, in which business he continued through life. He lived in Malden (now Melrose) until his death, February 20, 1852, aged 77.

He married Lois Howard, of Malden, about 1800. She died Sept., 1826.

They were both members of the Baptist Church, and are remembered as good and christian people.

FAMILY.

(205) **Ezra,** b. Jan. 31, 1803; m. Susanna Flint, of Reading, April 17, 1828.
(206) **Mary,** b. ———, 1808; died in 1826, aged 18.
Born in Malden.

Capt. William Tainter, (108)

Of Leominster, was born in Watertown on the old homestead, July, 1772. When he was seventeen years of age, his father, Eaires Tainter, sold the place and removed to Leominster.

He married Betsey Kilburn, of Lunenburg, Nov. 21, 1799, and took his father's farm and carried it on. His wife, who was "a most excellent woman," died Sept. 1, 1819, aged 41. He followed her in 1824, aged 52. They left seven children orphans, who were scattered in various directions.

FAMILY.

(207) **William C.,** (Capt.) b. June 21, 1800; m. Mary B. Hiscock, of Cambridgeport, April 15, 1827; d. March 30, 1853, æ. 52.
(208) **Eunice,**[*] b. April 4, 1802; resides in Leominster. When quite young she commenced teaching school, which vocation she pursued for twenty-nine years, much beloved and respected by her pupils.
(209) **Elmus,** b. March 11, 1804; m. Abigail Green, of Lexington, April 26, 1835.
(210) **Lewis,** b. Sep. 21, 1806; m. Lucinda Pierce, of Groton, April 5, 1831.
(211) **Elijah F.,** (Deacon) b. Aug. 11, 1808; m. Cordelia Bridges, of Watertown, Nov. 6, 1833.
(212) **Elizabeth,** b. Aug. 25, 1810; d. Dec. 9, 1811.
(213) **Daniel A.,** (Capt.) b. July 28, 1812; m. Sarah D. Willis, of Boston, March 18, 1833; d. April 4, 1854, æ. 41.
(214) **Elizabeth, 2d,** b. July 11, 1814; d. Aug. 26, 1834, æ. 20.
(215) **Solon S.,** b. June 2, 1816; m. Joanna Littlefield, of Holliston. She died July 30, 1858; m. 2d, Cynthia L. Littlefield, Nov. 10, 1859.
All born in Leominster.

Daniel A. Tainter, (110)

Of Watertown, son of Eaires Tainter, was born July 24, 1779. He was named David Adams, after a minister of Watertown. In 1789, his parents removed to Leominster, but on becoming of age, he returned and took charge of the farm of Miss Elizabeth Barnard, whom he married Dec. 1808.

He died June 22, 1839, in his 60th year. He was an overseer of the poor in Watertown.

Mrs. Tainter resides in Watertown on the farm where she was born, and is one of the oldest persons in town, being between 80 and 90.

FAMILY.

(216) **Susanna B.,** b. Jan 8, 1811; d. Jan. 30, 1812.
(217) **Dan'l Adams,** b. Nov. 3, 1812; m. Persis Richardson, of Watertown, Nov. 26, 1840.
(218) **Isaac B.,** b. March 7, 1816; d. Sep. 27, 1821.
(219) **Elizabeth,** b. May 7, 1820; d. Sep. 26, 1821.
(220) **George,** b. Oct. 13, 1822; m. Abby Sanger, of Watertown.
All born in Watertown.

[*] Petitioned the Legislature, and obtained leave, in 1837, to take the name of Elisabeth Eunice.

SEVENTH GENERATION.

1815 — 1854.

BEING THE CHILDREN OF

WILLIAM TAINTER, of Troy, N. Y. (112)
LUTHER G. TAYNTOR, of Philadelphia. (123)
JOEL TAYNTOR, of Framingham. (124)
ASA TAYNTOR, of New York. (128)
HOLLIS W. TAYNTOR, of Marlboro'. (132)
BENJAMIN TAYNTOR, of Eaton, N. Y. (139)
LORENZO TAYNTOR, of   "   "   (141)
JONAH TAYNTOR, of   "   "   (145)
Deacon JOSEPH TAYNTOR, of W. Eaton, "   (148)
Rev. ORASAMUS TAYNTOR, of Ashford, "   (150)
IRA B. TAYNTOR, of W. Eaton,   "   (152)
ERASTUS P. TAYNTOR, of Buffalo,   (153)
CYRUS K. TAYNTOR, of Eaton,   "   (154)
STEPHEN TAINTER, of Millbury, Mass. (155)
ABIJAH TAINTER, of   "   "   (156)
SIMON TAINTER, of   "   "   (160)
Adjt. HARVEY TAINTER, of Leicester. (162)
ELISHA L. TAINTER, of Medford. (171)
Deacon SAMUEL TAINTER, of Bradford, Me. (175)
SIMON TAINTER, of Carthage, Me. (177)
BENJAMIN TAINTER, of Bangor, Me. (178)
JOSIAH W. TAINTER, of Whitingham, Vt. (181)
Deacon JONATHAN TAINTER, of Kalamazoo, Mich. (185)
TIMOTHY TAINTER, of Pent Water, Mich. (186)
Deacon LOREN TAINTER, of Warsaw, Mo. (187)
STEPHEN G. TAINTER, of Prairie du Chien, Wis. (188)
Deacon EZEKIEL W. TAINTER, of   "   "   "   (189)
Rev. JOHN L. TAINTOR, of Cleveland, N.Y. (201)
WILLIAM L. TAINTER, of Boston. (202)
EZRA TAINTER, of Melrose. (205)
Capt. WILLIAM C. TAINTER, of Boston. (207)
ELMUS TAINTER, of Lexington. (209)
LEWIS TAINTER, of Lawrence. (210)
Deacon ELIJAH TAINTER, of Watertown. (211)
Capt. DANIEL A. TAINTER, of Boston. (213)
SOLON S. TAINTER, of Holliston. (215)
DANIEL A. TAINTER, of Watertown. (217)
GEORGE TAINTER, of   "   (220)

Families, 38.

William Tainter, (112)

Of Troy, N. Y., was born in Norwich, Conn., in 1781, learned the machinist trade, and married Elizabeth Jordan, in Albany. They had one son, who died at the age of 15.

He lived in Albany a part of his life, and died in Troy, a few years since, in advanced years.

FAMILY.

(221) **William**, b. ———; died, æ. 15.

The following comprises the services done by those of the name of Tainter, in the Massachusetts militia, during the Revolutionary War, but does not include services done by them in the Continental army.

The name of Abijah Tainter is borne on roll of Capt. James Greenwood's company, Col. Ebenezer Learned's regiment, on alarm of April 19, 1775. Three days and 90 miles travel as Sergeant from Sutton. Also on roll of Capt. Andrew Elliott's company, Col. Jonathan Holman's regiment, on alarm of Dec. 10, 1776. Service at Providence, 43 days. Rank not given.

The name of Aires Tainter is borne on roll of Capt. Samuel Barnard's company, Col. Thomas Gardner's regiment, on alarm of April 19, 1775. Six days from Watertown. Also on roll of men to guard the powder house at Watertown, from July 2, 1778, to July 17, 1779. Also on roll of Capt. Phineas Stearns's company, ordered by Gen. Washington to take possession of Dorchester Heights, March, 1776.

The name of Benjamin Tainter is borne on roll of Capt. Seth Morse's company, Col. Jonathan Ward's regiment, on alarm of April 19, 1775, as fifer from Westboro.' Also on roll of Capt. Timothy Brigham's company, Col. Job Cushing's regiment. Service at Bennington, from July 27th to August 29th, 1777. Also on roll of Capt. Nathan Fisher's company, Col. Nathaniel Wade's regiment, from July 20th to December 31st, 1778, as private from Westboro'. The name of Benjamin Tainter is borne on roll for service at Rhode Island, July 24th to December 31st, 1779, as private from Shrewsbury.

Also Benjamin Tainter, Jr. is borne on roll of Capt. Edmund Brigham's company, Col. Job Cushing's regiment, from Aug. 21st, 1777, 5 days, and 65 miles, as private from Westboro'. Also on roll of Capt. Ebenezer Belknap's company, Col. Wade's regiment, from June 20th to September 2d, 1778.

The name of Daniel Tainter is borne on roll of Capt. Elias Pratt's company from Sutton, stationed at Rutland, in 1779. Also on roll of Capt Benjamin Alton's company, Col. Rand's regiment, service at West Point in 1780, as private from Sutton.

The name of Jedediah Tainter is borne on roll of Capt. Daniel Barn's company, Col. Jonathan Ward's regiment, on alarm of April 19, 1775, of 8 mos. men, return of roll not dated, as Corporal, from Marlboro'.

The name of Joel Tainter is borne on roll of Capt. Andrew Elliott's company, Col. Ebenezer Learned's regiment, on alarm of April 19, 1775, thirteen days, as Corporal from Sutton. Also on roll of Capt. Bartholomew Woodbury's company, Col. Job Cushing's regiment, from August 13, 1777 (advanced from Corporal to Sergeant). Also on roll of Capt. Abijah Burbank's company, Col. Jacob Davis's regiment, from July 30th, 1780, as Sergeant.

The name of John Tainter is borne on roll of Capt Phineas Stearns's company, ordered by Gen. Washington to take possession of the Heights of Dorchester, March, 1776. Also as guard to the powder house at Watertown, from April 2, 1777, 6 months. Roll dated at Watertown. Also to guard the powder magazine from July 2, 1778, to July 17, 1779.

The name of Levi Tenter is borne on roll of Lieut. Jeremiah Blanchard's company, Col. Thos. Poor's regiment, of 8 months service from their arrival at Peekskill, North River, from May 16, 1778, to Jan. 29, 1779.

The name of Nahum Tainter is borne on roll of Capt. Andrew Elliott's company, Col. Ebenezer Learned's regiment, on alarm of April 19, 1775, as private from Sutton. Also on return of Capt. Isaac Bolster's company, Col. Learned's regiment of 8 months men. Name borne on coat roll dated Roxbury Camp, Dec. 26, 1775, as private, from Sutton. Also on roll of Capt. Abijah Burbank's company, Col. Jacob Davis's regiment, from July 30, 1780, as Corporal.

The name of Stephen Tainter is borne on roll of Capt. Timothy Brigham's company, Col. Job Cushing's regiment, service at Bennington, from July 27, to Aug. 29, 1777. Also on roll of Capt. Joseph Warren's company, Lt. Col. Wheelock's regiment, from Sept. 27 to Oct. 23, 1777, as drummer. Also on roll of Capt. Ephraim Lyon's company, Col. Wade's regiment, from June 24, 1778, as drummer. Roll dated Gratton. Also on roll of Capt. Nathan Fisher's company, Col. Nathaniel Wade's regiment, Rhode Island service, from July 20 to December 31, 1778, as drummer. Also mustered to serve at Rhode Island from July 24 to December 31, 1779, in Capt. Fisher's company, Col. Cushing's regiment, from Shrewsbury.

Stephen *and* Daniel Tainter are borne on roll of Capt. Joseph McNull's company, Lt. Col. Samuel Pierce's regiment, Rhode Island service, from May 12, 1779, two months each, as privates.

Luther G. Tayntor, (123)

Of Philadelphia, was born in Marlboro', Mass., March 21, 1792. He commenced learning the hatter's trade, in Marlboro', but buying his time, he went to Boston, and as clerk, entered the dry goods store of Robert Rogerson, who subsequently set him up in business. A few years after, he left Boston and went to Baltimore, forming a partnership with a man in Philadelphia, but not succeeding in business, he went to Lynchburg, Va., then to Fayetteville, N. C., where he staid a number of years, and then went to Charleston, S. C. In all these places he was engaged in mercantile business, and after visiting Massachusetts for the last time, in 1820, he returned to Charleston, S. C., and taught a school of young ladies, one of whom he procured for a help-meet. After staying awhile in Georgia, and N. York City, he entered the dry goods business in Philadelphia, where he continued until his death, March 19, 1836.

He married, Aug. 1, 1824, Mary Ann Hill, a native of Charleston, S. C., daughter of Capt. William F. Hill, a native of Spain. She died Oct. 25, 1852.

FAMILY.

(222) **Francis L.**, b. May 13, 1825; m. Elizabeth A. Thompson, of Warehouse-point, Ct., May 13, 1849; died July 20, 1853, æ. 28.

(223) **George W.**, b. March 6, 1827; entered the U. S. Navy when quite young, as a sailor, became schoolmaster on board the vessel. After serving five years he returned to Philadelphia, and died at Pittsburg, in 1854, æ. 27.

(224) **Henry C.**, b. Jan. 2, 1830; m. Harriet M. Knapp, of Phila., Dec. 19, 1832; d. Nov. 2, 1857, æ. 27.

(225) **John Q. A.**, b. March 18, 1832; died April 11, 1832.

(226) **Frederick A.**, b. July 8, 1834; entered the U. S. Army; is a recruiting officer, in Phila.

(227) **Marion J.**, b. Aug. 30, 1836; resides in Philadelphia.

(222) born in Augusta, Ga., the remainder in Philadelphia.

Joel Tayntor, (124)

Of Framingham, is a farmer. He was born in Marlboro', in 1796, and went to Framingham when seven years of age, where he was brought up by his uncle, John Nurse. In 1821, he married Lydia Leland, of Sherburne. He lives on a fine farm bought by him at that time, now about forty years ago. He and his family are all members of the Congregational Church.

FAMILY.

(228) **Lydia L.**, b. Feb. 7, 1822; m. Nathan H. Moore, of Framingham. They have four children, and reside in S. Braintree.

(229) **Lucy M.**, b. July 10, 1824; d. young.

(230) **Elizabeth**, b. March 20, 1826; m. John Boyd, Jr., of Marlboro'. They have two children, and reside in Boston.

(231) **Persis A.**, b. June 28, 1829; m. Warren Howe, of Sudbury. They have one child, and reside in Natick.

Born in Framingham.

Asa Tayntor, (128)

Of New York, was born in Marlboro', Mass., lived awhile in Medway and Holliston, Mass.; in the latter place was a leading one in establishing and building a Methodist Church. He has been afflicted many years with asthma. Being in New York one summer, and finding that his health was better, he removed thither. He lives at No. 364, Canal St., near Broadway, at which place he carries on a Bread and Cake Bakery.

He married Almira Trowbridge, of Marlboro', Nov. 1, 1825. They are both Church members in N. Y. City.

FAMILY.

(232) **Lucy W.**, b. Oct. 25, 1826; m. Isaiah F. Fay, of Southboro', Mass., Nov. 15, 1844; d. Jan. 20, 1852, æ. 25.

(233) **Edwin E.**, b. April 10, 1831; m. Eliza I. Edwards, of N. Y., June 25, 1851.

(234) **John W.**, b. Sept. 2, 1834; m. Elizabeth S. McDonnell, Feb. 9, 1858. (J. W. Tayntor & Co., Butter, 11 Clinton Market, N. Y.)

(235) **Emily F.**, b. Aug. 11, 1839.

(232) was born in Medway, the others in Holliston, Mass.

Hollis W. Tayntor, (132)

Of Marlboro', farmer and mill owner, lives on the old Tainter farm, settled upon one hundred and forty-two years ago by his great-grandfather, Deacon Joseph Taynter, from Watertown.* He married Olive W. Wiley, of Medway, June 12, 1855. Is a member of the Congregational Church. His mother, an aged lady, and his brother Henry (unmarried), are members of his family.

FAMILY.

(236) **Joseph I.,** b. July 14, 1857.

Benjamin Tayntor, (139)

Late of Russia, N. Y., was born in Worcester, N. Y., married Eliza Foster, of Sharon, N. Y., and died in Eaton, January, 1855.

FAMILY.

(237) **Guilford,** b. Oct. 31, 1820 ; m. Wealthy C. Wooden, of Russia, N. Y., Dec. 24, 1843 ; resides in Eaton, N. Y.
(238) **Mary A.,** b. ———— ; m. William Emory, of, and resides in Russia, N. Y.
(239) **Alanson,** b. Feb. 12, 1829 ; m. Mary Tayntor, of Eaton, July 4, 1852.
(237) was born in Sharon, N. Y., the others in Russia, N. Y.

Lorenzo Tayntor, (see 141)

Of Eaton, N. Y., owns a good farm and manages it well. He is a good economist, and has a peculiar faculty to turn every thing to the best account. He lives independent, and owes no man, makes butter, raises cattle, sheep and working oxen for market, and grows grain, fruit and garden vegetables to some extent. He has quite a numerous family of respectable and intelligent children, and every thing around him indicates thrift and prosperity. He married Louisa Foster, of Russia, N. Y., July 9, 1832.

FAMILY.

(240) **Mary L.,**   b. Feb. 17, 1835 ; m. Alanson Tayntor, July 4, 1852.
(241) **Olive U.,**   b. Aug. 13, 1837.
(242) **Marshall L.,** b. March 17, 1840.
(243) **Emma L.,**   b. Apr'l 28, 1842.
(244) **Helen C.,** b. Aug. 6, 1844.
(245) **Homer L.,** b. Jan. 25, 1847.
(246) **Margaret E.,** b. Sept. 2, 1849 ; died April 9, 1852.
(247) **Asa A.,**   b. Oct. 17, 1852.
(248) **Vivene,**   b. Oct. 26, 1855.
All born in Eaton.

Jonah Tayntor, (145)

Of Eaton, N. Y., farmer, is the only son of (76) Benjamin Tayntor that is now living. He is a plain man, rather retiring in his habits, and is a professor of religion ; is an independent liver, has a small family, works a small farm, and has a place for every thing and every thing in its place. He married Roby Luther, of Thuxton, N. Y., in 1835.

FAMILY.

(249) **Theresa,** b. in Lebanon, N. Y., Feb. 3, 1836.
(250) **Mary,**   b. in Georgetown, N. Y., Dec. 22, 1839.
(251) **Sarah L.,** b. in Eaton, N. Y., Aug. 24, 1851.

* April, 1717, Joseph Tainter buys of B. Bailey, for 200£, "27 1-2 Acres in that part of the town which was the Indian Plantation, called Agogonquemessett, on the westerly side of the Indian Hill, and on Cow Commons."

Deacon Joseph Taynter, (148)

Of West Eaton, N. Y., born April 3, 1803, was brought up under the instruction and discipline of pious parents, and was baptized into the fellowship of the Baptist Church in the place where he resided, in 1821. In 1834, he was appointed deacon in a branch of the second Baptist Church of Eaton, which was constituted in the immediate neighborhood of his residence. Subsequently, this branch was merged into the body of the Church in Eaton Village, where he was again appointed deacon, in 1840. In this Church he had the charge of a large Bible class and Sabbath School most of the time for fifteen years. In 1853, a Church edifice was erected, and a new Church formed at West Eaton, where he was re-appointed deacon.

At 20 years of age he engaged as a teacher in one of the District Schools in Madison County, and in the following year being resolved on pursuing this his favorite employment, he entered the Academical School in Hamilton, Madison Co. Here, at intervals, he spent a portion of his time up to 1829, laboring on a farm as a hired servant in the summer season, and teaching school winters. In this school he gave his attention mainly to the common English studies, and the higher branches of Mathematics, Elocution, Surveying and Astronomy. In 1828, he purchased a farm of one hundred and thirty acres, and married Ann Bennett, of the town of Eaton, who was also a teacher.

These changes did not, however, deter him at once from his favorite employment. He continued to teach during the winter seasons in some of the largest and most popular schools in the County, until the pressing cares of farm and family compelled him to abandon teaching altogether, in 1840.

In 1829, he was school inspector, and subsequently he was run three consecutive years for town superintendent of schools, but in this failed, not being, as the saying goes, "*on the right side in politics.*" In the military he served as Private, Corporal, Sergeant, Lieutenant and Captain. In 1836, he was one of twelve drawn from the Grand Jury box to appraise damages on a section of the N. Y. Central Railroad. He has since served a number of years as Grand Juror in the Courts of Madison County. In 1837, he was elected one of the Assessors of the town of Eaton ; again in 1844, for a term of two years ; and again in 1854, for a term of three years.

He owns a farm of 275 acres, raises some grain for market, keeps 25 head of cattle, 3 horses, and 200 Merino sheep. In 1854, he erected a new house, in which he now resides, while his son-in-law manages the farm for one half of the avails.

His family consists of a wife and two daughters, one of whom is married.

He is a life member of the Baptist Missionary Union, and also of the American and Foreign Bible Society, and has been a professor of religion nearly forty years.

FAMILY.

(252) **Ann A.**, b. March 13, 1831 ; died Feb. 3, 1855.
(253) **Eliza M.**, b. June 5, 1834 ; m. Jeremiah B. Wadsworth, of Eaton, June 16, 1853.
(254) **Homer B.**, b. May 4, 1836 ; died Aug. 28, 1844.
(255) **Amelia B.**, b. Sept. 14, 1845.
　　All born in Eaton, N. Y.

Rev. Orsamus Tainter, (150)

Of Ashford, N. Y., is a Baptist clergyman, and is in the strictest sense of the word a hard-working man. He lives in a new country, works a small farm, and is pastor of three churches, and in many instances does the work of an Evangelist, and the blessings of Heaven seem to attend his labors wherever he goes. He is scrupulously conscientious, and engages in no enterprise either great or small unless he is first satisfied that it is the will of the Lord. He has had many afflictions, but feels the assurance that they will work out for him " a far more exceeding and eternal weight of glory." In a letter just received he says, " I was blessed with having for a mother an honest and true-hearted daughter of *old Massachusetts*, who was the great instrument in the hands of God by which in early life I became religiously inclined."

He married Roxanna M. Daniels, of Eaton, Sept. 19, 1832. She died June 18, 1856. He married, second, Mrs. Sophia Denman, of Buffalo, March 4, 1857.

FAMILY.

(256) **Sarah L.,**   b. in Otto, N. Y., Sept. 20, 1834; died Aug. 8, 1836.
(257) **Caroline M.,** b. in "   "   Aug. 28, 1837; died Sept. 13, 1838.
(258) **Emma A.,**   b. in "   "   June 13, 1843.
(259) **Ellen A.,**   b. in "   "   June 25, 1847.
(260) **Lucy R.,**   b. in Ashford, N. Y., June 4, 1856.
        Flora,

Ira D. Tainter, (152)

Of West Eaton, N. Y., owns a delightful situation near that village, of 150 acres. The making of butter and cheese is the chief business of himself and household. He keeps some 30 cows, and has an interesting family, pleasant and courteous in all their social and domestic relations. He has obtained considerable celebrity as a teacher of common schools, having taught some twenty years. He and his wife and two of his daughters are members of the Baptist Church.

He married Thankful C. Darrow, of Eaton, March, 1837.

FAMILY.

(261) **Marion J.,**   b. Oct. 18, 1838.
(262) **Sarah L.,**   b. Dec. 6, 1840.
(263) **Albert I.,**   b. Feb. 25, 1844.
(264) **Rufus N.,**   b. Feb. 11, 1846.
(265) **Helen E.,**   b. Jan. 9, 1849.
(266) **Adelia S.,**   b. Aug. 29, 1852; died Sept. 25, 1852.
(267) **Charles E.,** b. Aug. 2, 1854.
        All born in Eaton, N. Y.

Erastus P. Tainter, (153)

Of Buffalo, N. Y., is a man of industry and energy. He has changed his residence several times within the space of a few years; now lives on the banks of Lake Erie, within the limits of the City of Buffalo, where he and his family have been subjected to great peril by inundations from the lake during the past season. He and his wife are both members of the Baptist Church. He is a man of all labor. Married Marietta S. Beebe, of Fenner, N. Y., Aug. 14, 1838.

FAMILY.

(268) **Mary E.,**   b. June, 1839.
(269) **Rufus A.,**   b. March, 1841.
(270) **Oscar J.,**   b. June, 1844.
(271) **Eugene M.,** b. Jan., 1847.
(272) **Ruth A.,**   b. July, 1849; died in Eaton, April, 1851, æ. 2.
(273) **Lewis M.,**   b. May, 1852.
(274) **Corrine D. F.,** b. Oct., 1854.
        (268) born in Lebanon, the others in Eaton.

Cyrus K. Tainter, (154)

Of Eaton, N. Y., is a farmer, a man that takes the world as it is, thinks soberly, acts prudently, lives well, brings up his children well, and is himself a good citizen and a member of the Baptist Church. He has owned several small farms at different times, and in different places, but now lives on one which he rents. He keeps a dairy and makes butter and cheese.

He married Ruth A. Beebe, of Fenner, N. Y., March 24, 1843. Married, second, Abigail Harris, of Thuxton, Sept. 8, 1851.

FAMILY.

(275) Eliza A.,	b. Oct. 2, 1846.	(277) Ruth L.,	b. May 7, 1853.
(276) Homer J.,	b. Sept. 3, 1849.	(278) Cyrus H.,	b. June 11, 1856.

(275) born in Lebanon, (276) in Ashford, (277) and (278) in Eaton.

Stephen Tainter, (155)

Of Millbury, was born in 1776, married Polly Dyke, by whom he had one child. She died July 4, 1834. He married, second, Lucretia Gates, Oct. 18, 1834, and died in 1843, æ. 67.

It is said that he possessed an ancient parchment, on which was written the pedigree of the Tainter family in various hand-writings, and running back a number of centuries. Several persons testify to having seen it, among them Dr. Gates, a brother of his second wife.

Stephen Tainter was an oldest son, his paternal ancestors were all oldest sons, and it is quite probable that such a paper was transmitted through the line; but he left no children, and at his death his papers fell into indifferent hands. All attempts to find it have been in vain.

FAMILY.

(279) Sumner, b. ——; died young.

Abijah Tainter, (156)

Of Millbury, was born in 1778. He married Mercy Shumway, of Oxford, who died Sept. 26, 1815. He married, second, Mrs. Hannah Smith, and died in 1830, æ. 52, leaving a large family of children.

FAMILY.

(280) Fanny,	b. Feb. 6, 1800; m. —— Burt.
(281) Lucy,	b. Jan. 7, 1801; died young.
(282) Leonard,	b. April 13, 1804; m. Lurenda Barnes, of Cato, N. Y., March 6, 1826.
(283) David,	b. Nov. 5, 1805; m. Mrs. Eliza T. B. Marble, Oct. 1, 1836.
(284) Daniel,	b. Aug. 28, 1807; m. Betsey M. Marsh, of Sutton, April 21, 1833.
(285) Sumner,	b. Jan. 16, 1810; d. in White Pigeon, Mich., Jan., 1845, æ. 35.
(286) Willard S.,	b. Feb. 20, 1812; m. Hannah Goddard, of Worcester; d. Jan. 28, 1859.
(287) Almira,	b. Oct. 29, 1819; m. Asa Burt, of Millbury, Dec., 1839.
(288) Sarah,	b. Aug. 22, 1824; m. —— Bates, of Franklin.
(289) Sybil,	b. July 8, 1825; m. Theodore Bowen, of Millbury.
(290) Lucy,	b. Jan. 29, 1826; died ——.
(291) Emeline,	b. July 10, 1830; died ——.

All born in Millbury.

Simon Tainter, (160)

Of Millbury, born Oct. 16, 1799, received a good farm at the death of his father, and carried it on some ten years, but he lost his property, and for a number of years took charge of a farm in Millbury, and the Town-poor farm one year. He afterwards lived in Sterling, Leicester, and other places. He was an overseer of the poor in Millbury, and in Leicester a Highway Surveyor and Prudential Committee man.

He m. Hannah Rice, Sept. 3, 1822. The family reside in Stafford Springs, Ct.

FAMILY.

(292) Joel E.,	b. June 8, 1823; m. Jane E. Taylor, of N. Becket, Mass., Mar. 4, 1850. She died Nov. 3, 1855; m., 2d, Nancy M. Engle, of Superior, Iowa,
(293) Harriet E.,	b. Aug. 10, 1826; died Oct. 25, 1847, æ. 21. [April 8, 1857.
(294) Charles A.,	b. April 20, 1834; m. Frances A. Hall, of Manchester, Conn., Nov. 26, 1857; is overseer in a woolen mill, Wales, Mass.
(295) Elbridge G.,	b. April 17, 1837; resides at Stafford Springs, Conn.

Harvey Tainter, (162)

Of Leicester, farmer, was born in Sutton, N. Parish, Jan. 9, 1784. When he was about a year old his parents removed to Leicester, and cleared the farm where he resides. He received an Academy education, and at the age of 21 commenced teaching school, which vocation he followed about fifteen years, teaching in Spencer, Worcester, &c. &c.

He married Lucy Copeland, of Leicester, Sept. 12, 1816. She is a lineal descendant of Gov. William Bradford, John Alden, and also of Rev. James Keith, who came from Scotland in 1662.

He has been chosen Assessor, Coroner, Treasurer and Selectman, in Leicester, was a number of years Adjutant of the regiment of Cavalry, in the First Brigade and 7th Division Massachusetts Militia; was appointed, in 1814, Marshal of a Court Martial holden in Brookfield, and one of three Commissioners for setting off and dividing the real estates of three of the largest land-holders in Leicester, among their heirs—has been juror to Courts holden at Worcester, and to the U. S. Court, at Boston; was one of a committee of three appointed to change the inside of Leicester meeting-house, in 1829, the cost of which was $3,484.

In 1840, he was appointed Assistant Marshal for taking a portion of the U. S. Census, Massachusetts District.

Years ago, when the temperance movement commenced, he was among the first in Leicester to sign the pledge and to banish liquor from the harvest-field; also one of the first who helped establish a sabbath school in the town. He has a number of mottoes, which being printed on cards, he presents to his friends. The following is one :—

> "Express your love to God,
> And charity for man,
> By doing always right,
> And all the good you can."

Mr. Tainter is an "old line democrat," but as such *must not be judged of by the company he keeps.* In fact it has proved a blessing to his neighbors that he is such.

A few years ago an ineffectual attempt was made to establish a Post Office in the village where he resides. This year it was renewed, and as it was deemed necessary to the success of the enterprise that a Democrat be named for Post Master, *and as there was but one Democrat in the place,* Mr. Tainter was obliged to be the candidate for that honor. It was promptly conferred upon him, and on the 22d of February last, a Post Master dispensed his postage stamps to the happy villagers of Cherry Valley.

FAMILY.

(296) **Isaac K.,** b. Jan. 9, 1818 ; m. Harriet N. Eddy, of Auburn, Mass., Oct. 6, 1845.
(297) **Daniel,** b. Sept. 8, 1819 ; m. Sarah E. Johnson, of Worcester, May 21, 1840.
(298) **Nahum,** (Rev.) b. June 14, 1821 ; m. Ann E. Pierce, of Smithfield, R. I., May 28, 1845.
(299) **Ephraim C.,** b. July 15, 1823 ; m. Elvira L. Parks, of Shirley, 1848.
(300) **Harvey S.,** b. April 28, 1825 ; died Sept. 28, 1827, æ. 2.
(301) **Lucy K.,** b. Dec. 3, 1827 ; died Sept. 16, 1844, æ. 16.
(302) **Harvey S., 2d,** b. Oct. 11, 1829 ; m. Sarah E. Burbank, of Worcester, Oct. 8, 1851.
(303) **Carver,** b. July 8, 1831 ; m. Emily E. Capron, of Worcester, May 5, 1857.
(304) **Laura,** b. April 19, 1836.
(305) **Cecelia L.,** b. Oct. 15, 1841.
All born in Leicester.

(A Copy). Birth day reflections, Jan. 9, 1805. This day brings me to the twenty-first year of my age; an age, at which I consider myself free.

It is natural for people on their birth day to make some reflections, and especially so, on the day of their freedom.

My present circumstances naturally lead me to reflect on the manner of my education, which may very fitly be compared to a young appletree. I at first sprung up in about middling soil, and was left, for a while, mostly to nature. At length, I had some attention paid me. I was pruned, and flourished for awhile, and then left for a while to be browsed down by forgetfulness. I was pruned again, and again browsed down. In this manner, I grew, like the appletree in the mowing land, starting in the spring, and growing through the summer : but in autumn browsed down by the cattle. In this manner I arrived to my present height in knowledge—learning one winter and forgetting the next summer.

But through the kindness and good attention of my parents, I have arrived to a height capable of bearing some fruit, and may I, by future application and attention, be enabled to bring myself to a state, capable of bearing *fruit* * *which shall prove an honor to myself,* a reward to my parents, *and a blessing to Society.*

In his youthful days, while prospecting as to the future, he gave utterance to his anxiety respecting a wife, in the following lines :—

Is my dear wife to be a "Scold,"	Is she to be a vixen "Drab,"	Will she be always making Strife
A termigant so fierce and bold,	A ragged and a dirty "Hag,"	With honest neighbors all her life,
As to be armed, both night and noon,	Ne'er known, or seen,	By dealing slander and deceit,
With boiling water, tongs, or Broom ?	Her clothes to wash, or house to clean ?	From house to house, thro' all the street?
Then I'll not marry.	Then I'll do my own baking,	I had rather—d——n it,
Alone I'll tarry—till death.	Mending and making—till death.	Live a hermit—till death. 1802.

* A crop of thriving sons, in Worcester and elsewhere, prove a fair realization of his ambition.

TAINTER GENEALOGY.

Elisha L. Tainter, (171)

A farmer, was born in Westboro', Feb. 5, 1777. When he was three years of age his parents removed to Watertown. He married Sarah P. Smith, of Lexington, Feb., 1800, and settled in Weston, afterwards lived in Stoneham, Cambridge, and Medford. He died at the latter place, Sept. 19, 1851, æ. 74. His first wife died in 1806, leaving two children. Aug. 26, 1810, he married Lydia Fessenden, of Lexington. He acquired a comfortable fortune by farming, and was an honest and exemplary man. About twenty years before his death, he was taken with the shaking palsy in one arm, which disease finally seized his whole frame, rendering him helpless, so much so, that he was unable to walk or use his hands without assistance.

FAMILY.

(306) **Mary A.,**   b. Aug. 23, 1801; m. John Clough, Feb. 17, 1820; resides in Medford.
(307) **Albert,**   b. May 4, 1803; m. Mary G. Tufts, Aug. 20, 1826.
(308) **Edwin,**   b. June 15, 1815; m. Charlotte B. Ewell, of Medford, Jan. 2, 1838.
(309) **Adaline M.,** b. Dec. 30, 1817; died March 8, 1819.
(310) **Emeline M.,** b. Dec. 16, 1819; m. Elijah S. Ewell, May 20, 1840; resides in Medford.
(311) **Lydia A.,**   b. Dec. 26, 1821; m. John A. Bartol. Sept. 17, 1843; resides in Marblehead.
(312) **Cordelia,**   b. Jan. 30, 1824; m. John E. Hutchins, Dec. 25, 1845; resides in Medford.
(306) and (307) were born in Weston, the others in Medford.

Deacon Samuel Tainter, (175)

Of Bradford, Me., farmer, was born in Vermont, in 1787. In the year 1790, his parents removed to Watertown, and, in 1803, to Jay, Me. When 19 years of age he bought his time from his father for one hundred dollars, and with his brother-in-law, Vose, purchased a farm on time, in W. Cambridge, Mass. His life has been a chequered one, he having three or four times lost his property, but "Phœnix-like," he has risen from the ashes, and now owns a pleasant place of 90 acres in Bradford, with a large orchard of 500 apple trees, in a bearing state, with pears, cherries and plums in abundance.

FAMILY.

(313) **Thomas D.,** b. May 19, 1814; m. Mary Black, of Sedgewick, Me., Oct. 28, 1837.
(314) **Margaret H.,** b. Dec. 2, 1816; m. Robert Bartlett, of Bethel, Me., Jan., 1835; resides at So. Aurora, N. Y. They have 8 children.
(315) **Samuel H.,** b. Oct., 1818; m. Joanna Black, of Sedgewick, Me., Aug., 1841.
(316) **Hannah S.,** b. Oct., 1821; m. Allen Hammond, of Hermon, Me.
(317) **Nancy D.,** b. July, 1823; m. Josiah Bartlett, of Bethel, Me., May, 1841; now a farmer in Wellsville, N. Y.; have 7 children.
(318) **Amasa D.,** b. Aug. 11, 1825; m. Louisa Dexter, of Independence, N. Y., June, 1857.
(319) **Amos L.,** b. Aug. 29, 1828; m. Mary E. Rolfe, of Wellsville, N. Y., Sept., 1855.
(320) **Sarah,** b. April 22, 1830; m. Alonzo Trim, of Charleston, Me., May, 1850; have 4 children.
(321) **Horace S.,** b. Oct. 31, 1832; died May 17, 1849, æ. 16.
(322) **Robert B.,** b. Nov. 21, 1834.
(323) **Marcia E.,** b. Sept. 8, 1837.
The last three born in Glenburn, the others in Bradford.

While at W. Cambridge, his brother-in-law failed, so he returned to Maine, and commenced on a farm there, farming in summer and lumbering in winter. By the time he was twenty-five he had nearly paid for it. May 10, 1812, he married Sarah Davis, of Lisbon, Me., and continued to live on his farm until 1832, where he met with good success up to 1814–15, at which time he went on a visit to Brewer, where a brother-in-law traded largely in merchandize, who offered him goods extremely low for produce, and he was induced to com-

mence an exchange trade with him, which he did on a large scale, carrying
him several one horse loads of butter, cheese, poultry, &c., taking in exchange
goods at very low rates, which he was able to sell at large profits. He then
drove him six fat oxen loaded with produce, poultry, &c., and took his goods
in exchange, but on his return home with the goods he was overtaken by a
Custom House Officer, who took all his goods, the duties not having been
paid, which explained why the goods had been bought so cheap. On getting
out of this difficulty, he found himself financially worse than nothing.

He purchased a tract of pine timber and went to lumbering, and at one
sweep placed himself where he was before he went into the trading speculation.
Finding the lumbering business profitable, he the next winter bought a larger
tract, and all the winter with a small gang cut and hauled the lumber. The
next spring there was a great freshet on the Androscoggin, which carried off
the mills owned by the parties to whom he sold the lumber (now carried out
to sea); they failed, and he has their notes to this day. This left him again financially worse than nothing. He called on his creditors and explained matters,
and told them if they would wait three years, he thought that he could then
settle. They had about agreed to, when one sued, then another, and within a
week every one sued, and all that he had was put up at auction. He managed to maintain his family until the spring of 1826, when buying a yoke of oxen
on credit, and borrowing another of his brother, he commenced teaming from
Jay to Augusta, taking merchandise one way and shingles the other. This
he found profitable, and in less than a year he had two six-ox teams on the
road all paid for. He remained in this business four years, then sold out,
bought back his old place, and paid up his old debts. He was induced by his
friends to exchange his ox teams for horses, which he did at good prices, and
again commenced teaming. He followed the business another four years, and
run behind with horses nearly as fast as he before went ahead with oxen. At
this juncture (1831), he was taken sick, and was unable to work for one year.
In the fall, being able to ride, he visited Brewer, and was induced to let his
farm, and move to that vicinity, which he did the following year, to the town
of Glenburn, and again went to lumbering on contract. He did an extra
winter's work, and in the spring parties offered to pay all expenses and one
thousand dollars besides, for his job. He could not get released from the parties with whom he first contracted, who wished to hold the lumber, as they
had saw-mills themselves, telling him that instead of one thousand, he should
eventually get two. The lumber was sawed, and during the business it became necessary (?) for him to endorse notes; the parties failed and died, and
he, to pay the notes which he had endorsed, was obliged to sell his farm and
the interest he had in a farm at Glenburn, and again he became worse than
nothing.

He then bargained for a piece of land (50 acres) with a shell of a house
which he could have by paying $260 in November following. He obtained
the $260 by cutting cord wood, peeling bark, &c., in season to obtain a deed
of the place, but about this time a relative died, and $1500 of his debts, with
a debt of $700 which he owed him, came against him. These heavy debts
induced him to go into bankruptcy, which he *did*, and his small place was
sold; but he got it back again and lived on it until 1845. Having in the mean-
while brought it under a good state of cultivation, and built good buildings
upon it, &c., he was offered $1500 for it, and exchanged for a farm in Bradford,
of 90 acres, where he now resides.

Simon Tainter, (177)

Of Carthage, Me., farmer, is an aged and much respected citizen, and the pioneer of that town. Fifty years ago, when but 19 years of age, and when this place was but a wilderness, he came here with an axe on his shoulder, with the hopes of some day seeing the fruits of his hard labor. He now lives on the farm that he then cleared and has since brought to a thriving state.

A happy old man, he sits by his own fireside in comfort and peace, and lives independent, his children all around him.

He has many years been Town Treasurer, Selectman, &c., and has done much public business. He has been run for town Representative, when there being no choice the first time, he withdrew his name.

He was born in Watertown, July 10, 1792; married Asenath Reed, of Weld, Me., May 6, 1816.

FAMILY.

(324) **Alsworth.** b. Sept. 27, 1816; m. Caroline Gould, of Carthage, Me., Jan. 9, 1844.
(325) **Wyman V.,** b. Jan. 1, 1822; m. Susan F. Wilson, of W. Cambridge, Mass., May 7, 1848; m., 2d, Mary Maxfield, of Carthage, Me., Aug. 2, 1855.
(326) **Gilbert L.,** b. June 13, 1825; m. Semantha O. Fuller, of Carthage, March 27, 1853.
(327) **Rosilla M.,** b. July 22, 1828; m. Dr. J. M. Corrison, of Standish, Me., Aug. 3, 1852. He died June 19, 1857, æ. 36, at Woodville, Miss. Mrs. Corrison resides in Portland, Me.
(328) **Christopher C.,** b. Feb. 8, 1836.
    All born in Carthage, Me.

Benjamin Tainter, (178)

Of Bangor, Me., merchant, was born in Watertown, Mass., May 22, 1795. His parents removed to Jay, Me., in 1817. He married Deborah Merritt, about the year 1820, and died in 1839, æ. 44.

FAMILY.

(329) **Caroline M.,** b. July 17, 1821; died March 3, 1845, æ. 23.
(330) **Benjamin,** b. July 10, 1822; died Aug. 10, 1822.
(331) **Thomas P.,** b. July 20, 1823; m. Josephine C. Brooks, of Apalachicola, Fa., May 15, 1851.
(332) **Charles B.,** b. July 4, 1826; lost at sea, from the Bk "Susan and Jane," Jan. 13, 1845, æ. about 19.
(333) **James H.,** b. Sept. 20, 1828; died Jan., 1832, æ. 3.
(334) **James H., 2d,** b. April 8, 1831; late of Apalachicola, Fa.; d. in New York City, Dec. 15, 1858, æ. 27.
(335) **Harriet A.,** b. June 15, 1833; m., Sept., 1857, Mr. Richard B. Watson, of Georgia. They reside in Apalachicola, Florida.
(336) **John M.,** b. 1835; clerk in a cotton Com. House, in Apalachicola, Fla.
(337) **Horace B.,** b. Dec. 4, 1837; clerk in the N. Y. and N. Haven Railroad Co.'s office, N. York City.
(338) **George Tainter Dale,** b. March 22, 1840; adopted son of Dea. Samuel H. Dale, of Bangor, Me.
    All born in Bangor, Me.

The following is an extract from a letter written by one of his sons, Thomas P. Tainter, Esq., of Apalachicola, Fla.

. . . . . "I regret that it is not in my power to furnish you with any facts or data of importance concerning my family, but I presume you would be pleased to learn the little that I can impart, however meagre. If it possesses no interest, it will serve to swell the book and to make the volume respectable in size, if not in matter, which I suppose is a desideratum. However, I will cheerfully aid you all that I can.

Some years since, while visiting Hartford, Conn., I made the acquaintance of Gov. Seymour, of that State, and was presented by him with a small pamphlet, entitled the "Genealogy of the Tainter family," which was the first that I knew of any attempt to collect the records of the name.

My father died suddenly in the summer of 1839, leaving my mother with a family of eight children, six boys and two girls. He had been engaged in active business as a merchant, the greater portion of his life, and was interested to a considerable extent in shipping. The financial storm of 1836–7, that swept over the country, making bankrupt three-fourths of the country, prostrated my father, and just as he was recovering from the blow, and the clouds that dimmed the commercial horizon were breaking away before the sunshine of prosperity, his labors were arrested by death.

Years have passed since that event, and from a child I have grown to manhood's estate, yet the scene is fresh and vivid in my mind. At his death, my mother was left with little to support her large family, and upon me, being the oldest boy, devolved the responsibility and care of mother, sisters and brothers. In this I was seconded nobly by a brother two years my junior. Unhappily he met a most untimely death. On his voyage home from Smyrna to Boston, he was lost over-board in the Mediterranean Sea, on the same day my mother died at home in Bangor. Previous to this, my oldest sister had died. My little brothers and one sister were left without a protector, but kind friends provided for them until my return the following year.

I had left home immediately after my father's death, and was absent at the time of the decease of my mother and sister.

At the age of sixteen I commenced life as a sailor, and for a few months sailed out of New York, but soon became tired of it and entered the office of a commission merchant, in N. York. In 1842, I came to Florida, where I have since resided with the exception of one year in New Orleans. For the last ten years I have been engaged in business as a merchant. Previous to that, I was clerk with my present father-in-law, in the commission and shipping business. I have a brother and a married sister living here. I enclose you a list of the names of our family, with all the facts that I possess, and regret that I am unable to furnish you with items of greater interest.

Respectfully and truly yours,

THOMAS P. TAINTER.

CHILDREN OF MAJ. JOHN WISWALL AND MARY TAYNTOR (166) HIS WIFE.

Luther Wiswall,   b. Jan. 9, 1801; m. Sophronia Kendall; is Pastor of the Congrega-
                       tional Church in Windham, Me.; has two children living, Luther
                       and Ellen K.
Mary Wiswall,   b. Aug. 22, 1804: resides in New Haven, Conn.
Elizabeth Wiswall,   b. April 18, 1807; m. Sumner Frost, of Marlboro', N. H., Oct. 1828;
                       died at Newport, Vt., June 3, 1835, leaving two daughters, Carrie E.
                       and Harriet A.
Louisa Wiswall,   b. Oct. 12, 1809; m. Levi Jones, of Marlboro', N. H., June 25, 1831;
                       have three children, Sarah M., Luther M., and Levi D. Wiswall.
Laurinda Wiswall,   b. Aug. 10, 1811; resides in Marlboro', N. H.
Henry Trowbridge Wiswall, b. April 13, 1816; m. Harriet Farrar, who died. He m., 2d,
                       Ruth Lawrence. They have five boys, named Osgood R., Henry
                       L., Oren H., Frank T. and Herbert Tayntor Wiswall.
John Tayntor Wiswall, b. Dec. 21, 1819; m. Mary W. Stebbins, of Roxbury, N. H., Dec.
                       19, 1849. She died Jan., 1856. He resides in Marlboro'.
Oren Wiswall,   b. Sept. 19, 1822; died in Lowell, Mass., Oct. 2, 1851.

Josiah W. Tainter, (181)

Of Whitingham, Vt., farmer, son of Dea. Jonathan Tainter, of Somers, Ct., was born in Dummerston, Vt., Jan. 26, 1782. He married Molly Davis, of Somers, Ct., Aug. 26, 1803, and settled in Whitingham, in which town he has been a member of the Baptist Church over forty years. His wife died March 22, 1848, æ. 67.

FAMILY.

(339) **Rebecca,**   b. Jan. 15, 1806; m. Benjamin Eames, of Halifax, Vt., May 15, 1825.
(340) **Betsey,**   b. Sept. 8, 1809; m. David Chase, Oct. 6, 1829; second, Isaac Allerd, of Whitingham, Vt.
(341) **Norris D.,**   b. March 6, 1812; m. Sarah Martin, of Whitingham, Sept. 2, 1834.
(342) **Lydia,**   b. July 5, 1814; m. Joseph Farnum, of   "   Feb. 14, 1837.
(343) **Josiah W.,**   b. March 1, 1818; m. Elizabeth Russell, of Northampton, Mass., Nov. 5, 1838; killed by falling between two cars at Holyoke, Mass., Feb. 20, 1854, æ. 35.
(344) **James M.,**   b. April 5, 1821; m. Catherine Lake, of Whitingham, Feb. 6, 1848.
All born in Whitingham, Vt.

Deacon Jonathan Tainter, (185)

Of Kalamazoo, Michigan, son of Dea. Jonathan Tainter, of Somers, Conn., was born in that place in 1791. At the death of his father, in 1801, he went to live with a farmer named Davis. In 1804, he went to Whitingham, Vt., and lived with John Cooley, who had married his oldest sister. They all removed to the western part of N. York State in 1805.

He married Eunice, daughter of Deacon Benjamin Bowman, from Marlboro', Vt., Dec. 31, 1821, and settled in the Genesee Valley, town of York, N. Y. He suffered from ill health a number of years, consequent on lifting, and working beyond his strength when young, and he is in feeble health now. He lived in York until the fall of 1850, when he removed to Michigan.

He was a deacon in the Christian Church of York.

FAMILY.

(345) **Rosetta,**   b. Sept. 28, 1822; m. Elder Samuel M. Fowler, of Riga, N. Y., July 10, 1842; resides in Spring(?)water, Mich.
(346) **Cyntha,**   b. Jan. 20, 1824; m. Peter A. Beebe, of Leicester, N. Y., July 10, 1842; resides in Brady, Mich.
(347) **Lucinda,**   b. Dec. 1, 1825; m. Gideon A. Mosher, of Covington, Wyoming Co., N. Y., Sept. 11, 1844; died May 5, 1848.
(348) **Edna,**   b. Oct. 31, 1827; died Dec. 28, 1828.
(349) **Edna M.,**   b. Aug. 26, 1829; m. Morris M. Thayer, of Oshtomo, Mich., May 12, 1851.
(350) **Jonathan,**   b. Jan. 17, 1831; m. Marancy Blakesley, Feb. 2, 1852. A miller, at Millburg, Mich.
(351) **Lucinda,**   b. Dec. 10, 1832; m. Lyman Blakesley, Feb. 2, 1852; d. Sept. 14, 1852.
(352) **Amanda,**   b. Nov. 8, 1834; died March 22, 1837.
(353) **Silas B.,**   b. July 25, 1840.
(354) **Merritt R.,**   b. May 2, 1845; died Sept. 22, 1847.
All born in York, N. Y.

Timothy Tainter, (186)

Of Pent Water, Michigan, trapper and hunter, was born in Somers, Conn., April 5, 1796, son of Deacon Jonathan Tainter, who died when the subject of this notice was but a few years old. At six years of age he went into the family of William Cook (his guardian), of Somers, where he remained until he was fifteen. Soon after he was bound to John Hunt, of the same place, to learn the blacksmith's trade. With him he emigrated to Ohio, in 1815, and remained with him two years.

In Feb., 1818, he married Louise Peck, from Massachusetts. She died in May, 1819, leaving a daughter. In Feb., 1821, he married Jemima Allen, also from Massachusetts.

In 1824, he built a saw-mill in Chardon, Ohio, and "lumbered" 14 years, then sold and bought a farm which he occupied 7 years, exchanged for property in Pennsylvania, where he farmed and kept a public house ten years, then sold and returned to Ohio, where he bought a farm and lived a year, when leaving Mrs. Tainter with Mr. Newcomb, their son-in-law, to provide and take care of the farm, he took up his rifle to which he has always been strongly attached, and betook himself to the trail. He lives and sleeps in the wilderness alone for weeks and months, killing deer, trapping bears, beaver, and the different kinds of furs. His home is a brush cabin, with a bed of hemlock; for food, venison, and a little corn bread "wet up" with water and baked on a chip. He has a strong constitution, and, to him, exposure is health.

FAMILY.

(355) **Cordelia,**   b. April 5, 1819; m. Orris Newcomb, of Chardon, Ohio.
(356) **Lovern,**   b. Nov., 1824; m. Eben Brown, of Bradford, Pa., Sept., 1848.
(357) **Charles L.,** b. Feb. 18, 1825; m. Orrian Newcomb, of Parkman, Ohio, Jan. 29, 1851,
                and Nancy Young, of same place, May 3, 1857; resides in Pent Water,
(358) **Orvil E.,**   b. June 16, 1827; died at sea.   [Mich.
All born in Chardon, Ohio.

Deacon Loren Tainter, (187)

Of Warsaw, Missouri, farmer, was born in Somers, Conn., April 18, 1799, son of Deacon Jonathan.

After his father's death he resided in the family of his brother-in-law, Joel Shumway, in Whitingham, Vt., until 14 years of age; then lived a short while with his brother-in-law, Ansel Winslow, of Leroy, N. Y. After serving a short period at Sackett's Harbor, as a substitute, in the last war with England, he apprenticed himself to the carpenter's trade in Watertown, N. Y., married Ruth C. Graves, of that place, Feb. 26, 1821, and settled in Rossie, N. Y. Five years after, he returned to Watertown, N. Y., and after living there five years, removed to Rutland, where he lived until the death of his wife (July 23, 1834), then removed to the western part of the State, Livingston Co., town of York. In Leicester, in the same County, he married Mrs. Mary Forbes, daughter of Theodore Norton, formerly of Conn.

He united with the Baptist Church in Watertown, in 1828. In 1836, he removed from New York State to Dryden, Michigan, where he was a Deacon in the Baptist Church sixteen years, and served as School Inspector and Town Supervisor. Almost all of his children are members of the Baptist Church.

He has just sold his place in Michigan, and bought a farm of 280 acres in Missouri, Warsaw, Benton County.

FAMILY.

(359) **Benjamin D.,** b. April 7, 1822; m. Nancy Hillard, of Almont, Mich., Oct. 10, 1849.
(360) **Angeline,**   b. Aug. 14, 1823; m. P. Moe, of Cole Camp, Missouri.
(361) **Jonathan O.,** b. March 24, 1825. At Indian Springs, Nevada Co., Cal.; "returns
                next summer if alive and well."
(362) **Cordelia,**   b. Oct. 25, 1826; died Dec. 12, 1826.
(363) **Othniel B.,** b. Jan. 29, 1827; died Feb. 28, 1827.
(364) **Rozell,**   b. April 7, 1830; died July 1, 1857.
(365) ——— f.,   b. May 15, 1834; died Aug. 10, 1834.
(366) **Lucinda J.,** b. Feb. 16, 1836; m. James Walton, of Mica, Mich.
(367) **Laura N.,**   b. June 26, 1838.
(368) **Loren,**   b. May 11, 1840.
(369] **Jared F.,**   b. June 16, 1842.
(370) **John,**   b. Oct. 29, 1845.
(359) (360) (361) born in Rossie, N. Y., (362) (363) (364) in Watertown, (365) in Rutland.

Stephen Gorham Tainter, (188)

Son of Dr. Stephen Tainter, was born in Amherst, Mass., Sept. 15, 1792. He married and settled in Sandgate, Vt., where he lived until 1836, during which time he was called upon to superintend various public works. He spent two summers building a section of the Farmington, Conn., canal, and four years on the Chesapeake and Ohio canal, in the District of Columbia, being absent from home almost six years. In 1836, he joined his brother Ezekiel, in Prairie du Chien, Wisconsin, where he lived until his death, Oct. 12, 1846, æ. 54.

FAMILY.

(371) **Julia Catherine**, b. Aug. 7, 1814; m. William S. Nickerson, of Sandgate, Vt., Nov. 12, 1835; 3 children; Prairie du Chien, Wis.

(372) **Stephen L.**, b. Feb. 28, 1818; m. Elizabeth Walker, of Manchester, Iowa, March 15, 1838; he died at Prairie du Chien, Sept. 12, 1846, æ. 28. His widow m. Hurley D. White, in 1849, and died April, 1850.

(373) **Anson G.**, b. Aug. 19, 1823; m. Rachel Jane Tobler, of Lancaster, Wis., March 8,
(374) **Milo B.**, b. April 21, 1825. [1852.
(375) **Rodolphus F.**, b. Feb. 16, 1835.
All born in Sandgate, Vt.

His wife, Anna Hurd, was born in Sandgate, Vt., May 15, 1795. She resides with her son, Anson G. Tainter, in Franklin, Bad Axe County, Wisconsin. To her we are indebted for letters containing details of the family history. Extracts from one, containing an interesting account of the family, with incidents of pioneer life, are here inserted.

Franklin, Bad Axe Co., Wis., Aug. 13, 1858.

D. W. TAINTER, Dear Sir,

Your letter dated Feb. 11th did not reach us until the latter part of June. Absence from home and sickness has compelled me to delay replying. The Good Being who is ever mindful of us enabled me to leave my couch yesterday, and I hope will strengthen me to finish this.

My son, with whom I live, left home the 16th of July, with his family, to visit his wife's friends in Lancaster, Grant County, about 60 miles distant, and to get 70 pounds of wool carded near the Wisconsin River. On their return to the prairie, in getting out of the wagon, near his sister's, his foot slipped off the hub and he fell. He laid at Catherine's three weeks, and was then brought home on his bed; and is now just able to walk about with his staff, to see 12 acres of wheat go back on the ground. He has the sowing of 130 bushels of oats good for this year, but not one hand can we get as yet to save it, until they have attended to their own. By that time ours will be past saving. But we have been fortunate enough to get 18 acres of wheat cut and stacked in good condition.

At the death of my dear husband, Anson and Milo were making a farm on the Kickapoo River, but sickness compelled them to relinquish it, and we concluded to live together. He rented a farm at the prairie for two years, until we got our business settled, and then came up here and put up a log house, and moved up in the spring (1848 or 9). Fayette and myself took care of the stock, and Anson went out a breaking prairie three seasons.

We live half a mile from the Black River road. Our nearest neighbors north, are distant 2¼ miles, where there are 3 or 4 log houses. They have raised a Liberty-Pole, which is a guide for travellers, who in passing inquire "how far is it to the pole?" *We call that up town.* Our nearest neighbor east, is 1 mile; west, 7 miles; south, towards Prairie du Chien, 12 miles.

We have 169 acres fenced, and all but 30 acres broke. * * * * * * * *

My husband was deprived of his mother at about nine years of age, and went to Sheldon, Vt., near Canada, to live with his uncle Samuel.

A few years after, while Dr. Tainter lived in Sandgate, Vt., he returned home, and buying his time, for which he paid, I believe, $140, remained in town, or near there, working by the month. In Oct., 1813, he married, and as I was an only daughter, it was agreed that he should never separate me from my parents. We remained at home about a year, and then moved upon a small farm a short distance from my father's. From here he would often go to Boston with a load of poultry, returning with provisions, and sometimes to Canada, returning with wheat. After some years he took the office of Constable. I opposed him, likewise my family connections. I told my neighbors that if they were friends to him or to me that they would not vote for him, but he came in at night laughing, and said, "there, wife, I have got it in spite of you."

He managed well for the public, but not for himself. He had much important business to transact, such as settling estates and apprising on property, which called him away from home so much that his own business was neglected, and he must fail, as I had predicted. He gave up his property, and April, 1827, left home to work on the Farmington, Ct., canal, expecting to return by the fall. The time arrived. I learnt by neighbors who did return, that he was not coming, whereupon I made him a visit, about 130 miles distant, which was quite a journey for those days. I need not tell you I took him by surprise. I was anxious for him to return with me, but he could not be spared. The following fall he wrote that he had received an invitation from the South, and wished me to visit him again, which I accordingly did in Sept., in company with two of my cousins. I staid with my dear husband until the last of November, then took the stage and returned to my lonesome home. He superintended a large culvert across the Farmington River, and in December went South. He remained silent so long, that we knew not what had become of him. In January, 1829 or 30, he wrote that he had been sick for nine months with bilious fever, was given up by his physicians, and must give up all hope of ever meeting me again, and wished me to do all that I could to supply the place of a father. But God saw fit to restore him to health.

In the spring of 1832, I was taken sick. My parents came and lived with me and took care of us. I kept my bed for nearly three years, and as my husband had not been heard from, I was advised to take out papers that I might hold or dispose of my property. In April, he wrote, saying that he should return in August, if he was alive, nothing more. But he came not. In December, as I did not expect to live long, I got a friend to write to the Postmaster, in Georgetown, for information. The answer was privately handed to Catherine at an evening meeting.

In January (22d, 1833), as the villagers were going to an evening meeting, he met them, amid exclamations of great surprise. The school teacher, a stranger, exclaimed, " who is this ? Is it Washington or Lafayette ?" " It is Uncle Gorham," was the answer, " the father of the sick family in yonder house." " O, I will rejoice too," was his rejoinder. My physician advised him not to go home, as his wife was so low, so they went to my brother's. " Where have you come from ?" asked he, " from the clouds, or out of the ground? We thought that you were buried long ago, with the cholera, but dared not mention it before Anna. But come in, I will send her word. We thought that she was dying last night."

Catherine came into my room and said, "Mother, the Squire is coming, his staffs are flying like drum sticks" (he had walked with two staffs for years). O, I little thought he was coming with such glorious news. He came to the door and spoke, and then they all rushed into my room (they had just left for the evening meeting). " What is the matter," asked I, " is grandfather kill d ?" " No." " Is Stephen killed ?" " No." " Is any one hurt ?" " Pa is down to uncle Josiah's. You dont believe it, but the Squire said it is old GOR., for I have shook hands with him."

My sick mother left her bed and came into my room for the first time for five months, forgetting that she was sick. " O Anna, I have come to rejoice with you. Do they say that Gorham Tainter is alive and coming home ? Praise the Lord for his goodness."

When he came into my room, mother was the only one that could speak, our feelings more plainly felt than told.   . . . .

It lacked only from the 22d of Jan. to the 8th of April, of being six years since he took leave of home.

We lived in that house 22 years, but my husband was not contented, and thought best on account of our boys to come West. Ezekiel kept writing for us, and finally we started. May, 1836, and I have never had it to regret. We arrived at Prairie du Chien on the 26th of July. The two brothers went into partnership in mercantile business. After that, Ezekiel was High Sheriff and Gor. was Deputy. An outlandish chap went once into a tavern, threatening the two landlords (who ran for their lives), and brandishing his bowie knife in one hand, and a loaded pistol in the other, saying, let no one come in here, or I'll kill them. Ezekiel said to Gorham, I command you to take this man, dead or alive. "Try it, and you are a dead man," cried the man, attempting to stab him. Gorham hit his arm with a billet of wood, and the knife flew over the counter. They seized him before he could bring his pistol to bear, and he was disarmed and tied.

When he resigned the office, my son, Stephen L., accepted it. They were both jailors, and both farmed at the Prairie. The Indian Agent, Rev. Mr. Lowrie, came to get Stephen L. to do a job for Government. Elizabeth said to him, " why do you always call on the Tainters to do such work ?" " Well, madam, I will tell you," replied he, " we know that if we get a Tainter to take hold, we shall have no farther trouble about it."

We put up a large two-story house and barn, and all three of the families kept a boarding-house until after the Chippewa Indians were removed and the contract up.

In November, 1843, Mr. Tainter went to New Orleans, for his health, and returned in the spring with health much improved. I think he joined the Temperance Society in the winter of 1840, was soon appointed PRESIDENT, and the good Lord set his sins in order before him, and he and my son-in-law both experienced religion in one week. Our children all professed religion in their youth, except one, and not one is a slave to any bad habit.

I visited Vermont two years ago this summer. If I had known of your attempt to prepare a history of the family, I would have liked to have called upon you. If you could come and make us a visit I could tell you better than I can write. You have liberty to put this in your own language (not have my name before the public). Add or diminish as you think proper.

This from your aged friend,

ANNA TAINTER.

Deacon Ezekiel W. Tainter, (189)

Of Prairie du Chien, Wisconsin, was born in Shelburne, Mass., in 1793. He lived, in early life, in Salina, N. Y., where he was married, Sept. 29, 1822, to Ruth Burnham, of Lysander. He afterwards lived two years in New Jersey. In 1828 (his family remaining at Salina), he went to Wisconsin, and helped build Fort Crawford. Intending to remain, he sent for his family, a wife and three children, who, accompanied by her father and two brothers, performed the journey. It required at that time ten weeks. It is now performed in two days. Arriving at Portage, they went down the Wisconsin River in a bark canoe. On getting to a sand-bar they would all have to step out into the water and hold the children until they could launch the boat again. She mixed her bread in the barrel, and going ashore would bake it on the river bank. Arriving at Prairie du Chien, they at first lived in a cabin until unitedly they could build a log house. The old stump which at that time served Mrs. Tainter as a fire-place (30 years ago) is still standing.

During the thirty years that he has lived in Wisconsin, considerable money has passed *through* Mr. Tainter's hands. He has tilled the soil, taken contracts, merchandized, kept public house, done the business of a High Sheriff, and returned to farming again. He lives now on a good dairy farm of 200 acres, in Utica, Crawford Co., which he went upon in 1844, at which time there was not a neighbor within five miles. Now they are plenty.

Mr. Tainter was a Deacon in the Presbyterian Church at Salina, N. Y. But since removing to the frontier he, with several of his children, has joined the Methodist persuasion.

It appears from a catalogue of the Fort Edward, N. Y. Seminary, that one of his daughters is being educated at that institution.

In a paper on the "Early Times and Events in Wisconsin," read by Hon. James H. Lockwood before the Wisconsin Historical Society (Collections, Vol. 2), he thus speaks of

"EZEKIEL TAINTER, THE PRAIRIE DU CHIEN PIONEER."

"I must not omit to mention another of the early American settlers of Wisconsin. In 1833, the quartermaster of Fort Crawford advertised in Galena, for proposals for a contract to furnish the fort with a year's supply of wood. EZEKIEL TAINTER, and a man by the name of REED, got the contract, and came here and supplied the first contract together, at the end of which, Mr. REED left the country. MR. TAINTER remained, and continued for several years to take the wood contract, together with that for supplying the fort with beef; and at this business, which he well understood, in connection with the cultivation of a farm on the bluff where he cut his wood, he made money quite fast, as he was industrious and saving. He sent for his family, which he had left in the State of New York, and paid off some old scores which he had previously been unable to do, and had some money left for which he had no immediate use. Notwithstanding he knew nothing about merchandizing, he concluded, as he expressed it, "that the merchants were coining money, and that he must have a hand in," and borrowing some means in addition to his own, went to St. Louis and purchased a small stock of goods, which, as might be expected, were not very judiciously selected for the market. During this time his brother Gorham (Stephen Gorham Tainter) arrived to his assistance. Him he took into partnership; but knowing as little about mercantile affairs as his brother, the business was not very well conducted. Both had large families to support, and it appears that they kept no account of expenses, or of what each took from the store. If one wanted an article, the other took something else to balance it. They continued business for about two years, when they took account of stock, and found a deficiency of about three thousand dollars, for which they could not account; and as goods to this amount had been taken from the store without keeping any account of them, it did not at first occur to their minds that their families had consumed them. This satisfied MR. TAINTER that money was not so easily gained by merchandizing as he had supposed, and he returned to farming, and is now a resident and a worthy citizen of our county."

He was a Sheriff in Madison County, Wis., in 1839, and a Deacon in the Presbyterian Church in Salina, N. Y., at the time of his removal to the West.

FAMILY.

(376) **Andrew,**   b. July 6, 1823.
(377) **Sarah A.,**   b. Sept. 24, 1825; m. Margerum Mitchell, of P. du Chien, June 5, 1846.
(378) **Emeline A.,** b. Sept. 11, 1827; m. Alonzo Pelton, of P. du Chien, Nov. 29, 1845.
(379) **Eliza R.,**   b. June 9, 1832; m. Francis Marion Flick, of Utica, Wis., Jan. 14, 1853.
(380) **Mary E.,**   b. Feb. 24, 1834; m. Clinton Pardon, of Bl'k River, Wis., April 9, 1852.
(381) **Jeremiah B.,** b. Jan. 6, 1836.
(382) **Harriet,**   b. Oct. 24, 1837; m. Robert C. Larabee, from Berkshire, Vt., in Utica,
(383) **Martha,**   b. July 21, 1839; died June 20, 1840.   [Wis., July 4, 1855.
(384) **Emily,**   b. April 13, 1841.
(385) **David L.,**   b. Oct. 7, 1842.
(386) **Lewis H.,**   b. Sept. 4, 1844; died Oct. 2, 1844.
(387) **Ellen M.,**   b. Sept. 6, 1846.
(388) **Marilla,**   b. July 28, 1848.
(389) **Stephen G.,** b. Dec. 7, 1850.

(376) (377) born in Salina, N. Y., (378) in   N. Y., the remainder in Wisconsin.

Rev. John L. Tainter, (201)

Of Cleveland, N. Y., was born in Boston, Dec. 8, 1798, of poor but industrious and pious parents. About the year 1809, his parents removed to Pembroke, N. H., where they resided until after the war of 1812.

He spent the years of 1813–14, with his uncle Timothy Lewis, at Plattsburg, N. Y., where he witnessed the battle of Lake Champlain. He with some other boys stood upon pine stumps, their curiosity to see overcoming their fear of danger, notwithstanding the balls were flying past in every direction, but they were observed by some American officers and ordered off. Soon after leaving the stumps, they saw some 15 or 20 British soldiers who in the heat of the battle had taken refuge in a log hut on the outskirts of the field. Drawing an old cannon down the hill, they fired at the building to the best of their ability, until their firing attracted the attention of a company of riflemen who had been secreted in the grass hard by, and who came to their assistance, taking prisoners those who were alive.

In a letter he says :—

" A few days after the battle, in company with other lads, I wandered over the blood-stained fields. Here and there lay the bodies of the slain—mangled—and stripped of their most serviceable clothing and arms. We gathered up a quantity of bullets, with the *patch* or *paper* still remaining on them *unburnt*. It was accounted for in this manner. The deserters who were questioned as to the cause of their firing into the ranks of the Americans in time of battle, replied, ' we were compelled to, or suffer the penalty. Hence, not wishing to kill, *we bit off the ball*, dropped it on the ground, and fired *a blank cartridge*.' The British army had possession of the village and suburbs some two or three days previous to the battle of the 11th of Sept. On the east side of the Saranac River, near the pond, stood a large stone grist-mill. In this mill were quartered daily a company of riflemen (sharp-shooters). Through holes made in the walls, hour after hour, with unerring aim, I saw them discharge their rifles upon the enemy who attempted to cross the naked timbers of the bridge, but were dropped off into the water below. The day after the battle, I visited a large building (a barn, I think) occupied as a hospital. Here I saw the living and dying commingled together under surgical operation. From this scene of pain and anguish I turned away and followed the funeral of some officers who fell in battle, and whose bodies were now borne away to their final resting place."

In the spring of 1815, he received a letter from Boston, requesting him to return home. At the present day, a lad might start from the northern part of New York State, after breakfast, and get to Boston in time to take tea; but forty years ago, it was a journey on foot ; which, as he was desirous of spending the 4th of July with his brother and sister, on the Common, was accomplished in about a week.

Soon after his return home, his parents removed to the neighboring town of Charlestown. He was soon after taken by Rev. Dr. Morse, into his family, where he did such work as is usually allotted to boys, between school hours. He remained in Dr. Morse's family about three years, and was sent by him to Mr. Evarts' Seminary, and to the Foreign Mission School, at Cornwall, Conn. While residing with Dr. Morse, he became a member of his church, and was engaged with his friend and class-mate, Rev. John Todd, D.D., of Pittsfield, Mass., in establishing Sabbath Schools in the neighboring towns. (The one at Rev. Mr. Morse's Church was among the first, if not *the* first, established in New England).

He was sent to the Mission School by Dr. Morse, in 1818, with a view to the Missionary service. At this school there were natives of different countries, Sandwich Islands, Malay, Chinese, Indians of our own forests, and a few select American students. He here formed an intimate acquaintance with George, the young Prince and son of the old King of the Sandwich Islands, and they adopted each other for mutual companions. Eventually George wrote home, saying, that when he returned to his native land he should select a companion to accompany him. He had previously exacted a promise from John, who was now returning to Charlestown, to be the one. They corresponded with each other, until George finished his education. Arrangements were made, and a sea captain paid, by George's father, $900, to take them both at New York, and leave them at Honolulu, but as the subject of our notice was about to leave Boston, news came from George, saying that Capt. Davis had received sailing orders and had left without them. This intelligence was most disheartening. All his hopes of future life and success had been built upon his expectations of going to the Sandwich Islands. They had encouraged and urged him on in his studies, but they were now crushed, and the world looked dark indeed.

About this time, and while pondering over his misfortune, his situation came to the knowledge of some philanthropic individuals connected with the Universalist Church in Charlestown, who consoled and comforted him. By their invitation he attended evening lectures in their chapel, to which he listened with interest. Pleased with their liberal views on religious subjects, his case was made known to their pastor, Mr. Turner, the matter was talked over, and arrangements were made to place him under his care. This was in the fall of 1819. The following year he began to lecture in Charlestown, Salem, Boston and vicinity, and after that was encouraged to travel and preach in various parts of New England.

In a letter he says :

"I still retain with grateful remembrance the *kind care and attention* which I received, both in Dr. Morse's and Mr. Turner's family. I owe them a debt of gratitude, also many other friends whom I left in Charlestown. I believe that all my old and worthy teachers have gone the way of the earth, Dr. Morse, Rev. Edward Turner and Rev. Mr. Brown of Charlestown, Pres. Daggett of Cornwall, Dr. Livingston of Philadelphia (formerly of Coxsackie, N. Y.), and Dr. Richards, Pres. of Auburn Theological Seminary. PEACE BE TO THEIR ASHES."

In the spring of 1821, he went to Hudson, N. Y., where he preached a part of the time, and had charge of a select school. Here he became acquainted with Miss Judith Ann Dean, a member of the Society of Friends, and an accomplished and popular teacher of young ladies, whom he afterwards married.

During the ensuing summer, *a change took place in his religious sentiments.* For three or four weeks he retired from public exercises, and divesting himself of religious prejudices as much as possible, he contemplated and investigated the subject of the salvation of man. He wrote a discourse on justification through faith in Christ. The conditions of this doctrine presented new difficulties in the way to prove the salvation of all. Not satisfied with this, he wrote another on the doctrine of the Atonement, in which he endeavored to prove its universal application with respect of persons. On reviewing, he thought the weight of argument against his own position. Finally, he arrived at the following conclusion : "That the Atonement opened the way for God to *propose* mercy and even to *dispense* mercy to all who would *believe.* When this *end* of Christ's *death* is considered, thought he, it is proper to say that "He died for all." He understood the Bible as asserting this when it says, "He gave himself a ransom for all, and that he is the propitiation for our sins, and not for our sins only, but for the sins of the whole world." But when the *ultimate end* of Christ's death is spoken of, it is to be understood in a restrictive sense—then he is said to lay down his life for his sheep—his friends—the church; Acts 20 : 28, "Feed the Church of God which he hath purchased with his own blood." John 10 : 15, "I lay down my life for the sheep." Eph. 5 : 25, "Christ also loved the Church and gave himself for it."

A public renunciation followed these conclusions, and no little persecution and misrepresentation was the result.

In June, 1822, he married Judith Ann Dean. Her mother was a Palmer, and one of the nine emigrants from England, who purchased a tract of land in Duchess County, and gave it the name of the "Nine Partners."*

In the fall they left Hudson and settled in Coxsackie, where they took charge of another school for some thirty years, and where he renewed his Theological studies with the Rev. G. R. Livingston. His health failing, he retired for one or two years, and employed his time in going through a thorough course in Greek, Exegesis, Theological and Sacred History, while at the same time he prepared and wrote a short system of doctrines and Church Government, for a Text-book, about 200 pages ; and while at the Auburn Theological Seminary, a Vol. of Notes on Didactic Theology and Church Government, also a course of Lectures on Sacred History.

Soon after closing these studies, a question was agitated, whether he held to the fundamental doctrines of the Presbyterian Church. It was well known that he had rejected three cardinal points in the Calvinistic creed, viz., Election, Predestination and particular Redemption or Atonement. To avoid being drawn into the labyrinth of another religious controversy, he withdrew his connection with the Presbytery and took a decided stand upon the broad platform, that in the suffering and death of Christ, an Atonement was made, sufficient for the salvation of all who believe. I John 2 : 2, "He is the propitiation for our sins, and not for ours only, but also for the sins of the whole world. " John 3, 35, "He that believeth on the Son, hath everlasting life ; and he that believeth not on the Son, shall not see Life."

He spent a few years in mercantile business, and then sold his place in Coxsackie, and emigrated in company with three other families to the western part of the State, to Cleveland, Oswego Co., and located about two miles north of Oneida Lake, living the first season in a log house, in the midst of the forest.

The writer had the pleasure of spending several days at his humble but pleasant home in the winter of 1858. It commands a prospective view of the Lake, a young orchard *and a forest of pine stumps*, with the blue hills of Lawrence stretching far in the distance.

Mr. Tainter is short in stature, with curly iron-gray hair, but not bald, and though 60 years of age, he is as active as any young man that we ever saw, performing whatever he does with a sort of *steel-trap* accompaniment, which peculiarity it is understood extends to his sermons, his hearers seldom indulging in sleep.

He lives in a locality about a hundred years behind the older portions of the country, where one horse uncovered cutters are *called mail stages*, and a distance of twelve miles to the railroad "*a short cut.*" Mr. Tainter thinks nothing of starting on foot to visit one of his daughters and son-in-law, at Camden, twelve miles distant, walking into their house as though he had simply crossed the road. His occupation is cultivating the soil, preaching or lecturing whenever there is an opportunity of doing good and aiding Sabbath Schools. His leisure hours are devoted to reading and writing.

Since our visit, good Mrs. Tainter has finished her labors on earth. She died Nov. the 10th.

FAMILY.

(390) **Olive C.,** b. May 3, 1823 ; m. Samuel Alexander (a native of Scotland), Feb. 22, 1843, a farmer ; resides in Cleveland, N. Y. ; has four children, Ann Alida æ. 16, Egbert William æ. 15, Sarah Chrystina æ. 11, Judith Evangeline æ. 7.

(391) **Mary E.,** } b. July 15, 1824 ; d. Aug. 19, 1824.
(392) **Alida B.,†** } m. William C. Wells, Jan. 17, 1850 ; of Camden, N. Y. ; ornamental and landscape painter ; musical character, &c. ; has two children, Emma Chrystina æ. 7, and another younger.

* They were relatives of Oliver Cromwell.   † Studied Latin at six years of age.

William L. Tainter, (202)

Son of John Tainter, of Boston, was born Nov. 27, 1800. He married Sophronia Bachellor, of Billerica, in 1825, and was engaged in mercantile business in Boston. He kept a store in Milk St., about three years, when his partner proved untrustworthy, and decamped with the available funds of the concern, leaving him a prey to the creditors. It was too severe a blow for him to bear, having previously sustained an independent position in circles that he was now unable to frequent, and he became an intemperate man, a *wreck* of what he had once been. He possessed a fine education, and in his sober moments was in every respect a gentleman.

He met his death while bathing at Braman's baths. He dove into the water, we believe for a wager. The water not being so deep as he expected, his head struck the bottom, and he was taken out dead.

His widow, now widow of Anthony Martis, whom she married in 1836, resides in Boston.

FAMILY.

(393) **Maria E.,** b. Nov. 28, 1826; m. Charles Furlong, of Boston, W. I. Goods dealer. They have two children.
(394) **Hannah T.,** b. Oct. 12, 1828; m. John Elkins, of Boston; have one child.
(395) **Helen M.,** b. April, 1830; m. George Fisher, of Falmouth; have two children.
(396) **Sophronia,** b.   1832; died 1841, æ. 9.
All born in Boston.

Ezra Tainter, (205)

Of Melrose (formerly a part of Malden), was born in that place, in 1803; married Susanna Flint, of Reading, April 17, 1828, and the following year removed to Duxbury, where he opened a country store, and manufactured ladies' boots and shoes. After living here about twenty-five years, with the exception of a year or two at South Reading and Pocasset, he returned to Melrose, where he now resides, engaged in the manufacture of ladies' shoes.

FAMILY.

(397) **Edward,**   b. April 10, 1830; m. Sarah C. Blakeley, of Melrose, Sept. 26, 1854; d. July 5, 1859, æ. 29.
(398) **George F.,** b. July 19, 1832; died Dec. 13, 1837, æ. 5.
(399) **George A.,** b. July 3, 1840.
(397) born in Melrose, (398) in Duxbury, (399) in Pocasset.

Capt. William C. Tainter, (207)

Of Boston, was born in Leominster. When about nineteen years of age, he went to Cambridgeport, and lived awhile with Deacon Livermore, soap manufacturer, then went into the Market in Boston, and did business there a number of years; afterwards opened a Restaurant opposite the market, where he did considerable business, as he was a man whom every one liked, was widely known, and possessed a host of friends. His Restaurant was a great place of resort for farmers and drovers who came in from the country in those almost anti-railroad days, to market. Among these, it had its reputation for *"good steaks"* and a smiling host.

At an early day a large number of the market men used annually to indulge in a target shoot and dinner, at Brighton or Cambridge. A medal was usually presented for the best shot, which he could never make. Year after year the "target shoot" would come off, and to the great sport of the company, he would come in *second* best. He was about to give up, when a 2d medal was furnished, to suit his case. This called him from retirement, and on the appointed day, amid much hilarity and interest on the part of his friends, he fired *as before*, taking the second medal.

This company was afterwards organized under the title of "The Boston Veteran Association," and adopted the style of uniform worn by the officers of the Continental Army.

He was a man of good business qualities, of middling height, heavy but well-proportioned. His was a countenance where a smile of genial good nature seemed always to rest.

He was an active member of the Order of Odd Fellows, Masons, and the Militia, and was a commander in the above-mentioned company.

He died March 30, 1853, æ. 52, and was buried with military honors. Mrs. Tainter resides in Watertown, in the family of her son-in-law, Mr. Brigham.

FAMILY.

(400) **Mary E.,** b. Jan. 3, 1830; m. John Brigham, Jr., of Watertown, Jan. 5, 1852.
Children, Cora E., b. Oct. 7, 1852; Annie Maria, b. 1857, d. 1858.
(401) **William H.,** b. May 13, 1832; went to California in 1849; is in Sacramento City.
(402) **Daniel W.,** b. Sept 9, 1836; died Jan. 17, 1839.
Born in Boston.

Elmus Tainter, (209)

Of Lexington, was born in Leominster, March 11, 1804, and when a young man went to Lexington, where he has since resided.

He married Abigail Green, of Lexington, April 6, 1831.

His occupation is principally dressing and preparing furs.

FAMILY.

(403) *Harriet Spaulding, b. April 23, 1835; m. Abel Simonds, of Burlington, Mass., Feb. 9, 1854. They have two children.

Lewis Tainter, (210)

Of Methuen, was born in Leominster, Sept. 21, 1806. When a young man, he went to Groton, to learn the hatter's trade, and married Lucinda Pierce, of that place, April 5, 1831. A few years ago he removed to Methuen, quite near Lawrence, where he follows his trade a part of the time, and cultivates a quantity of land. He lives remote from the village, and is much troubled by pilferers from the city. Last summer, he discovered, one sabbath afternoon, three Hibernians very industriously engaged with basket and hoes in his potato field. He went out, and in a tone of voice becoming the day, *inquired* what they were about. They made no reply, but matters at once assumed a warlike aspect. Mr. Tainter stood the odds against him until a black eye, a bloody nose and rent garments reminded him that discretion was the better part of valor, and he retreated — though defeated, still unconquered. Harnessing a horse he pursued them into Lawrence, where they were arrested and afterwards dealt with to the extent of the law.

But deeds like his, it appears, go not long unhonored in the little town of Methuen. The following sabbath found him raised to the dignity of a constable, which unexpected honor he seems to sustain with becoming modesty.†

FAMILY.

(404) **George L.,** b. June 22, 1832. Is in Chicago, Ill.
(405) **Frances L.,** b. Dec. 14, 1835.
(406) **Willard H.,** b. Jan. 15, 1839; learned the hatter's trade, which being dull, he went on a voyage to the Pacific, from which he has just returned.
(407) **Lydia A.,** b. Aug. 26, 1843.
(408) **Elizabeth C.,** b. Aug. 27, ; died Aug. 17, 1847.

* Adopted. † Since writing the above, he has removed a short distance, and is now within the limits of Lawrence.

Deacon Elijah F. Tainter, (211)

Of Watertown, was born in Leominster, Aug. 11, 1808. His parents dying when he was young, he was, at the age of twelve years, put out on a farm, but soon went to Watertown and learned the baker's trade ; afterwards did business in Holliston, Lynn and Hingham. He finally settled in Watertown, and after carrying on a bakery awhile, bought out (about ten years since) the line of expresses running between Boston and Watertown, Newton Corner and Brighton. He owns a good house and establishment in the centre of the village, is a Deacon in the Universalist Church of Watertown, and is interested in the cause of temperance, and the reforms of the day.

(Uncle Elize is a man of 50 years, quite short in stature, with a head topped with gray. One of his lower limbs is an *eighth* of an inch shorter than the other, which tho' not a deformity, adds a a peculiarity of gait to his shortness of stature. The possessor of a temper that a tornado might not ruffle, he is in the broadest sense of the word a "*first rate*" man. He is a christian of the practical school, and is *Universally* respected.)

He married Cordelia Bridges, of Watertown, Nov. 6, 1833.

FAMILY.

(409) **Frederick E.**, b. Aug. 25, 1834 ; died Nov. 16, 1834.
(410) **Ellen E.**,   b. Nov. 2, 1835 ; died Aug. 15, 1842.
(411) **Adelia A.**,   b. June 20, 1837.
(412) **Alfred B.**,   b. Oct. 6, 1839.
(413) **Harriet A.**,   b. July 18, 1841.
(414) **Francis L.**,   b. July 2, 1843 ; died Aug. 18, 1844.
(415) **Theron E.**,   b. June 11, 1845 ; died Feb. 6, 1847.
    (409) born in Holliston, (410) (411) in Lynn, (412) (413) in Hingham, (414) (415) in Watertown.

Capt. Daniel A. Tainter, (213)

Of Boston, was born in Leominster, July 28, 1812. Being left an orphan at an early age, he was put out on a farm, where he remained several years.

"When about sixteen, he walked to Lunenburg, on a 'training day,' to visit his grandmother Kilburn, and sister Eunice, who not liking the appearance of his '*visiting suit*,' resolved that he should not return. Purchasing some gingham for coat and pants and a piece of '*calico for a vest*,' Eunice soon had him neatly attired and on his way to Boston."

In Boston, his brother William had engaged him a situation in the provision store of Dean Willis. He continued in the provision business the greater part of his life.

In 1833, he married Sarah, daughter of Mr. Willis, and embarked in business with him.

In 1837, he went to New York, and engaged in the business there, but the financial revulsions of that year created so many bills which he could not collect, that he lost money and shortly returned and opened a stall in Faneuil Hall Market.

He held a commission in the Massachusetts Militia, and was a Ward officer in Boston in 1844. He removed to Newton Corner in 1845, where he lived five years, then returned to Boston and Charlestown, and died at the latter place, April 4, 1854, æ. 41. He was buried with military honors by the Boston Veterans, of which company he was a past commander.

FAMILY.

(416) **Frances J.**, b. Jan. 29, 1834 ; m. W. L. Harris, Dec. 15, 1851 ; died Nov. 14, 1853. He died Aug. 7, 1854.
(417) **Dean W.**,   b. Jan. 27, 1836 ; m. Sarah S. Adams, of East Lexington, Jan. 23, 1859.
(418) **Daniel W.**,   b. Feb. 22, 1838.
(419) **Margaret W.**, b. Aug. 29, 1839 ; died May 22, 1841.
(420) **George W.**,   b. July 26, 1841.
(421) **Mary E.**,   b. Nov. 13, 1843 ; died Dec. 22, 1844.
(422) **William H. H.**, b. Dec. 27, 1845.
(423) **Sarah H.**,   b. Dec. 19, 1847.
(424) **Marshall**,   b. Dec. 9, 1849 ; died Dec. 5, 1850.
(425) **Charles M.**, b. Jan. 19, 1851 ; died Aug. 20, 1851.
    All but (423) (424) were born in Boston ; they in Newton.

Solon S. Tainter, (215)

Of Holliston, was born in Leominster, June 2, 1816. When about six years of age he was taken by a Mrs. Barrett, who owned a large and good farm in Lunenburg. The family consisted of but these two. Here he was well cared for, and much petted for being a "poor motherless boy." Many a morning would find her out in the barn with *boots* on and shovel in hand, while Solon was comfortable in bed. When he got to be sixteen, he left to learn a trade, and went to Holliston, where he worked for his brother Elijah, who was engaged in the baking business. He finally learned the boot-making business, which is still his occupation. A neat house and lot are the visible fruits of his industry.

In 1816, he married Joanna Littlefield, of Holliston. She died July 29, 1858. Nov. 10, 1859, he married Cynthia L. Littlefield, a sister of his former wife.

FAMILY.

(426) **Alvah Ayers,** b. Sept. 29, 1847; died Sept. 14, 1849.
(427) **Alma Jane,** b. Oct. 11, 1851.
(428) **Emma Lizzie,** b. Feb. 26, 1855; died Sept. 21, 1855.
(428½) **Ella Louisa,** b. " " "
Born in Holliston.

Daniel Adams Tainter, (217)

Of Watertown, was born in Watertown, Nov. 3, 1812. Married Persis H. Richardson, of W., Nov. 26, 1840. He is engaged in the lumber business in Watertown, firm of R. Gilkey & Co. He also carries on a farm of from twenty to thirty acres, is or has been an Overseer of the Poor, also Assessor in Watertown, is a member of the Baptist Church, and one of the parish committee in the same. Is a man of few words and superior judgment.

FAMILY.

(429) **Elizabeth B.,** b. Aug. 25, 1841.
(430) **Henry A.,** b. July 19, 1845; died Feb. 25, 1850.
(431) **Mary J.,** b. March 16, 1848.
(432) **Newell J.,** b. Sept. 5, 1851.
All born in Watertown.

George Tainter, (220)

Of Watertown, was born in Watertown, Oct. 13, 1822, and married Abby Sanger, of W.

He carries on a Door, Sash and Blind Manufactory.

FAMILY.

(433) **Georgetta,** b. Oct. 24, 1850.
(434) **Charles S.,** b. April 25, 1854.
Born in Watertown.

VERSES, (CONTINUED FROM PAGE 48).

13 He makes ye mortals for to know
When he commands his wrath shall go,
And may ye tremble at the day
When he did snatch your friends away.

14 That day the sun in splendor rose
To wake each soul from its repose—
It was in April ninety-nine,
These four young Maidens did combine.

15 A visit they had thought to make,
And for that end their ways did take
To Mr. Bliss's, in the street,
Where they in harmony did meet.

16 O there they sat and spent away
The golden hours of that day,
Not thinking that they should run their race
Before the sun would hide his face.

17 They being young, they thought to speed,
Not knowing what God had decreed.
A sailing voyage they did propose,
And there each one his party chose.

18 O, Mr. Gordon Bliss made one,
With him Miss Nabby Merrick run;
And Miss Assenith Bliss made three,
With her Miss Warriner did agree.

19 These four with hasty stride,
While Leonard Bliss before did ride;
For they across their Lot set out,
While others ran another route.

20 How swift and dreadful was their flight
From Mr. Bliss's out of sight;
At length they came upon the shore,
And view'd their pleasures as before.

21 They, their companions did outrun,
At length unto the Boat they come,
Where they with Folsom leaped in,
And hoisted sails up to the wind.

22 With fresh delight and pleasant breeze,
They ran acrost their little seas;
And as atempting to turn round,
A gale of wind did cast them down.

23 O solemn, solemn, solemn scenes,
To hear their screaches and their screams,
While sinking down in gaping graves,
And drinking death amidst the waves.

24 Great God! how must these creatures feel,
When their dear souls began to reel,
And their companions on the shore,
To see them sink to rise no more.

25 There each of them they lost their breath
In the cold arms of icy death,
And bid their last a long farewell
To all this side of Heaven and Hell.

26 O what a sudden change took place,
It spread a gloom on every face;
And through the Town the news did fly
Swift as the Lightning from the sky.

27 There was a running to and fro,
The real truth they wish to know;
With aching hearts and weeping eyes,
It seemed tho' heaven was pierced with cries.

28 They to the pond did soon repair,
But O, alas, when they came there,
Could do no more than stand and gaze,
For half of them were in a maze.

29 To get to them was all their care,
Allthough no other boat was there,
Yet by industry reaching round,
Within few hours three were found.

30 To gain their lives was all their aim,
But all attempts did prove in vain;
This was an instance verry rare,
That three good swimmers drowned there.

31 Not more than six rods from the shore,
On the next day they found two more;
Then they conveyed these five away,
To be prepared for funeral day.

32 Now swadling bands their bodies close,
To fit them for their last repose.
The sable coffin and the grave
Is all the dwelling nature gave.

33 Behold the solemn day is come,
The mourning hours are begun,
Which was the second day of May,
Prepared to bear their Corpse away.

34 From Neighboring Towns vast numbers
The solemn mourners for to greet, [meet,
And take their final last survey
Of these pale lumps of lifeless clay.

35 They did unto God's house repair,
To hear the sacred warning there,
By Christ's embasendor was given,
To be prepared for Death and Heaven.

36 Here it was set before there Eyes,
As mortals they were born to die,
And soon to leave this world of woe—
And then unto the judgment go.

37 Pursue the paths that lead to joys,
Dont daily with these earthly toys,
All carnal joys in gold array
Will take them wings and fly away.

38 You cant forget that solemn day,
When your dear children took their way,
Left you, their parents and their friends,
Expecting to return again.

39 The Eternal God had fixed the place
Where they must go and end their race,
And pay the debt, that great demand
That nature ows to sovereign hand.

40 Their voices you will hear no more,
For favours they cant you implore.
Because their powers they cease to move,
They know no hatred, grief, or love.

(Continued on a future page.)

THOSE BORN UP TO THE PRESENT TIME OF THE
EIGHTH GENERATION.

BEING THE CHILDREN OF

HENRY C. TAYNTOR, OF PHILADELPHIA, PA. (224)

FREDERICK A. TAYNTOR, OF U. S. ARMY. (226)

EDWIN E. TAYNTOR, OF N. Y. CITY. (233)

JOHN W. TAYNTOR, OF N. Y. CITY. (234)

GUILFORD TAYNTOR, OF EATON, N. Y. (237)

ALANSON TAYNTOR, OF EATON, N. Y. (239)

LEONARD TAINTER, OF WHITE PIGEON, MICH. (282)

DAVID TAINTER, OF MILLBURY, MASS. (283)

DANIEL TAINTER, OF MILLBURY, MASS. (284)

WILLARD S. TAINTER, OF MILLBURY, MASS. (286)

JOEL E. TAINTER, OF FAIRBANK, IOWA. (292)

CHARLES A. TAINTER, OF WALES, MASS. (294)

ISAAC K. TAINTER, OF PROVIDENCE, R. I. (296)

DANIEL TAINTER, OF WORCESTER, MASS. (297)

REV. NAHUM TAINTER, OF MINNESOTA, (298)

EPHRAIM C. TAINTER, OF WORCESTER. (299)

HARVEY S. TAINTER, OF WORCESTER. (302)

CARVER TAINTER, OF WORCESTER. (303)

ALBERT TAINTER, OF MEDFORD. (307)

EDWIN TAINTER, OF MEDFORD, MASS. (308)

THOMAS D. TAINTER, OF SO. BROOKVILLE, ME. (313)

SAMUEL H. TAINTER, OF BROOKLINE, ME. (315)

AMASA D. TAINTER, OF AUGUSTA, WIS. (318)

AMOS L. TAINTER, OF AUGUSTA, WIS. (319)

ALSWORTH TAINTER, OF CARTHAGE, ME. (324)

WYMAN V. TAINTER, OF CARTHAGE, ME. (325)

GILBERT L. TAINTER, OF DIXFIELD, ME. (326)

THOMAS P. TAINTER, OF APALACHICOLA, FLA. (331)

NORRIS D. TAINTER, OF WHITINGHAM, VT. (341)

JOSIAH W. TAINTER, OF WHITINGHAM, VT. (343)

JAMES M. TAINTER, OF WHITINGHAM, VT. (344)

JONATHAN TAINTER, OF MILLBURGH, MICH. (350)

Francis L. Tayntor (222)

Was born in Philadelphia, in 1825. Being left without a father at an early age, he was bound out for a term of seven years to learn the tobacconist business. In the middle of the seventh year, having been kept on one branch of the trade, from the first, he requested to be put on some other part, which request not being complied with, he ran away and went to N. York City. Being advertised for, he assumed the name of Turner, which he retained through life.

He married Elizabeth A. Thompson, of Warehouse Point, Conn., May 13, 1849 ; was a segar manufacturer, in Connecticut and Portland, Me., and died at the latter place, July 20, 1853, æ. 28, of consumption. Mrs. Turner resides in Boston. No children.

Henry C. Tayntor (224)

Was born in Philadelphia, Jan. 2, 1830 ; was married Oct. 31, 1848, to Harriet M. Knapp, a native of P. Her parents were natives of France. He carried on the tobacconist business. Died Nov. 2, 1857, æ. 27. His family reside in Philadelphia.

FAMILY.

(435) Matilda K., b. June 14, 1852.
(436) Amelia V., b. July 19, 1854.
(437) Mary A., b. June 15, 1856.
Born in Philadelphia.

Frederick A. Tayntor, U. S. A., (226)

Of Philadelphia, was born July 8, 1834. Commenced learning the trade of cigar making, but not liking it he enlisted in the army, Oct. 30, 1849, and served five years ; was sent to Carlisle Barracks to learn music, and was sent from there to Fort Hall, Oregon Territory ; joined Company C., Regiment of mounted Rifles, as First Bugler. Two years after was ordered to Texas, where he served out his time, having been through all the Western States and parts of Mexico, Kanzas, Missouri, Nebraska, Utah, Washington and Oregon Territories. After returning home to Philadelphia, he again went into the cigar business—again enlisted in the army, May 15, 1855, and is at this time a recruiting officer in Philadelphia. It is his intention to leave the army at the expiration of his term, next May. He married Elvira L. Fell, April, 1856.

FAMILY.

(438) Elvira Marion.
(439) Anne.

Edwin E. Tayntor, (233)

Of New York City, carries on a bakery, in Greenwich Avenue. He was born in Holliston, Mass., son of Asa Tayntor, April 10, 1831. Married Eliza J. Edwards, of N. York, June 25, 1851.

FAMILY.

(440) Edward F., b. in New York, Oct. 9, 1852.
(441) Mary E., b. " Dec. 26, 1855.

John W. Tayntor, (234)

Of New York City, was born Sept. 2, 1834, son of Asa, of New York. He married Elizabeth S. McDonnell, Feb. 9, 1858, and is engaged in the produce business in Clinton Market.

Guilford Taynter (237)

Of Eaton, N. Y., farmer, is a man of sterling qualities, and is quite successful as a farmer. Has formerly been employed in teaching school in Russia, N. Y. He married Wealthy C. Wooden, of that place, Dec. 24, 1843.

Alanson Taynter, (239)

Of Eaton, N. Y., is a young man of industrious habits, and has just commenced business in life. He has a farm, and raises some stock for market. Was born Feb. 12, 1829; married Mary Taynter, of Eaton, July 4, 1852.

FAMILY.

(442) **Luella E.,** b. in Eaton, June 14, 1856.

Leonard Tainter, (282)

Of White Pigeon, Michigan, was born in Millbury, Mass., April 13, 1804. In Feb., 1824, he went to Cato, Cayuga Co., N. Y.; married Lurenda Barnes, March 6, 1826. In 1830, he went to Auburn, in the same County, where he remained until 1837, at which time he settled in Michigan. He is a wagon maker by trade, which has been his busines in former years. For the last thirteen years has been Deputy Sheriff and Constable in White Pigeon.

FAMILY.

(443) **Electa A.,** b. Dec. 16, 1826; m. William Bycroft, May 24, 1843; d. Feb. 7, 1853.
(444) **Rufus,** b. Dec. 15, 1828; died July 7, 1832, æ. 3 years 7 months.
(445) **Cynthia A.,** b. June 19, 1833; m. Hiram C. Ellsworth, Nov. 14, 1849; resides in Garden Grove, Decatur County, Iowa.
(446) **Melissa A.,** b. March 1, 1837.
(443) (444) were born in Cato, N. Y., (445) in Auburn.

David Tainter, (283)

Of Millbury, Mass., was born Nov. 5, 1805; married Mrs. Eliza T. B. Marble. Her maiden name was Eliza Tainter Bancroft, daughter of Simon Bancroft and Mehitable Tainter (160).

FAMILY.

(447) **Hannah Eliza,** b. July 31, 1838; died April 26, 1840.
(448) **Mary Elizabeth,** b. Aug. 31, 1841.
(449) **Abijah S.,** b. Nov. 14, 1843.
(450) **Simon Bancroft,** b. April, 1852; died July 17, 1859.
All born in Millbury.

Daniel Tainter, (284)

Of Millbury, was born Aug. 28, 1807; is a member of the Baptist Church. Married Betsey M. Marsh, of Sutton, April 21, 1833. He is a carpenter by trade, but works at boot-making a part of the year.

FAMILY.

(451) **Louisa,** b. June 9, 1834; m. Henry Woodruff, May, 1855.
(452) **George F.,** b. April 13, 1842; died Jan. 6, 1854.
(453) **Eldoretta M.,** b. Feb. 2, 1848.
(454) **Lillia M.,** b. June 7, 1852; died Aug., 1852.

Willard S. Tainter, (286)

Of Millbury, farmer, was born Feb 20, 1812, and married Hannah Goddard, of Worcester. He died Jan. 28, 1859, in his 47th year.

On the 25th of January last, he was called from his work in the woods at noon, to go to Worcester on business. He left his family in health and cheerfulness, but never to return to them alive. The following account of his untimely death is taken from the newspapers of the day.

The *Spy* states that on Tuesday evening Mr. Willard S. Tainter, a farmer of Millbury, was assaulted in the house upon the Millbury road, known as the Half Way House, by a party of Irishmen who are supposed to belong to Millbury, and beaten over the head so violently that he died of the wounds inflicted, at about two o'clock on Friday afternoon. It appears that Mr. Tainter, while returning from Worcester to Millbury, broke the shaft of his wagon, and stopped at the Half Way House, kept by J. Senter, Jr., for the purpose of borrowing another vehicle. Mr. Senter was absent, and Mr. Tainter went into the bar room to await his return. While there, three partially intoxicated Irishmen entered and called for liquor, which the boy in attendance declined to furnish. They then proceeded to demolish the glasses, when Mr. Tainter remonstrated with them for their conduct, whereupon the three Irishmen commenced assaulting and abusing him in an outrageous manner, pulling his beard and hair. The sequel is thus stated :

" At this stage of the proceedings, Mr. Senter entered the room, having just returned from the city, and asked Mr. Tainter's assistance to clear the premises. Mr. Tainter accordingly, with the help of Mr. Senter, seized Duggan, who appeared to be the ringleader, and ejected him from the room ; and they were in the act of thrusting out another of the ruffians, when he fell to the floor, Tainter being uppermost, and his head projecting out of the doorway. At this juncture, and while he lay in this prostrate condition, Duggan returned with a cart-stake, five feet long and two and a half inches in diameter, of green oak, and with all the force he could muster, struck a blow directly upon Mr. Tainter's head. The ruffian aimed a second blow at Mr. Senter, who partially evaded it, and the main force of the blow fell upon the door, which was broken down. The villains then ran off together, leaving their coats and hats behind, and also their team.

Mr. Tainter was immediately taken up and cared for, and medical aid was sent for, but he never recovered his consciousness or spoke a word, and died, as we have stated, yesterday afternoon, leaving a wife and children to mourn his sudden and untimely end."

The police were not notified of the affair until several hours after it occurred, and at last accounts Duggan and his accomplices had eluded arrest.— *Worcester Transcript.*

IMPORTANT ARREST.—On Monday, Thomas Malone, one of the Irishmen concerned in the murder of Mr. Willard S. Tainter, at the " half-way house," on the Millbury road, on Tuesday last, was arrested in Dudley, by constable Geo. Hastings, of Sutton.

It appears that information had reached the ears of the city police, which induced a suspicion that Malone had been secreted in the house of one Dennis Murphy, in Sutton. Accordingly, the house was visited, on Monday morning, by Deputy Marshal Studley and officer Davis, of this city, in company with officer Hastings, of Sutton. Murphy was not at home, and a thorough search of his premises gave no clue to the whereabouts of Malone.

The officers then proceeded to a wood lot, where Murphy was at work, and questioned him as to his knowledge of the place where Malone was. At first, he resolutely denied that he had seen him for several weeks, but subsequently confessed that he *had* seen him on the night of the murder. He was accordingly arrested and given in charge of officer Hastings, with instructions to take him to Worcester, while the other officers continued their search.

Upon Mr. Hastings' arrival with his prisoner at Sutton Centre, Murphy expressed considerable reluctance to proceed to Worcester, and indicated a wish to regain his own liberty by revealing where Malone was, confessing, at the same time, that he carried him to Webster on Sunday morning. After some parleying, he consented to go with Mr. Hastings, taking him to Webster, and thence to the house of an Irishman named Lyon, in Dudley, near Webster, where Malone was found in a room in the second story, under lock and key. He was immediately taken into custody by officer Hastings, brought to Worcester, and placed in the lock-up, and will probably be brought up for examination this morning.— *Worcester Transcript, Feb.* 1, 1858.

VERDICT.—The jury summoned by Coroner Day, to hold an inquest over the body of the late Willard S. Tainter, killed at the " Half Way House," on Tuesday of last week, concluded its investigations, yesterday. After examining all the witnesses, they found the following verdict :

That the said Willard S. Tainter came to his death in consequence of a murderous blow upon the head, inflicted by a heavy, green chestnut sled-stake, in the hands of Cornelius Doogan, on Tuesday, Jan. 25th, 1859, at a house called the Half Way House, in Worcester, on the Millbury road, and that the said Tainter did linger until the following Friday, when he died. And the jury aforesaid further find, that Thomas Malone and Michael Brett were accomplices before the fact, by being present, aiding, and abetting in the homicide aforesaid.

FAMILY.

(455) **John H. N.**, b. in Millb'y, Sept. 12, 1843.   (457) **Almeda E.**, b. in Millb'y, Oct. 13, 1849.
(456) **Ellen M. M.**, b.   "   Aug. 21, 1846.   (458) **Frederick W.**, b.   "   Nov. 18, 1858.

Joel E. Tainter, (292)

Of Fairbank, Iowa, farmer, was born in Millbury, Mass., June 8, 1823, on the place where his father and grandfather lived and died. He married Jane E. Taylor, of North Becket, Mass., March 4, 1850. In the spring of 1854, he bought a tract of land in Iowa, and removed thither. Previous to his removal from Massachusetts, he resided at North Becket, and was Superintendent of repairs on a section of the Western Railroad. His wife died in Iowa, Nov. 3, 1855. He married, second, Nancy M. Engle, of Superior, Iowa, April 8, 1857. He has served as juryman, also as Treasurer of a School District, in Iowa, and is a Justice of the Peace for the County in which he lives.

FAMILY.

(459) **Lewis E.,**			b. at North Becket, Mass., Sept. 23, 1853.
(460) **Emma J.,**			b. at Fairbank, Iowa, March 27, 1858.
(461) **Lindsey K.,**	b.			"			"		Aug. 29, 1859.

Capt. Charles A. Tainter, (294)

Of Wales, Mass., was born in Millbury, Mass., April 20, 1834, and married Frances A. Hall, of Manchester, Conn., Nov. 26, 1857. Has lived in Stafford Springs, Conn., where he was a Capt. in the Conn. militia. He is an overseer in a woolen-mill, in Wales.

Isaac B. Tainter, (296)

Of Providence, R. I., son of Harvey Tainter, of Leicester, Mass., learned his trade in Worcester, and worked at it in several places in Massachusetts ; finally settled in Providence, where he owns a small house. He is a stair-builder. Married Harriet N. Eddy, of Auburn, Mass., Oct. 6, 1845.

FAMILY.

(462) **Berthier,**			b. in Providence, R. I., Oct. 20, 1855.
(463) **Isaac Willis,** b.			"			"		Jan. 14, 1858.

Daniel Tainter, (297)

Of Worcester, Mass., was born in Leicester ; went to Worcester in 1836, and learned the trade of a machinist ; commenced business in 1847, and is extensively engaged in the manufacture of woolen machinery, which is in use in all of the manufacturing States of the Union. He is a member of the Congregational Church, owns property in Worcester, and has been a member of the City Government.

Married Sarah E. Johnson, of Worcester, May 21, 1840.

FAMILY.

(464) **Calista B.,**		b. in Worcester, Nov., 1840.
(465) **Charles E.,**		b.			"			Feb. 20, 1846.
(466) **Edward,**			b.			"			died young.

Rev. Nahum Tainter, (298)

Of Minnesota, was born in Leicester, Mass. He educated himself for the ministry, keeping school winters, in Worcester, East and West Bridgewater, and Westport, Mass. He commenced preaching in 1843, being 22 years of age. He has preached in various places in New England ; being a member of the Methodist Conference, he changed once in two years. In 1856, he bought a section of land in Minnesota, Chatfield, Fillmore Co., and went thither, with the intention of farming, but has since resumed preaching. He married Ann E. Pierce, of Smithfield, R. I., May 28, 1845.

FAMILY.

(467) **Henry A.,**		b. in Chilmark, Mass., June, 1846.
(468) **Laurilla A.,**		b. in So. Coventry, Mass., Nov., 1850.

Ephraim C. Tainter, (299)

Of Worcester, was born in Leicester. He learned the cabinet maker's trade in Worcester, and went into business in Fitchburg, about the year 1846, continuing there about a year. He then went to Springfield, where he married Elvira L. Parks, of Shirley; soon after went to Philadelphia, and engaged in the manufacture of car seats, in which he was successful. He returned to Worcester in 1852, and is of the firm of J. A. Fay & Co., Machinists, in Worcester, Mass., Keene, N. H., Norwich, Ct., and Cincinnati, Ohio. Is a member of the Congregational Church.

FAMILY.

(469) **Dora,**   died young.
(470) **Carrie,**   "   "
(471) **Mary E.,**   b. Sept. 10, 1858.

Harvey S. Tainter, (302)

Of Worcester, was born in Leicester. Is connected, indirectly, with his brother Daniel, in building machinery. He married Sarah E. Burbank, of Worcester, Oct. 8, 1851. Is a member of the Methodist Church.

FAMILY.

(472) **Lucy M.,**   b. Oct. 3, 1851.
(473) **Edward E.,**   b. June 22, 1853.
(474) **David E.,**   b. Nov. 1, 1854.
(475) **Frederic H.,** b. Jan. 1, 1856.
(476) **Julia A.,**   b. March 31, 1857; died April 6, 1858.
(477) ———, son,*   b. June 27, 1859.

Carver Tainter, (303)

Of Worcester, was born in Leicester, July 8, 1831; is a machinist by trade. Married Emily E. Capron, of Worcester, May 5, 1857.

FAMILY.

(478) ———, son,*   b. June 27, 1859.

Albert Tainter, (307)

Of Medford, has lived in Boston, also in Charlestown. Has been in former years a W. I. goods dealer, in Boston, and owned property there. Was born in Weston, Mass., May 4, 1803, son of Elisha L. Tainter. He married Mary G. Tufts, of M., Aug. 20, 1826. They are members of the Congregational Church in Medford.

FAMILY.

(479) **Albert,**   b. June 4, 1827; m. Delia Wheeler, June 18, 1856; car inspector
                         F. R. R.; resides in Fitchburg, Mass.
(480) **Andrew E.,**   b. June 20, 1829; died in Cambridge, Dec. 11, 1847, æ. 18.
(481) **John H.,**   b. May 20, 1832.
(482) **Alonzo E.,**   b. Nov. 23, 1837.
(483) **Mary J.,**   b. June 1, 1842.
  First three born in Boston, last two in Charlestown.

Edwin Tainter, (308)

Of Medford, was born in that place June 15, 1815; married Charlotte B. Ewell, of the same town, Jan. 2, 1838. Owns a line of expresses between Medford and Boston. Is a member of the Congregational Church.

FAMILY.

(481) **Charlotte M.,** b. in Medford, June 21, 1840.
(482) **Elisha E.,**   b.   "   Nov. 18, 1845.

* Both born on the same day

Capt. Thomas D. Tainter, (313)

Master mariner, of South Brookville, Me., was born in Jay, May 19, 1814. He has been master of various vessels during the past twenty years, sailing between Bangor and the West Indies, or to New York and Boston and along shore. He owns four small coasting vessels at the present time, one of which, the "President Jackson," he sails himself. Another, the "Victory," is navigated by his oldest son, who sailed from Boston last week (Oct. 14), for Bangor.

He married Mary Black, of Sandwich, Oct. 28, 1837.

FAMILY.

(483) Edwin S.,	b. Dec. 7, 1838, in Sedgwick, Me.
(484) Frederick A.,	b. March 10, 1843, in Camden, Me.
(485) Thomas D.,	b. Dec. 12, 1844, in Glenburn, Me.
(486) Mary H.,	b. Jan. 10, 1847, in Sedgwick, Me.
(487) Emma L.,	b. April 9, 1849, in Bluehill, Me.
(488) Willard O.,	b. Dec. 7, 1853, in Brooksville, Me.
(489) Winfield S.,	b. Aug. 20, 1855, in "

Samuel H. Tainter, (315)

Of Brookline, Me., mariner, was born in Jay, Oct., 1818; married Joanna Black, of Sedgwick, Aug., 1841, and resided in that town awhile, also in Glenburn, Penobscot Co., several years before removing to Brookline.

FAMILY.

(490) Samuel W.,	b. Sept. 3, 1844.
(491) Edward B.,	b. June 7, 1847.
(492) Horace S.,	b. Oct. 19, 1850.
(493) Mary S.,	b. April 22, 1852.
(494) Charles H.,	b. Oct. 28, 1854.
(495) Allen H.,	b. April 29, 1857.

(490) (491) born in Glenburn, (492) (493) (494) (495) in Brookline, Me.

Amasa L. Tainter, (318)

Of Augusta, Wisconsin, was born in Jay, Me., Aug. 11, 1825. May 7, 1855, he went to New York State, Allegany Co., town of Wellsville, and engaged in the lumbering business, remaining there until Sept., 1856, at which time he went to Weston's Rapids, Clark Co., Wisconsin, where he was also engaged in lumbering. While residing here he returned to New York, and married Louisa Dexter, of Independence (June 5, 1857). He has held the office of High Sheriff of Clark Co., being appointed by the Governor to fill the vacancy occasioned by the death of the incumbent. Since last March, he has resided in Augusta, connected with the lumber business, while also farming.

FAMILY.

(496) Chandler A.,	⎱ b. at Weston's Rapids, Sept. 7, 1858.
(497) Chauncey D.,	⎰

Amos L. Tainter, (319)

Of Augusta, Wisconsin, was born in Jay, Me., Aug. 29, 1828. In April, 1852, he went to Wellsville, N. Y., where he married Mary E. Rolfe, of Willing, N. Y., Sept. 28, 1854. In Oct., 1856, he went West, and settled in Augusta, Bride Creek, Eau Claire Co., Wis., where he owns a farm and is connected in the lumber business.

Alsworth Tainter, (324)

Of Carthage, Me., is a farmer. Was chosen one of the Selectmen, Assessors and Overseers of the Poor in 1845-6 and 9; also in 1855-6-7-8-9; was also chosen Collector and Constable in 1849, which offices he has held up to the present time. He married Caroline Gould, of Carthage, Jan. 9, 1844.

(A little that we omitted to say of his father, on page 61, we will say here.)

Simon Tainter, son of Benjamin, started in life for himself at the age of 19, having bought his time of his father, then residing in Jay, Me. He, together with Jonathan Morse, bought 180 acres of land, giving their notes for $300 each, and commenced felling trees July 4, 1811, in an unbroken wilderness. After felling ten acres they left to await the coming spring, when they were to resume their labors. The first duty after their return was to select a spot whereon to erect a log cabin, but before that was accomplished a heavy rain came on; consequently they sought shelter in a *hollow tree*. His furniture consisted of one three-legged stool—two broken iron kettles—one broken fork—a knife made from a part of a grass scythe—one broken spoon, and a plank supported by wooden pins driven into the logs, was his only table. In the absence of his partner, he always cooked his three meals in the morning by making mush and filling up the broken kettle with milk. It was thus he buffeted the trials and hardships of a forest home—with a view of some day obtaining a competency. In the year 1813, he and Mr. Morse dissolved partnership, and divided the land. He then leased his land, and went to Stoneham, Mass., and worked two years. In 1815, he returned; and in 1816, married. He has never moved from that place. It has wholly been brought to a thriving condition by his own indefatigable industry and perseverance. Notwithstanding all the trials and hardships to which all pioneers must submit, they found much enjoyment. They looked with admiring wonder on the rapid progress of affairs, and with brave hearts and strong arms they kept up courage and toiled on. His young and energetic wife made sugar from the maple trees, and with her own hands spun and wove their garments. Soon their lodge assumed an air of comfort and convenience, and now the forest has given place to green fields of waving corn and grain, and a beautiful orchard attests their industry. Where was once the log cabins, are comfortable dwellings for man and beast.

FAMILY.

(498) **William H.,**   b. in Carthage, Dec. 1, 1846.
(499) **Emma,**   b.   "   May 26, 1848.
(500) **George G.,**   b.   "   July 5, 1851.

Wyman V. Tainter, (325)

Of Carthage, Me., nurseryman, was Postmaster from 1851 to 1855; has been Town Treasurer, Selectman, Assessor, Justice of the Peace, &c., in that town.

He married Susan F. Wilson, of West Cambridge, Mass., May 7, 1848. She died Dec. 8, 1854, leaving two children. He married, second, Mary Maxfield, of Carthage, Aug. 2, 1855.

FAMILY.

(501) **Albert W.,**   b. Feb. 18, 1850.
(502) **Elmar E.,**   b. April 14, 1854.
(503) **Willis L.,**   b. May 15, 1857.

Gilbert L. Tainter, (326)

Of Dixfield, Me., is a farmer, honest and industrious, and respected by all with whom his business relations in life bring him in contact. He married Semantha O. Fuller, of Carthage, March 27, 1853.

FAMILY.

(504) **Frank E.,** b. in Dixfield, April 5, 1856.

Thomas P. Tainter, (331)

Of Apalachicola, Florida,. merchant, was born in Bangor, Me., July 20, 1825; married Josephine C. Brooks, of A., May 15, 1851. (See letter on page 61.)

FAMILY.

(505) **Charles B.,** b. in Apalachicola, Fla., March, 1852.
(506) **Alice D.,** b. " " April, 1854.
(507) **Josephine M.,** b. " " April, 1856.

Norris D. Tainter, (341)

Of Whitingham, Vt., farmer, was born in that place March 6, 1812. Married Sarah Martin, of the same town, Sept. 2, 1834. They are members of the Methodist Church.

FAMILY.

(508) **Loren,** b. in Whitingham, Vt., June 26, 1838.
(509) **Lucinda,** b. " Feb. 20, 1843; died Sept. 3, 1845.
(510) **Sarah L.,** b. " June 13, 1845.
(511) **Norris D.,** b. in Governor, N. Y., July 5, 1851; died Sept. 5, 1852.

Josiah W. Tainter, Jr., (343)

Born at Whitingham, Vt., March 1, 1818; married Elizabeth Russell, of Northampton, Mass., Nov. 5, 1838. At Holyoke, Mass., while on a train of cars, his foot slipped, and he fell, being instantly killed, Feb. 20, 1854, æ. 35.

FAMILY.

(512) **Mary E.,** b. at Whitingham, Oct. 12, 1839.
(513) **Laura E.,** b. " Jan. 28, 1842.
(514) **Edward J.,** b. " Sept. 24, 1846.

James M. Tainter, (344)

Of Whitingham, Vt., farmer, was born in that town April 5, 1821. He married Catherine Lake, of the same place, Feb. 6, 1848.

FAMILY.

(515) **James H.,** b. Jan. 25, 1849.
(516) **Addison C.,** b. Oct. 26, 1851.
(517) **Norman F.,** b. March 18, 1854.
(518) **Frank A.,** b. Oct. 28, 1856.

Jonathan Tainter, (350)

Of Millburgh, Michigan, son of Deacon Jonathan, of Kalamazoo, was born in York, N. Y., Jan. 17, 1831; married Marancy Blakesley, Feb. 2, 1852. He rents a grist and saw-mill, in Millburgh.

Charles L. Tainter, (357)

Of Pentwater, Michigan, was born in Chardon, Ohio, Feb. 18, 1825. He married Orrian Newcomb, of Parkman, Ohio, Jan. 29, 1851. She died Oct. 28, 1853(?), leaving an infant son. He married, second, Nancy Young, of Parkman, May 3, 1857. He lived a number of years in Lafayette, Pa., and was Postmaster in that place. Is a Justice of the Peace in Pentwater.

FAMILY.

(519) **Orlow E.,**   b. at Lafayette, Pa., Aug. 29, 1853.

Benjamin D. Tainter, (359)

Of Thornville, Michigan, was born in Watertown, N. Y., April 7, 1822. His parents removed to Michigan when he was fourteen years of age. He remained at home, clearing and improving the soil, until of age, when he went into the carpentering business, which he followed some ten or twelve years. During the last three years he has been engaged in improving a new farm. The winter of 1849 he spent at Fort Wayne, Indiana, at his trade, and the eighteen months following he spent at Fond du Lac, Wis.; from thence returned to Michigan. He married Nancy Hillard, Oct. 10, 1849. She was born in Salem, Conn., Nov. 19, 1828, and at the age of 18 emigrated to Michigan.

FAMILY.

(520) **Darwin E.,**   b. July 18, 1852.
(521) **Ebenezer G.,**   b. Dec. 4, 1854.
(522) **Phebe E.,**   b. April 25, 1859.
    Born in Lapeer Co., Michigan.

Stephen L. Tainter, (372)

Of Prairie du Chien, Wisconsin, died of five days sickness, Sept. 12, 1846, æ. 28. He left a wife and two children. She remained a widow two years, then married Hurley D. White, of Point Douglass, Minnesota, and died April 20, 1850, æ. 33.

FAMILY.

(523) **Richard K.,**   b. Dec. 15, 1839; lives in St. Paul, Minnesota.
(524) **Martha A.,**   b. Dec., 1842; died Aug., 1844.
(525) **Emma E.,**   b. May, 1845; died May, 1848.

Anson Gorham Tainter, (373)

Of Franklin, Bad Axe Co., Wisconsin, was born in Sandgate, Vt., Aug. 19, 1823. He is a farmer, one of the Board of Town Supervisors, Treasurer of School District, Postmaster, and a member of the Methodist Church. He married Rachael Jane Tobler, of Lancaster, Wis., March 8, 1852.

(See letter on page 65.)

FAMILY.

(526) **John M.,**   b. Feb. 17, 1853.
(527) **Daniel F.,**   b. Aug. 18, 1854.
(528) **Aaron N.,**   b. July 29, 1856.
    Born in Franklin, Wisconsin.

Andrew Tainter, (376)

Of Dunn County, Wisconsin, was born July 6, 1823; took for a wife a Chippewa Indian girl, named Poskin, and has four likely children. He is of the firm of Wilson, Tainter & Co., extensive and wealthy operators in lumber.

FAMILY.

(529) **Charlotte.**   (Not knowing his Post-office address, we are unable to give any
(530) **Julia.**   dates respecting his family.)
(531) **William.**
(532) **Thomas.**

Edward Tainter, (397)

Of Melrose, Mass., son of Ezra Tainter, of the same town, was born in Duxbury, Mass., April 10, 1830. He married Sarah C. Blakeley, of Melrose, Sept. 26, 1854, and died July 5, 1859, æ. 29.

FAMILY.

(533) **Edward F.,**   b. May 4, 1855. His mind is impaired, having suffered with congestion of the brain, when three years of age.

(534) **Sarah S.,**   b. Dec. 18, 1857; died Jan. 13, 1857.

VERSES, (CONTINUED FROM PAGE 74).

41 Now they have joined that silent throng,
Where it will not be very long
Before you'l leave this world of care,
And go to your dear offsprings there.

42 Look to your children that remains,
O do your duty, spare no pains
To train them up now for the Lord,
Then you'll receive divine reward.

43 Come see you do those things thats right,
With your lamps trim'd and your loins girt,
Now waiting till your change shall come
To go to your eternal home.

44 And join that glorious throng above,
Where nothing reigns but perfect love,
Where you can never wear away
That blessed, long, Eternal day.

45 Dear children of the mourning flock,
Tis at your door Christ Jesus knocks,
Arise and leave your darling sin,
And let the sun of Glory in.

46 Behold him coming from above
With open arms of heavenly love,
Desiring you might see his face,
And taste the riches of his grace.

47 He, by his awful providence,
Calls you aloud to diligence,
In the improvement of your time,
While gospel sun holds out to shine.

48 Dear youth improve these golden hours
While you have life and vital powers;
The day of grace will soon be past,
And where will you appear at last.

49 Remember well that fatal day,
When your dear friends were call'd away;
You might have been where they are laid,
Had not your hasty steps been staid.

50 O may the sovereign God of love,
Send down his comforts from above,
And teach you while in youthful days,
To know his name and sing his praise;

51 To sound his praise while here on earth,
And triumph in the hours of Death,
Then take a joyful launch away,
To glorious realms of brightest day;

52 And join the millions round the throne,
Where pain and grief are never known,
There you the Angels will out-sing,
And strike the notes on grace's string.

53 Now there is one thats left behind,
Miss Nabby Merrick was confined,
Her Body under water lay,
Till the revolving sixteenth day.

54 Tho' day and night they searched around,
Yet nothing of her could be found,
Until some travellers passing by,
They saw her on the water lye,

55 A floating back towards the shore,
From whence she sailed few days before.
From there conveyed back to the town,
And laid in the cold and silent ground.

56 Sinners, attend the solemn call,
For your damnation waits your fall,
For you have either got to stand
Or fall before the son of man.

57 The Gospel Jubilee trumpet sounds,
The blessed voice echoes round,
And cries poor sinners come away,
Dont stop one moment nor delay.

58 Dont feast yourselves on false Ideas,
That you can live here as you pleas,
While you have God's word in your hand,
You must believe or else be damned.

59 Dont think that Christ the Son of God,
Came down to earth and spilt his blood,
To save you sinners in your sins,
And afterwards you'l reign with him.

60 Dont speak so bold with your bare face,
That Christ will save all Adam's race.
If so, what need there be, I say,
Of that great Solemn Judgment day.

61 Behold, our God is on his way—
Let sinners hear or disobey.
Come, blessed Jesus, quickly come,
Amen, and take thy children home.   A.D. 1799.

MASONRY.

Dr. Tainter was a strong anti-mason, as the following verses, written during the Morgan excitement, attest.

1 Free Masonry bears ancient date,
No one on earth the time can state;
Some do affirm it took its rise
Before the sun rolled through the skies.

2 How could there be a *Lodge* in Heaven ?
There were no sins to be forgiven.
How could that Holy, Heavenly place,
With such an *Order* be disgraced.

3 No "*Apprentices*" nor "*Fellow Craft*,"
Nor master masons in the "*Staff*,"
'Twould make the fallen angels stare,
To hear the "Oath," such masons swear.

4 Go range the heavens all around,
No "*Constitution*" can be found,
No "*Lambskins*" that the masons wear
Hang in the shining mansions there.

5 Old lucifer the great "*Arch Knight*,"
He with his legions out of spite,
Rebelled against the sovereign crown,
Like masons now are tumbling down.

6 They reached the doleful shades of hell,
In flaming caverns there to dwell,
But in the awful chamber there,
A Mason's "Altar" they did rear.

7 They found they were all taken in,
The pass word was, they all had sinned,
Doomed to prison they must be,
Like Morgan in Niagarie.

8 No cutting throats nor vital parts,
No tearing tongues nor bleeding hearts,
Such horrid murderers could not be
In hell with that "fraternity."

9 No house of timber to pull down,
To hang thereon a purged clown,
No human shape to act like gulls,
To drink wine out of human skulls.

10 No human hearts there to be got
To throw on dung-hills for to rot,
No head struck off in that hot fire
To be placed upon a lofty spire.

11 No present Grips could there be shown,
Whereby free masons might be known,
Such grips as these would surely fail
For the want of fingers and thumb nails.

12 'Tis by permission Satan roams,
Through the wide world his ways are known,
To frustrate eternal plans
To make all masons where he can.

13 To Eden's garden he went in,
Being clad in the old serpent's skin ;
Adam and Eve he found alone,
To them he made his errand known.

14 I've come, said he, you to invite,
You with our "Order" to unite,
Full-blooded masons you may be,
And go with our "Fraternity."

15 You are hood-winked in a sense,
Nothing you know but innocence,
And if you wish more light to see,
Eat fruit of that forbidden tree.

16 In "Buffs" you are already dressed,
To meet a "Compass" at your breast,
Or the sharp corner of the "Square,"
And hear the word, and "who comes there ?"

17 You'll answer there, a poor blind fool,
I've come to this masonic school,
To know how simple I must be,
To understand freemasonry.

18 Now round the lodge-room you must go,
And form a square with heel and toe,
Till at the Altar you will kneel,
With conscience seared with hardened steel.

19 Your nakedness will then appear,
Shall fill your breast with panting fear,
With cable tow around your neck,
And you must swear or have a check.

20 The little "Gavel" at your head,
With horrid Oaths you will be fed ;
You must look sharp and have good care,
You'll know how old mans catched the mare.

21 By crook of elbow you must swear
By the "Compass and the Square,"
Your obligations for to keep,
Or you'll be plunged in the deep.

22 You'll be murdered in the dark,
And make a breakfast for the shark,
With your throat cut and bowels out,
You'll make a dinner for the trout.

23 As you from the Altar rise,
Your hood-wink falls from off your eyes,
You'll think that bedlam has broke loose,
You'll know how the fox catched the goose.

24 And as you to "Higher Orders" go,
More mason secrets you will know,
After them you'll make strict search,
We three can raise the "Living Arch."

25 Now as you go from place to place,
Your poverty is no disgrace ;
And if you wish to hide your sins,
Fig leaves will do as well as skins.

26 And when you meet your "Fellow-Craft,"
Sit down and take a hearty laugh,
That you have been to mason schools,
Till all the rest the world are fools.

27 You'll meet with gamblers on the way,
Tell them to come without delay ;
And if they wish a game to take,
We'll stand them up until day break.

28 Sabbath breakers you will know,
They will ramble to and fro,
When on that day you'll often see,
And hear hollo, haw and gee.

29 They will go from house to house,
And keep the neighbors in a touse ;
Divine commands they can't endure,
But in your lodge will be secure.

30 You'll see the staggering drunkards come,
For they pretend that we keep mum ;
But surely they will find
We have no whiskey, rum nor wine.

31 We'll make such senseless mortals know
That in our lodge it is not so,
For in our lodge we mean to be
A temperate society.

32 See the old world come in a throng,
Through boundless billows launch along,
And at the doors to rap and stare,
Till we can answer, who comes there.

33 The Sodomites come in full gale,
With fire and brimstone raise their sail,
The " Sign " and " Secrets " they well know,
As they to " Higher orders " go.

34 Bold blasphemers, let them go,
They meet in the dark below ;
Yet if they our lodge offend,
We'll send them to Niagara's den.

35 Let their masonry in these parts,
Tear out their tongues and bleeding hearts,
Cut their throats and vital parts,
And bury them at low water mark.

36 But if they cannot keep them there,
They need not run into despair,
Send Lucifer word and they shall go
Into old Lake Ontario.

WATERTOWN.

Presuming that same account of Watertown would be interesting to families at a distance, the following is inserted from " *Barber's Historical Collections.*"

THIS is an ancient town, it being settled the same year as Boston, in 1630. The first Englishmen who are known to have visited the place were Mr. Wareham and some of his people, who afterwards settled Dorchester. The place in Watertown where they remained a few days is stated yet to bear the name of Dorchester Fields. Shortly after their removal, a permanent settlement was effected by another company. A party of the adventurous emigrants who came in Winthrop's fleet, with Sir Richard Saltonstall and Rev. George Phillips at their head, selected a place on the banks of Charles river for their plantation. On the 7th of Sept., 1630 (O. S.), the court of assistants, at Charlestown, " ordered that Trimountain be called Boston, Mattapan, Dorchester, and the town on Charles river, Watertown."

The first church in Watertown was gathered on the 30th of July, 1630, upon a day set apart for " *solemn fasting and prayer,*" which had been appointed by Gov. Winthrop, on account of the prevailing sickness in the settlements. Cotton Mather says that Rev. Mr. Phillips, with about 40 men, settlers of Watertown, on that occasion subscribed the covenant, in order unto their coalescence into a church estate. The Hon. James Savage, in a recent investigation of the subject, makes the first church in Boston and the Watertown church precisely coeval, assigning the origin of both to the 30th of July, 1630.

" The first minister of Watertown was the Rev. George Phillips, who continued in that office 14 years. At the first court of assistants, held at Charlestown, on board the Arabella, it was ordered that, as speedily as might be convenient, houses should be erected for the ministers at the public charge. Sir Richard Saltonstall ' undertook to have this done for Mr. Phillips,' and for salary he was to have £30 annually. The first meeting-house stood on the north side of the road to Cambridge, near the old burying-yard ; there was a common before it, which was used as a training-field. Mr. Phillips was sole minister of Watertown till 1639. In that year, Rev. John Knowles, ' a godly man, and prime scholar,' arrived in New England, and in December was ordained second pastor of the church, in connection with Mr. Phillips. In 1642, Mr. Knowles went to Virginia, where he preached a short time, but returned again to Watertown. He remained there a while after his return, but finally returned to England, after an absence of 11 years. He died in London, in 1685, at a very advanced age. On the 1st of July, 1644, died Rev. George Phillips. He is said to have been an able controversial writer. Mr. Phillips was succeeded in the ministry by Rev. John Sherman, a native of Dedham, Essex county, England. He preached his first sermon at Watertown under a large tree, as an assistant to Mr. Phillips. * * * Mr. Sherman was the father of 26 children, by two marriages, 6 by the first and 20 in the other. He died in 1685, aged 72, and was succeeded by Rev. John Bailey, who was ordained in 1686,

12

He was assisted for a time in the ministry by his brother, Mr. Thomas Bailey, till his death, in 1689; after which, Mr. Henry Gibbs was engaged as teacher. In 1692, Rev. John Bailey left Watertown and returned to Boston. Mr. Gibbs was now the only minister in the town, and was engaged from time to time, but not ordained. About 1692, there was much excitement on the subject of the location of a new meeting-house. In opposition to the wishes of the inhabitants of the eastern part of the town, it was located in the middle part. This caused a separation of the church. Mr. Gibbs continued to preach in the old meeting-house, and appears to have been settled in 1697. The part of the society who had built the new meeting-house obtained a pastor, Rev. Samuel Angier, who was also ordained in 1697. In 1720, a committee, appointed by the general court, to run the dividing line between the societies, decided that the western or new meeting-house should be removed to an eminence in the present town of Waltham, and that the old or east meeting-house should be removed to the hill back of the present meeting-house of the society, then called *School-house Hill.* Both societies soon erected new meeting-houses at the places directed by the committee. The western parish, in 1787, was incorporated a distinct town, by the name of Waltham. Mr. Gibbs died in 1723, in the 56th year of his age, and in the 27th of his ministry, reckoned from the date of his ordination. He was interred in the old burying-yard. The successor of Mr. Gibbs was Rev. Seth Storer (of Saco, Maine, and a graduate of Harvard in 1720), who was ordained in 1724. He died in 1774, aged 73."

The ministry of Mr. Storer was the longest which occurs in the history of Watertown, being half a century. The situation of the meeting-house was removed during his ministry from the summit of the hill, but not without much opposition. Rev. Daniel Adams was the next minister in succession from Mr. Storer, and was ordained in 1778. His ministry was short, as he died in August following his ordination. The next pastor of this church was Rev. Richard Rosewell Eliot, a native of New Haven, Conn., and descendant of Rev. John Eliot, the memorable teacher of the Indians. He graduated at Harvard, in 1774, and was ordained at Watertown in 1780. He died in 1818, aged 66, and was succeeded by Rev. Convers Francis; ordained in 1819.

Watertown village is large and compactly built, about 6 miles from Boston. The *United States Arsenal,* occupying a site of 40 acres, is about a mile eastward of the village, on the Boston road. The arsenal consists of several large brick buildings, enclosed by a high fence, on the north bank of Charles river. Watertown, in extent of territory, is one of the smallest towns in the state, containing but about 3,000 acres, including land and water; the soil is generally remarkably good. A portion of the southeastern extremity of the town is sandy, poor, and barren; but with this exception the land is some of the most productive in the commonwealth. Population, 3,500.

"It seems a very remarkable complaint so early as 1635, that 'all the towns in the Bay began to be much straitened by their own nearness to one another, and their cattle being so much increased.' This is said to be accounted for by the government having at first required every man to live within half a mile from the meeting-house in his town. The want of room appears from some cause to have been peculiarly felt in Watertown; and on several occasions the inhabitants emigrated and formed new settlements. The first of these was in 1635, at the place afterwards called Wethersfield, in Connecticut, where, as we are told, some people of Watertown, before they had obtained leave to go beyond the jurisdiction of the Massachusetts government, 'took the opportunity of seizing a brave piece of meadow,' which it seems was also coveted by their neighbors of Cambridge. This Watertown plantation at Wethersfield was for a long course of years a scene of dissension within and without. In the course of three or four years the church at that place fell into such a state of discord that the plantation divided, and a part removed and settled in combination with New Haven.

"Watertown in early times received but little trouble from the Indians. One remarkable instance, however, of Indian vengeance on a citizen of this town, was the melancholy fate of Capt. John Oldham. Before the settlement of Massachusetts Bay, he had resided in Plymouth, from which place, for some misconduct, he was expelled. He, however, was highly respected in Watertown, and was a deputy from the town to the first general court, in 1632. He became a distinguished trader among the Indians, and went to traffic with them at Block Island. The Indians got possession of Oldham's vessel, and murdered him in the most shocking manner. Two boys and two Narragansett Indians the murderers had spared. This atrocious deed excited great indignation in all the English settlements, and was one of the immediate causes of the Pequot war. In 1639, an order is found in the records by which 'the meeting-house is appointed for a watch-house for the use of the town,' which may lead to the inference that it was thought necessary to maintain a patrol in the night for fear of the Indians."

In the early wars of the country, and in the revolutionary war, the inhabitants of Watertown took an active part. In the time of excitement preceding the war of American independence, the article of tea was proscribed in this town, in the following words :

"That we consent to lay aside all foreign teas, as expensive and pernicious, as well as unnecessary ; this continent abounding with many herbs of a more salubrious quality, which, if we were as much used to as the poisonous bohea, would, no doubt, in time be as agreeable, perhaps much more so ; and whilst, by a manly influence, we expect our women to make this sacrifice to the good of their country, we hereby declare we shall highly honor and esteem the encouragers of our own manufactures and the general use of the productions of this continent ; this being in our judgment, at this time, a necessary means (under God) of rendering us a happy and free people."

The second and third sessions of the provincial congress were held at Watertown, in the meeting-house, within the first six months of the year 1775. General Warren, the early and lamented martyr in the cause of freedom, on the memorable 17th of June, presided at their deliberations. The congress was busy in adopting such measures as the distracted state of the colony required. Among the few newspapers printed at that time was "The Boston Gazette and Country Journal," published at Boston, by Edes and Gill, and was distinguished by the spirited and fearless tone in which it defended the American cause. The press of this paper was removed to Watertown, and the Gazette was there published for more than a year, from June 5, 1775, to Oct. 28, 1776, when, the British having evacuated Boston, the office was moved back.

The inhabitants of Watertown bore their part of the losses and burdens of the country at this perilous period. One of their number was killed on the 19th of April, and many others, during the war, either died by sickness in camp, or fell on the field of battle.

INDEX TO CHRISTIAN NAMES.

Name		Name		Name		Name	
Aaron,	126	Alvah Ayers,	426	Benjamin,	139	Charles Linole,	357
Abigail,	147	Amanda,	349	Benjamin,	178	Charles Melville,	425
Abigail Beals,	134	Amasa Davis,	318	Benjamin,	330	Charlotte,	529
Abigail Beals,	135	Amelia B.	255	Benjamin Darwin,	359	Charlotte M.	481
Abijah,	79	Amelia Virginia,	436	Bethier,	462	Chauncey D.	497
Abijah,	156	Amos Livermore,	319	Betsey,	120	Christopher C.	325
Abijah Shumway	449	Andrew,	376	Betsey,	169	Clarinda,	198
Adaline M.	309	Andrew E.	480	Betsey,	197	Clarissa,	173
Addison Carlton,	516	Angeline,	360	Betsey,	340	Clarissa K. W.	192
Adelia Ann,	411	Anna,	85	Calista Brainard,	464	Cordelia,	312
Adelia Minerva,	193	Ann,	3	Calvin,	125	Cordelia,	355
Adelia S.	266	Ann,	49	Caroline Maria,	257	Cordelia,	362
Alanson,	239	Ann Augusta,	252	Caroline M.	329	Corrine D. F.	274
Albert I.	263	Ann Maria,	137	Carrie,	470	Cyntha,	351
Albert,	307	Anna,	200	Carver,	303	Cynthia Almira,	445
Albert,	479	Anne,	61	Catherine,	59	Cyrus,	142
Albert Wyman	501	Anne,	439	Catherine Sparh'k	167	Cyrus H.	
Albovin,	55	Anon N.	528	Cecelia Lothrop,	305	Cyrus K.	154
Alfred Bridges,	412	Anson Gorham,	373	Chandler A.,	496	Daniel,	60
Alice Dale,	506	Asa,	128	Charles Austin,	294	Daniel,	87
Alida Bronk,	392	Asa A.	247	Charles Baker,	332	Daniel,	118
Allen H.	495	Benjamin,	6	Charles Brooks,	505	Daniel,	284
Alma Jane,	427	Benjamin,	12	Charles E.	267	Daniel,	297
Almeda E.	457	Benjamin,	30	Charles Emery,	465	Daniel Adams,	110
Almira,	287	Benjamin,	38	Charles H.	494	Daniel Adams,	213
Alsworth,	324	Benjamin,	88	Charles L.	204	Daniel Adams,	217

Name	No.	Name	No.	Name	No.	Name	No.
Daniel F.	527	Emeline M.	310	Henry Augustus,	430	Julia A.	476
Daniel Webster,	402	Emily,	384	Henry Adams,	467	Laura,	304
Daniel Webster,	418	Emily Frances,	235	Henry Clay,	224	Laura Eugenia,	513
Darius,	115	Emma,	499	Hollis Wood,	132	Laura Norton,	337
Darwin E.	520	Emma A.	258	Homer B.	254	Laura Augusta,	468
David,	31	Emma E.	525	Homer J.	276	Lavina,	143
David,	86	Emma Lizzie,	428	Homer L.	245	Leonard,	282
David,	283	Emma Jane,	460	Horace B.	337	Lewis,	210
David E.	474	Emma Louisa,	243	Horace Stone,	321	Lewis Edgar,	459
David Lowry,	385	Emma Louisa,	487	Horace S.	492	Lewis Hurd,	386
Dean Willis,	417	Ephraim Copel'nd	299	Ira B.	152	Lewis M.	273
Dolly,	105	Erastus P.	153	Isaac,	463	Lillia Maria,	454
Dora,	469	Eugene M.	271	Isaac Bond,	218	Lindsey K.	461
Dorothy,	10	Eunice,	208	Isaac Keith,	296	Lois,	183
Dorathy,	22	Ezekiel Wood,	189	James Henry,	333	Loren,	187
Eaires,	51	Ezra,	205	James Henry,	334	Loren,	368
Edna,	353	Fanny,	113	James Henry,	515	Loren,	508
Edna Melinda,	346	Fanny,	280	James Madison,	144	Louisa Ann,	451
Edward,	397	Flora,	261	Jared Forbes,	369	Lovern,	356
Edward,	465	Fordice,	190	Jedediah,	58	Lucinda,	184
Edward B.	491	Frances Jane,	416	Jedediah,	117	Lucinda,	199
Edward E.	473	Frances Lucinda,	405	Jemima,	180	Lucinda,	352
Edward F.	440	Francis Luther,	222	Jeremiah B.	381	Lucinda,	354
Edward Fay,	533	Francis Leath,	414	Joel,	81	Lucinda,	509
Edward Josiah,	519	Frank Augustus,	518	Joel,	124	Lucinda Jemima,	366
Edwin,	308	Frank Edgar,	504	Joel Emery,	292	Lucy,	66
Edwin Eugene,	233	Frederick A.	226	Johanna,	47	Lucy,	107
Edwin Stone,	483	Frederick August.	484	Johanna,	35	Lucy,	127
Elbridge Gilbert,	295	Frederick E.	409	Johanna,	98	Lucy,	151
Eldoretta Parthia,	453	Frederick W.	458	John,	19	Lucy,	281
Eleanor,	83	Frederick H.	475	John,	23	Lucy,	290
Eleanor,	163	George,	220	John,	48	Lucy Keith,	301
Electa Almira,	443	George A.	399	John,	63	Lucy Maria,	472
Elijah Fairbanks,	211	George F.	348	John,	102	Lucy R.	260
Elisha E.	482	George Franklin,	452	John,	129	Lucy Warren,	232
Elisha Livermore,	171	George Gould,	500	John,	194	Luella E.	442
Eliza,	130	George Lewis,	404	John,	370	Luther Goodnow,	123
Eliza A.	275	George T. Dale,	338	John H. M.	455	Lydia,	62
Eliza M.	253	Geo. Washington,	223	John Lewis,	201	Lydia,	342
Eliza Richards,	379	Geo. Washington,	420	John Marshall,	336	Lydia A.	311
Elizabeth,	14	Georgietta V.	139	John M.	526	Lydia Ann,	407
Elizabeth,	24	Gilbert Lafayette,	326	John Q. Adams,	225	Lydia Leland,	228
Elizabeth,	40	Guilford,	237	John Wesley,	234	Marcia Ellen,	323
Elizabeth,	53	Hannah,	25	Jonah,	145	Margaret E.	246
Elizabeth,	67	Hannah,	44	Jonathan,	7	Margaret Hines,	314
Elizabeth,	100, 106	Hannah,	84	Jonathan,	11	Margaret Davis,	
Elizabeth,	120	Hannah,	93	Jonathan,	26	MargaretWaldron	419
Elizabeth,	169	Hannah,	94	Jonathan,	37	Maria Elizabeth,	393
Elizabeth,	191	Hannah,	101	Jonathan,	89	Marion J.	261
Elizabeth,	197	Hannah,	174	Jonathan,	136	Marion Jessie,	227
Elizabeth,	212	Hannah Eliza,	447	Jonathan,	185	Marilla,	388
Elizabeth,	214	Hannah Stone,	316	Jonathan,	350	Marshall L.	242
Elizabeth,	219	Hannah True,	394	Jonathan Oscar,	351	Marshall,	424
Elizabeth Eunice,	108	Harriet,	165	Joseph,	4	Martha,	383
Elizabeth Barnard	429	Harriet,	382	Joseph,	13	Martha A.	524
Elizabeth Carter,	908	Harriet Abby,	335	Joseph,	27	Mary,	2
Ella Louisa,	428	Harriet Augusta,	413	Joseph,	56	Mary,	18
Ellen A.	259	Harriet Elvira,	293	Joseph,	64	Mary,	21
Ellen Elizabeth,	410	Harriet Spaulding	403	Joseph,	148	Mary,	32
Ellen Madora,	387	Harvey,	162	Joseph I.	236	Mary,	43
Ellen M. M.	456	Harvey Sibley,	300	Josephine M.	507	Mary,	80
Elmar Eugene,	502	Harvey Sibley 2d,	302	Joshua,	41	Mary,	95
Elvira Marion,	438	Helen C.	244	Josiah Wood,	90	Mary,	116
Elmus,	209	Helen E.	265	Josiah Wood,	181	Mary,	144
Emeline,	291	Helen Maria,	395	Josiah Wood,	343	Mary,	158
Emeline Adelia,	378	Henry	131	Julia,	530	Mary,	179

Mary,	. 195	Olive Christina,	390	Samuel, .	. 92	Stephen Lewis,	372
Mary,	. 206	Olive U. .	. 241	Samuel, .	. 99	Sumner, .	. 285
Mary,	. 250	Orlow Eldridge,	519	Samuel, .	. 175	Sumner, .	. 279
Mary Ann,	. 238	Orsamus, .	. 150	Samuel Hinds,	315	Sumner, .	. 434
Mary Ann,	. 306	Orvil Eldridge,	358	Samuel W.	. 490	Susanna, .	. 16
Mary Ann,	. 437	Oscar J. .	. 270	Sarah,	. 8	Susanna, .	. 36
Mary E. .	. 268	Othniel Bennett,	363	Sarah,	. 39	Susanna, .	. 46
Mary Eliza,	. 391	Patty,	. 149	Sarah,	. 65	Susanna, .	. 96
Mary Elizabeth,	386	Persis Ann,	. 231	Sarah,	. 97	Susanna, .	. 176
Mary Elizabeth,	400	Philetta, .	. 146	Sarah,	. 114	Susanna Bond,	216
Mary Elizabeth,	421	Phœbe E.	. 522	Sarah,	. 121	Sybil,	. 289
Mary E. .	. 441	Polly,	. 158	Sarah,	. 140	Theresa,	. 249
Mary E. .	. 448	Polly,	. 179	Sarah,	. 288	Theron Elijah,	. 415
Mary E. .	. 471	Randall, .	. 15	Sarah,	. 320	Thomas,	. 532
Mary E. .	. 512	Rebecca, .	. 5	Sarah Ann,	. 377	Thomas Davis,	313
Mary Helen,	. 486	Rebecca, .	. 20	Sarah Beals,	. 138	Thomas Davis, .	485
Mary Josephine,	481	Rebecca, .	. 34	Sarah Davis,	. 400	Thomas Phillips,	131
Mary L. .	. 240	Rebecca, .	. 45	Sarah Lewis,	. 203	Thomas Sparh'k,	168
Mary S. .	. 498	Rebecca, .	. 109	Sarah L. .	. 251	Timothy, .	. 186
Matilda Ketler,	435	Rebecca, .	. 182	Sarah L. .	. 256	Vivene, .	. 248
Melissa Ann,	. 446	Rebecca, .	. 339	Sarah L. .	. 262	Willard O.	. 488
Mehettable,	. 161	Richard K.	. 528	Sarah Lucinda	510	Willard Howard,	406
Merritt Root,	. 348	Robert Bartlett,	322	Sarah H. .	. 423	Willard S.	. 286
Milo Burdick, .	374	Rodolphus Fay'te	375	Sarah S. .	. 534	William, .	. 52
Miriam, .	. 29	Rosetta, .	. 350	Silas Burt,	. 347	William, .	. 57
Miriam, .	. 54	Rosilla Hubbard,	327	Simon,	. 9	William, .	. 108
Nabby, .	. 159	Roxa,	. 166	Simon, .	. 17	William, .	. 112
Nahum, .	. 82	Rozell, .	. 364	Simon, .	. 33	William, .	. 119
Nahum, .	. 298	Rufus, .	. 444	Simon, .	. 78	William, .	. 221
Nancy, .	. 122	Rufus A. .	. 269	Simon, .	. 160	William, .	. 531
Nancy, .	. 164	Rufus H.	. 155	Simon, .	. 177	William Coolidge,	207
Nancy, .	. 170	Rufus N. .	. 264	Simon B.	. 450	William Henry,	401
Nancy Davis, .	317	Rufus Willard,		Solon S.	. 215	William H.	. 498
Nathaniel, .	. 104	Ruth A. .	. 272	Sophia, .	. 133	William H. Har.	422
Newell Josiah,	432	Ruth L. .		Sophia, .	. 172	William L.	. 202
F. Norman Francis		Sally, .	. 111	Sophronia,	. 396	Willis Leroy,	. 503
Norman A.	. 517	Sally, .	. 157	Stephen, .	. 91	Winfield S.	. 489
Norris Davis, .	341	Sally, .	. 196	Stephen, .	. 155	Wyman Vose,	. 325
Norris Davis, .	511	Samuel, .	. 42	Stephen Gorham,	188	Zerviah, .	. 28
Olive, .	. 141	Samuel, .	. 50	Stephen Gorham,	389		

THE TAINTER SPOONS.

Mr. Dean W. Tainter,   *Leslie, Michigan, Nov. 26, 1859.*

Dear Sir, — I have received your letter dated the 16th inst., in which you express a disappointment in not getting one of the silver spoons. Yet, dear sir, you shall have one of them. Your proposition is accepted, and the spoon shall be forthcoming as soon as I can accomplish the business. In the first place, my sister, Mrs. Du Bois, lives 15 miles from here, north and a little east. I shall have to go there for the spoon, and will next week. I shall then have to go to Jackson, 15 miles south of this, to an Express office, and I have business that will call me there in a few days, and the spoon shall be forwarded to you with all proper diligence.

I have no certain date when the buttons were made into spoons, but I should think it was in the year 1818, or thereabouts.

You state, in your letter, that you have inserted into the book my letter containing the captivity of my grandfather and the Indians, and you say you presume that I have no objections. *No, Sir.* If I can in any way contribute anything of interest to its pages, it will be a pleasure to me to do so.   Yours with great respect,

SAMUEL T. RICE.

(See letter on pages 36 and 46.)

The receipt of the spoon is gratefully acknowledged, and that it may carry its story itself, from this time henceforth, the following has been engraved on the back :

" This spoon is one of six, made
in the year 1818 from 24 silver
buttons worn by the 1st Tainter,   A.D. 1638.
on his vest & short clothes,
when he came over from England."

The spoon is almost perfect, and of very white silver, quite small and symmetrical, to be seen by the curious who may be pleased to call on the writer.

PEDIGREE OF THE OTHER

TAINTOR FAMILY,

Descending from Charles Taintor, who was in Connecticut as early as 1643, and who (tradition says) came from Wales. He was a trader to Virginia, and was lost at sea in 1654. Supposed by some to be the father of Joseph Taynter, who came over in the Confidence, A.D. 1638.

(A Genealogy of the family is in course of compilation by Charles M. Taintor, Esq. It was the intention of those concerned, to have both Genealogies published in the same volume, but having disposed of his farm in Shelburne, Mass., and removed to Colchester, Conn., as this was about going to press, Mr. Taintor has been unable to devote the necessary time to preparing the copy; consequently its publication is deferred awhile.)

Charles A.D. 1643 — { Michael, Charles, Marie }

Michael — { John, Micaiell, Elizabeth, Johana, Sarie }

John — { Micael, John, Mary, Joseph, Sarie }

Micael — { Eunice, Michael 1, Charles 2, John 3, Mary, Prudence, Sarah 2, Anne, Mary, Joseph 4, Elizabeth, John 5, Michael 6, Nathaniel 7 }

3 Gershom, Roger 6, Solomon 7, Sally, Polly, 4 Joseph 8, Elizabeth, 5 Benjamin, Jared 9, Abigail, Michael 10, 6 Mary, Medad 11, Elizabeth, Nathaniel, Rebecca, 6 Eunice, Submit, Isaac

1 Sarah, Michael 1, Anne, Eunice, 2 Charles, Sarah, Betsey, Sophia, Newhall 3, Eudocia, Esther 2, Betsey, John 4, Charles 5

1 Lydia, Michael 1, Sarah 1, Asa 2, Mary, Alfred 3, Charles 4, John R. 5, Maria 2, Charles 6, Sophia, Jesse F. 7, Morton, Giles S., John S. 3, William, Mary S., Ralph S. 8, Sophia D., Harriet N. 4, Charles, Abigail B., Charlotte, Roger, Ruth C., Solomon, Ruth C. 5, Addison C., Sarah, Abbe, Eliza, Giles 9, Clarrissa, John A. 10, Edwin B. 11, Caroline, Henry G. 12, Joseph 13, Mary, Eunice, Joseph 7, Eli 14, Harvey 15, John 9, John, Nathaniel 16, Lucy 8, Sally, Alanson 17, Olive, Abigail, Lucretia 9, Alanson, Sarah, Reuben, Anne, Eunitia, Henry 18, Grace 11, Hannah

Joanna, Josiah, Alexander T., Mary M.
Lydia, Asa L., Damaris, Elizabeth C., John W., Harriet
Anne, Mary A., Eliza A., Sarah, Lydia A.
Mary H., Harriet E., Charles M., David W., Henry G.
Charlotte, John B., Mary E., Sarah A., Baxter M., Lydia C., Roxana C., Charles A. L.
Charles M., Henry F., George R., Giles E., Edward C., Sarah M.
Susan P., Anna M., Sarah B., Mary L., Issabella
Joseph L., Ralph S., Phebe L., Charles N., James W., Michael
Frank L., Charles, Abby L., Henry S.
Louisa A., Alice
Lucy P., Caroline, Susan, Eugenia

12 — Henry E.

13 — { Hiram, Cleopatra, Edward, Charles W., Samuel J. }

14 — { Jason A., Phineas W., Erving, Eli N., Albert J. }

15 — { Fidelia, Mahala }

16 — Hiram

17 — { Olive, Mary, Lucy }

18 — { Grace, Henry R., Almira }

In Colchester, Conn., at the house of Addison C. Taintor, there is to be seen a carved oaken chest, "brought by the family from England," or rather perhaps Wales.

The writer had the pleasure of making a pilgrimage to this relic, in the fall of 1859, and of receiving from its present owner, Miss Sophia D. Taintor, a small remnant thereof, being the lid to a small division inside. This has been duly converted into a frame for a document written by the Watertown emigrant in 1654, and measures 9 by 11 inches.

The farm of Mr. Taintor has never been sold, it having remained in the family since the tract was bought from the Indians. The house was built about 150 years ago—the sash, window-glass, &c., being brought from Boston on ox-teams. Situated at the top of " Taintor Hill," it commands a pleasant view of the surrounding country. A large, old-fashioned mansion, its contents consist *principally of a chimney*, though *there are rooms* on each side of it. The largest chimney that that we have ever seen in any old-fashioned house, we will not thus allude to it without respectfully adding the apology, "*They built it large, that the house* (being on a hill) *might not blow away.*"

One of the *many* anecdotes related to us by Miss Taintor, we will fill out the page by inserting here. Not remembering which ancestor it was, it will suffice to say, that he was "*one of the oldest inhabitants*," and was considered infallible in weather wisdom, never having been known to prophesy wrong, and was often consulted by his neighbors when any business depended on the weather. He was a man, too, who seldom said more than " yes," and " no," though he *looked* more, when occasion required.

A neighbor came to him one day, and asked him if the weather would hold fair until the morrow, while he harvested his field of wheat "Yes !" was the reply. But noon came, and with it a torrent of rain, and the wheat lay on the ground, destroyed. As Mr. Taintor had never been known thus to err in his judgment, the neighbor attributed it to malice, and he was duly arraigned before a jury, for " *maliciously deceiving, with intent to injure his neighbor*," &c. But whether with the dignity attributed to the early New England fathers, or whether through the love of fun, suggested by the charge, *we know not*, but the jury pronounced him guilty—fining him 4 shillings and 6 pence," *and it is thus recorded on Colchester records.*

TAINTER FAMILIES, AND WHERE LOCATED.

Descendants of the Watertown Emigrant — numbering 66 families and about 300 persons.

Massachusetts.

Elijah F. Tainter (211), Watertown.
Daniel A. Tainter, (217),   "
George Tainter (220),   "
Hollis W. Taynter (132), Marlboro'.
Harvey Tainter (162), Leicester.
Joel Tainter (124), Framingham.
Daniel Tainter (297), Worcester.
Ephraim C. Tainter (299),   "
Harvey S. Tainter (302),   "
Carver Tainter (303),   "
David Tainter (283), Millbury.
Daniel Tainter (284),   "
Mrs. Willard S. Tainter (286), Millbury.
Charles A. Tainter (294), Wales.
Solon S. Tainter (215), Holliston.
Lewis Tainter (210), Lawrence.
Elmus Tainter (209), Lexington.
Mrs. Elisha L. Tainter (171), Medford.
Albert Tainter (307), Medford.
Edwin Tainter (308),   "
Albert Tainter, Jr. (479), Fitchburg.
Ezra Tainter (205), Melrose.
Mrs. Dan'l A. Tainter (213), Charlestown.

Maine.

Samuel Tainter (175), Bradford.
Simon Tainter (177), S. Carthage.
Thomas D. Tainter (313), S. Brookville.
Sam'l H. Tainter (315), Brooklyn.
Alsworth Tainter (324), S. Carthage.
Wyman V. Tainter (325),   "
Gilbert L. Tainter (326), Dixfield.

Vermont.

Josiah W. Tainter (181),   Whitingham.
Norris D. Tainter (341),   "
Mrs. Josiah W. Tainter, Jr. (343) "
James M. Tainter (344),   "

Rhode Island.

Isaac K. Tainter (396), Providence.

Connecticut.

Simon Tainter (160), Stafford Springs.

New York.

Asa Tayntor (128),   N. Y. City.
Edwin E. Tayntor (233),   "
John W. Tayntor (234),   "
Jonah Tayntor (145), Eaton.
Joseph Tayntor (148),   "
Lorenzo Tayntor (141),   "
Ira B. Tayntor (152),   "
Cyrus K. Tayntor (154),   "
Guilford Tayntor (237),   "
Alanson Tayntor (239),   "
Rev. Orasamus Tayntor (150), Ashford.
Erastus P. Tayntor (153), Buffalo.
Mrs. Hepzebah Tainter (99), Lebanon.
Rev. John L. Taintor (201), Cleveland.

Pennsylvania.

Mrs. Henry C. Tayntor (224), Philadelphia.
Frederick A. Tayntor, U.S.A. (226),   "

Florida.

Thomas P. Tainter (331), Apalachicola.

Michigan.

Jonathan Tainter (185), Kalamazoo.
Timothy Tainter (186), Pentwater.
Charles L. Tainter (357),   "
Leonard Tainter (282), White Pigeon.
Benj. D. Tainter (359), Thornville.
Jonathan Tainter (350), Millburgh.

Missouri.

Loren Tainter (187), Warsaw.

Minnesota.

Rev. Nahum Tainter (298).

Wisconsin.

Ezekiel W. Tainter (189), Prairie du Chien.
Andrew Tainter (188), Dunn Co.
Anson G. Tainter (373), Franklin.
Amasa D. Tainter (318), Augusta.
Amos L. Tainter (319),   "

Iowa.

Joel E. Tainter (292), Fairbank.

TAINTOR FAMILIES,

Descendants of the Connecticut Emigrant—numbering 32 families.   A full and correct list would number about 40.

Charles M. Taintor, Colchester, Conn.
Ralph S. Taintor,   "   "
Addison C. Taintor,   "   "
John A. Taintor, Hartford,   "
Henry G. Taintor, Hampton,   "
Henry Taintor, Clinton,   "
Giles Taintor, Windham,   "
Edward Taintor, Colebrook,   "
Josiah Taintor, ——,   "
Nathaniel Taintor, East Haven,   "
Hiram Taintor, ——,   "
Joseph Taintor, Colebrook,   "
Edward Taintor, ——,
Edwin B. Taintor, Brookfield, Mass.
Eli Taintor, Lee, Mass.
Jason A. Taintor, ——

Phineas W. Taintor, ——
Rev. Erving Taintor, Harford, N. Y.
Eli N. Taintor, ——
Albert J. Taintor, ——
Charles Taintor, Buffalo,   N. Y.
Dr. John R. Taintor, Avon,   "
Jesse F. Taintor, Cleveland, Ohio.
Alanson Taintor, Euclid,   "
O. H. Taintor, ——
Alexander S. Taintor, Canterbury, N. H.
Charles Taintor, ——, Pa. (?)
Giles S. Taintor, Natchez, Miss.
William Taintor, near Michigan City, Ind.
Morton Taintor, Natchez, Miss.
Jesse Taintor, Hartland, Ohio.
Augustus Taintor, (?) E. Troy, Wis.

INDEX TO FAMILY NAMES ALLIED BY MARRIAGE.

	Page.		Page.		Page.		Page.
Adams,	. 72	Dexter,	. 59	Hutchins, .	. 59	Randall, -	- 11
Alexander,	. 69	Dyke,	. 44	Hurd,	. 47	Reed, -	- 45
Allen,	. 46					Rice,	34, 36, 44, 46
		Eames,	. 63	Jacobs,	. 35	Richardson,	47, 50
Bachellor, .	. 49	Eaton,	. 35	Jarvis,	. 29	Rolf, -	- 59
Bailey,	. 34	Eddy,	. 58	Jenkins,	. 38	Root, -	36, 42
Baker,	. 23	Edwards, .	. 53	Johnson,	. 58	Rugg, -	- 45
Bancroft,	35, 44	Eldridge,	. 45	Jordan,	. 41	Russell, -	- 63
Barnard,	. 38	Elkins,	. 70				
Barnes,	. 57	Emory,	. 54	Kendall, .	. 23	Sadler, -	- 23
Barrett,	. 17	Engle,	. 57	Kilburne, .	, 38	Sanger, -	- 50
Bartlett,	59, 59	Ewell,	59, 59	Kingsbury,	. 34	Sawyer, -	- 35
Bartol,	. 59			Knight,	. 42	Shedd,	29, 29
Bates	. 57	Fairbanks, .	. 38	Knapp,	. 53	Shumway,	44, 46
Beers,	. 15	Farnum,	. 63			Sibley,	35, 44
Beebe,	43, 43, 63	Fay,	. 53	Lake,	. 63	Simonds, -	- 71
Bennett,	. 43	Fessenden, .	. 45	Larabee,	. 67	Small, -	- 35
Black,	59, 59	Fisher,	. 70	Leland,	. 42	Smith,	21, 41, 44, 45
Blakesley,	63, 63, 70	Flick,	. 67	Levaughn, .	. 41	Stone,	15, 29, 45
Bond,	. 43	Flint,	. 50	Lewis,	. 35	Symmes, -	- 42
Bowen,	. 57	Follansbee,	. 38	Libbey,	. 44		
Bowker,	. 23	Forbes,	. 46	Littlefield, .	. 50	Taylor, -	15, 57
Bowman,	. 46	Foster,	. 42	Loring,	. 42	Tayntor, -	54, 54
Boyd,	. 53	Fowler,	. 63	Luther,	. 42	Thayer, -	- 63
Bridges,	. 50	Fuller,	34, 61			Thompson,	- 53
Brigham,	21, 71	Furlong,	. 70	Marble, -	- 57	Tobler, -	- 65
Brooks,	. 61			Marsh, -	- 57	Treat, -	- 42
Brown,	. 64	Gammon,	. 35	Martin, -	- 63	Train, -	- 59
Bruce,	. 23	Gates,	. 44	Maxfield, -	- 61	Trowbridge,	- 42
Burbank,	. 58	Gibson,	. 35	Maynard, -	- 33	Tufts, -	- 59
Burdick,	. 47	Goddard,	35, 35, 57	McDonnell,	- 53		
Burnham,	. 47	Goodell,	. 21	Merriam, -	- 45	Vose, -	- 45
Burt,	57, 57	Goodnow, .	. 34	Merritt, -	- 45		
Bush,	. 34	Gorham,	. 36	Mitchell, -	- 67	Wadsworth,	- 55
Butcher,	. 17	Gould,	34, 61	Moe, -	- 64	Walker, -	- 65
		Graves,	. 46	Moore, -	- 53	Walton, -	- 64
Capron,	. 58	Green,	. 50	Morse, -	- 44	Ward, -	- 21
Carter,	. 44	Guy,	15, 20	Mosher, -	- 63	Warren,	15, 23, 42
Chase,	. 63					Watson,	29, 29, 61
Clark,	. 49	Hall,	. 57	Newcomb,	64, 64	Wellington,	- 43
Clough,	. 59	Hammond,	. 59	Nickerson,	- 65	Wells, -	- 69
Cooley,	. 46	Harrington,	17, 17, 44			White,	- 65
Coolidge, .	. 29	Harris,	43, 72	Pardon, -	- 67	Whitney, -	17, 45
Copeland, .	. 44	Hastings, .	. 17	Parks, -	- 58	Wiley, -	- 42
Corning,	. 41	Hewett,	. 47	Peck, -	- 46	Willis, -	- 50
Corrison,	. 61	Hill,	29, 42	Pelton, -	- 67	Wilson, -	- 61
Curtis,	. 20	Hillard,	. 64	Perry, -	- 34	Wilkins, -	- 34
Cushing,	. 44	Hinds,	. 36	Pierce,	35, 50, 58	Winslow, -	36, 46
		Hiscock,	. 50	Pollard, -	- 15	Wiswall, -	21, 62
Dale,	. 61	Houghton,	34, 35	Pond, -	- 42	Wooden, -	- 54
Daniels,	. 43	Howard,	. 35	Popenbury,	- 35	Wood, -	21, 23
Darrow,	. 53	Howe,	17, 34, 34, 42, 53	Popple, -	- 42	Woodruff, -	- 77
Davis,	45, 46	Hubbard, .	. 34	Post, -	- 33	Wyman, -	- 35
Dean,	. 49	Hunt,	. 46	Potter, -	- 34		
Denman,	. 43					Young, -	- 64

FAMILY RECORD.

Name of Father.   Date of birth.

Name of Mother.   Date of birth.

Married.   Father died.   Mother died.

CHILDREN.

Names.   Born when and where.

FAMILY RECORD.

Name of Father,   Date of birth,

Name of Mother,   Date of birth,

Married,   Father died,   Mother died,

CHILDREN.

Names,   Born when and where.

1

2

3

4

5

6

7

8

FAMILY RECORD.

———✦❖✦———

Name of Father,   Date of birth,

Name of Mother,   Date of birth,

Married,   Father died,   Mother died,

CHILDREN.

     Names,   Born when and where,

FAMILY RECORD.

—◦◦◦◦◦◦◦—

Name of Father,   Date of birth,

Name of Mother,   Date of birth,

Married,   Father died,   Mother died,

CHILDREN.

Names,   Born when and where.

1

2

3

4

5

6

7

8

, Names of Children should be written on the numbered lines, with date and place of birth; their date of marriage, and whom, or the date of their death, on the blue lines.

DIED,

In Charlestown, Jan. 20, of typhoid fever, Sarah, wife of
Dean Willis Tainter, aged 19 years, 6 mos. 24 days.

THE writer cannot close without alluding to the death of a young and beloved companion. Earnestly she watched the preparation and completion of the greater number of these pages, until sickness and death freed her from the cares and responsibilities of earth.

From time to time the writer has been gratified on receiving from the various branches of the family, new items of birth and marriage, as they transpired, and has been pleased to insert them in their proper places. But little thought he that the *last* item would be furnished by *himself—* that the last stroke of his pen, in this family record, would be to record the death of a lovely and affectionate wife.

SARAH SARGENT ADAMS was born in Lexington, June 26, 1840, second daughter of Winthrop ?. and Maria S. Adams. The father dying when Sarah was but three months old, Mrs. Adams was dependent upon her own industry for the support of herself and two daughters through eleven long years of widowhood. Successfully and blamelessly did the young mother this, though the widow's mite, after the expenses of each succeeding week, was often small. Under the careful training of a mother tried in adverse circumstances—whose only thoughts were the welfare and happiness of her two children—Sarah acquired a disposition peculiar for firmness of principle, earnestness, and a desire to please those first with whom her lot in life placed her. With an active and matured mind, for one of her years, she was ever agreeable to all, maintaining a high character as a christian, as a friend, as a wife. Taken in marriage when scarcely eighteen years of age, with every prospect of a long and happy career, one year passed swiftly by, like the flight of a midsummer's day, the memory of which is but sunshine. With but a short season of sickness, and ere she had scarcely said, "I am going to heaven," "life's fitful fever was o'er;" and as the hour came round that had been marked, just one year before, by her nuptials, there had assembled in large numbers her friends and relatives, and the members of Temperance Lodge (of which she had been a member), to view for the last time her cold remains in death.

Charlestown,
Jan. 27, 1860.

"GREEN BE THE TURF ABOVE THEE,
WIFE OF MY EARLY DAYS,
NONE KNEW THEE BUT TO LOVE THEE,
NONE NAMED THEE BUT TO PRAISE."

DIED, in Charlestown, Jan. 20, Mrs. Sarah, wife of D. Willis Tainter, in her 20th year. The death of one so amiable and so truly a Christian, as was the subject of this notice, calls for something more than the simple announcement that he has departed. It was the happy privilege of the writer to act for a season as her religious teacher. She was a member of my Bible Class ; and never have I known a young lady of her age so deeply interested in religious subjects, and especially in the study of the Scriptures, as she was at that time. Soon after she left my class, she was married and moved to Charlestown ; and in just one year from her wedding day she was carried to her tomb. A few moments before she expired, she engaged in prayer. She thanked God for the year of happiness she had enjoyed in the society of her husband, and asked for patience and resignation to await a reunion in the spirit land. Those who heard that prayer present it as being angelic. She called her sister and smilingly said, "Emma, I am going to heaven." Lovingly she took leave of her husband, and in a moment departed. The religion she loved so well, and the instruction she sought earnestly in the Sunday school, were sweet to her in the close of a beautiful life, and transformed the bed of death into a Mount of Ascension. O, what an example do we here behold for the young to imitate ! A little while before her last illness she said to a friend, "I do not know as I was ever unhappy." May her faith be ours ; our lives like her life; her death like hers.—*Christian (Universalist) Freeman.* L. J. F.

At a meeting of Crescent Lodge, No. 2, Independent Order of Good Templars, the following resolutions were unanimously adopted :—

Whereas, God in his divine wisdom has called home our dear sister Sarah S. Tainter (wife of Dean W. Tainter, Esq.), in deep grief must mourn a sad parting with one whose short sojourn in our midst, like a ray of heavenly sunshine, warmed us with an assurance of our Father's love, for she was indeed sent to make others happy. And now that the light of our dear Sister's life has gone out in the cold gloom of death, the memory of her many virtues points us, like a monument of faith, to the throne of the great Jehovah, where we know our gentle Sister in radiant immortality enjoys the triumph of her earnest faith in the promises of Christ.

We thank God, who has chosen to cloud the scenes so lately warmed by the bright, sun-lit nature of our lost Sister, that we can sympathise with those upon whom this affliction falls heaviest ; we cannot lighten the weight of sorrow that darkens the home so early robbed of its treasure ; we can only pray that the Almighty, who has sent this great grief, and give to our sympathy the power to comfort them in their bereavement. Therefore,

Resolved, That with heavy hearts we mourn the loss of an earnest, warm-hearted Sister, a noble, disinterested worker, and a high-minded, Christian woman, whose whole life was ever marked with the divine principles of *Faith, Hope* and *Charity.*

Resolved, That we will strive to sustain our Brother in this his sad bereavement, bringing all the power of sympathy and friendship to our aid, to cheer the husband of our lost Sister in this his time of trial.

Resolved, That we condole with the relatives and friends of the deceased, hoping that in this sore affliction, the memory of the Christian resignation with which our dear Sister responded to the call of her Father, will give them strength and comfort in their sorrow.

Resolved, That a copy of these resolutions be forwarded to the husband of the deceased, and the same be published in the "Temperance Visitor" and "Bunker Hill Aurora." [*Temperance Visitor.*

MAXIMS

(To fill a spare page.)

I never saw an oft-removed tree, nor yet an oft-removed family, that throve so well as thos that settled be.—*Franklin.*

He that is ambitious for his son, should give him untried names.

Esteem more those who begin the nobility of their families, than those in whom and not b whom it is continued.

Hereditary honor is accounted the most noble; but reason speaketh in the cause of him wh hath acquired it.

Godliness with contentment—these be the pillars of felicity.

Endeavor to be first in thy calling, whatever it be; neither let any one go before thee in wel doing: nevertheless, do not envy the merits of another, but improve thine own talent.

Least said, quickest mended.

He who waits for good luck to come to him, is destined to die in poverty.

A young man idle, an old man needy.

For age and want, save while you may; no morning sun lasts a whole day.

A pin a day, is a groat a year.

A man without money is a bow without an arrow.

A rolling stone gathers no moss.

Forget others' faults by remembering your own.

Let another's shipwreck be your sea-mark.

All complain of want of memory, but none of want of judgment.

Error is a hardy plant; it flourisheth in every soil.

He preaches well who lives well; example teaches more than precept.

Feet warm, head cool, and bowels open, will keep doctors poor.

The best physicians are Dr. Diet, Dr. Quiet, and Dr. Merryman.

A letter timely written is a rivet in the chain of affection, but a letter untimely delayed is a rust to the solder.

He who liveth after nature, shall never be poor; after opinion, shall never be rich.

He that considereth he is to die, is content while he liveth; he who striveth to forget it, ha no pleasure in anything.

Pain that endureth long is moderate, blush therefore to complain of it: — that which is viole is short; behold, thou seest the end of it.

He who giveth away his treasure wisely, giveth away his plagues; he that retaineth their i crease, heapeth up sorrows.

The soul of the cheerful forceth a smile upon the face of affliction, but the despondence of t sad deadeneth even the brightness of joy.

To bear adversity well, is difficult; but to be temperate in prosperity, is the height of wisdor

"Keep good company or none. Never be idle. If your hands cannot be usefully employe attend to the cultivation of your mind. Always speak the truth. Make few promises. Li up to your engagements. Keep your own secrets, if you have any. When you speak to a pe son, look him in the face. Good company and good conversation are the very sinews of virtu Good character is above all things else. Your character cannot be essentially injured except l your own acts. If any one speaks evil of you, let your life be such that no one will believe hi Drink no kind of intoxicating liquors. Ever live, misfortunes excepted, within your incom When you retire to bed, think over what you have been doing during the day. Make no has to be rich, if you would prosper. Small and steady gains give competency, with tranquillity mind. Never play at any game of chance. Avoid temptation, through fear you may not wit stand it. Earn money before you spend it. Never run into debt. Never borrow, if you can po sibly avoid it. Do not marry until you are able to support a wife. Never speak evil of any on Be just before you are generous. Keep yourself innocent, if you would be happy. Save when y are young, to spend when you are old."